Remembering

Palgrave Studies in Oral History

Series Editors: Linda Shopes and Bruce M. Stave

Sticking to the Union: An Oral History of the Life and Times of Julia Ruuttila, by Sandy Polishuk; Foreword by Amy Kesselman (2003)

To Wear the Dust of War: An Oral History, by Samuel Iwry, edited by Leslie J. H. Kelley (2004)

Education as My Agenda: Gertrude Williams, Race, and the Baltimore Public Schools, by Jo Ann O. Robinson (2005)

Remembering: Oral History Performance, edited by Della Pollock (2005)

Postmemories of Terror: A New Generation Copes with the Legacy of the "Dirty War," by Susana Kaiser (forthcoming)

Growing Up in The People's Republic: Conversations between Two Daughters of China's Revolution, by Weili Ye and Ma Xiadong (forthcoming)

Creating Choice: A Community Responds to the Need for Abortion and Birth Control, 1961–1973, by David P. Cline (forthcoming)

Life and Death in the Delta: African American Narratives of Violence, Resilience, and Social Change, by Kim Lacy Rogers (forthcoming)

Voices from This Long Brown Land: Oral Recollection of Owens Valley Lives and Manzanar Pasts, by Jane Wehrey (forthcoming)

In the Wake of Kent State: Campus Rhetoric and Protest at the University of Nevada, by Brad Lucas (forthcoming)

Sisters in the Brotherhoods: Organizing for Equality, by Jane Latour (forthcoming)

Remembering

Oral History Performance

Edited by Della Pollock

Afterword by Jacquelyn Dowd Hall

First published in 2005 by
PALGRAVE MACMILLAN™
175 Fifth Avenue, New York, N.Y. 10010 and
Houndmills, Basingstoke, Hampshire, England RG21 6XS
Companies and representatives throughout the world.

PALGRAVE MACMILLAN is the global academic imprint of the Palgrave Macmillan division of St. Martin's Press, LLC and of Palgrave Macmillan Ltd. Macmillan® is a registered trademark in the United States, United Kingdom and other countries. Palgrave is a registered trademark in the European Union and other countries.

ISBN 1–4039–6374–6
ISBN 1–4039–6347–9

Library of Congress Cataloging-in-Publication Data

Remembering : oral history performance / edited by Della Pollock.
    p. cm.—(Palgrave studies in oral history)
Includes bibliographical references and index.
ISBN 1–4039–6374–6—ISBN 1–4039–6347–9 (pbk.)
    1. Oral history. 2. Performing arts. I. Pollock, Della. II. Series.

D16.14.R46 2005
792.02′2—dc22   2005043100

A catalogue record for this book is available from the British Library.

Design by Newgen Imaging Systems (P) Ltd., Chennai, India.

First edition: Ocotber 2005

10 9 8 7 6 5 4 3 2 1

Printed in the United States of America.

Transferred to digital printing in 2007.

For Dwight

Contents

Acknowledgments

It is simply impossible to acknowledge directly all of the people who contributed to this volume. Each essay is layered in practices of performative co-witness. Each variously reflects collaboration among interviewees, interviewers, artists, scholars, research and activist collectives, students, community participants, audience members, and projected readers. Each author is embedded in conversations that far precede and extend beyond these pages. Let me then begin by extending my deepest thanks broadly to all of the contributors to the work represented here and to the authors who have each struggled so eloquently (and patiently) to embed their voices among the many that have shaped and informed their own.

Linda Shopes provided invaluable commentary on all aspects of the project. Many thanks to Linda, Bruce Stave, Airie Stuart, Erin Ivy, Petrina Crockford, and Maran Elancheran for shepherding the book into production. Lesley Williams, Rivka Eisner, and Jules Odendahl provided critical assistance. I am endlessly grateful to Bill Balthrop, my colleagues at UNC, and the many groups of students who have supported the years of experimentation that made such a volume possible.

Jacquelyn Hall is in many ways at the center of this volume, not only in her willingness to participate in wildly unpredictable collaborations but in her open curiosity about how people make their histories and so make ours worth living. Jacquelyn inspires by the expanse of her vision and by the passionate particularity of each of the questions she asks, questions that continually, rigorously, and insistently renew our compact with histories of social change.

Dwight Conquergood taught that thinking and doing the performance of cultural politics in ethical action or *praxis* was simply necessary. No one better exemplified this commitment than did he. I humbly offer this book in the spirit of his commitment, as a gathering of insurgent and divergent interventions. Dwight, I'm sure you'd have lots to say.

Preface

Oral historians often claim that ours is an interdisciplinary practice. Certainly the kinds of deeply researched, in-depth, and historically focused interviews we typically do are also done by colleagues in fields other than history. Just as certainly, we have learned much about the craft of interviewing and the interpretation of interview texts from scholars working in a range of disciplines. Yet true interdisciplinarity is hard to come by. Often invoked, scholars in different fields just as often talk past each other, sliding over differences in their underlying assumptions, governing questions, and methodologies, as well as in the language they use to speak about their work.

This collection of essays, conceived of and edited by Della Pollock, is thus exemplary in the ways it connects the fields of history and performance studies through the medium of oral history. As many oral historians know intuitively, the telling of stories is inherently performative: an interviewee puts on a show, creates an identity, within the context of talking to the interviewer. The stories told, often deeply expressive of history's burdens, lay claim on us for retelling so that history may be known, shared, perhaps overcome. Performance, operating in the liminal space between then and now, you and me, what happened and what someone said happened, is an especially powerful means of doing so.

The nine essays included in this volume describe in detail the development of oral history-based performances on a range of topics, in a variety of settings: autobiographies of inmates in a medium-security prison in North Carolina and of a Vietnamese immigrant to the United States; a strike at a Wisconsin meat packing plant; community life in working class Boston; the Ghanaian practice of *trokosi*, whereby a young girl is surrendered to a shrine in reparation for a crime committed by a family member. We read too of students using performance to enrich their understanding of oral history. What links the essays is an introspection about process and a deep ethical concern for both representing narrators well and extending the reach of their stories.

A cautionary word is in order. Historians will perhaps find many of these essays quite challenging, as they encounter a theoretical framework and a language that may be unfamiliar to them. Moreover, explanations about performance can only approximate the actual experience of a performance; as with reading oral history narratives, the reader must use his imagination to see and hear the actual performances. We urge patient attention to the essays, however, for there is much to learn from them—about the body as a medium of expression, about *doing something* with interviews, about the hard work of creation. And there is one fundamental point that historians and performance scholars certainly agree on: that stories about the past matter deeply in the present, indeed they only exist in the present.

Remembering: Oral History Performance makes an important, substantive contribution to an interdisciplinary understanding of oral history. We are pleased to include it in Palgrave's *Studies in Oral History* series, designed to make work based on oral history interviews available to students, educators, scholars, and the reading public. The series includes both work that is deeply grounded in interviews and work that approaches oral history theoretically, as a point of departure for an exploration of broad questions of cultural production and representation.

Linda Shopes
Pennsylvania Historical & Museum Commission

Bruce M. Stave
University of Connecticut

ONE

Introduction: Remembering

Della Pollock

While scholars and practitioners in any number of fields, across the university and public humanities, are turning to performance as both an analytic and a practice—as a way of both describing and entering into the creative work of social transformation—oral history and performance enjoy a unique synergy. Oral historians and performance scholars/practitioners are increasingly discovering shared and complementary investments in orality, dialogue, life stories, and community-building or what might more generally be called *living* history. By which I don't mean reenactments or heritage theater exactly but the process of materializing historical reflection in live representation as both a form (a container) and a means (a catalyst) of social action. Performance—whether we are talking about the everyday act of telling a story or the staged reiteration of stories—is an especially charged, contingent, reflexive space of encountering the complex web of our respective histories. It may consequently engage participants in new and renewed understandings of the past. It may introduce alternative voices into public debate. It may help to identify systemic problems and to engage a sense of need, hope, and vision. As live representation, performance may in effect bring imagined worlds into *being and becoming*, moving performers and audiences alike into palpable recognition of possibilities for change. Through the incorporation of oral histories into public memory, it may most fundamentally ensure that "those who have given up their time to talk, know that their words have been taken seriously" (Slim and Thompson, 2).

Remembering is intended to introduce some of the work currently being done at the intersection of performance and oral history.[1] It is not a manual.[2] Recognizing the specificity of oral history and performance in local contexts, it does not provide instructions for developing oral history performances, although it does emphasize the unique integration of theory and practice, research and poetics, in each case represented here.[3] Each of the essays in this volume focuses intensively on specific, sensuous *processes of production and reception* and is methodologically and theoretically suggestive rather than, in any sense, prescriptive.

In turn, the essays reflect the peculiar resistance of performance to logics of cause and effect. Each author is concerned with work driven to make a difference; each moreover is working with the symbolic fabric of language, narrative, image, bodies in artful motion, and their respective interaction and interplay. As oriented as a performance may be toward change, performance does not work instrumentally. In the symbolic field of representation, effects are unpredictable, even uncontrollable. They may be fleeting or burrow deeply, only to emerge in an unexpected place, at another time. They may unfurl slowly, even invisibly, on affective currents that may compete with what we think a given performance is or should be doing. Or they may refuse to come out altogether, preferring instead to rest in the discourses of "mere" entertainment or passing pleasure.

The performance of oral history is itself a transformational process. At the very least, it translates subjectively remembered events into embodied memory acts, moving memory into re-membering. That passage not only risks but endows the emerging history/narratives with change. Accordingly, this volume turns on a promise, what I would call the essential of promise of oral history performance: that the body remembering, the bodies remembered, and the bodies listening in order to remember ("you remember, I told you . . .") will be redeemed in some kind of change—the small changes that come with repetition in different moments with different listeners; the large changes that might result from entering the memories of a whole body politic (medium-risk prisoners in Rouverol's work; striking laborers in Gordon's) into the human record of daily living. In this sense, performance is a promissory act. Not because it can only promise possible change but because it catches its participants—often by surprise—in a contract with possibility: with imagining what might be, could be, should be. As much as we may want to determine its effects—whether as a matter of intention or retrospection, it would consequently be counter-productive to do so. Whatever effects performances may have live beyond scientific controls and measures, in the ongoing reckonings of human understanding.[4]

What joins all the chapters is a sense that performance as promise and practice is at the heart of oral history. That insofar as oral history is a process of *making history in dialogue*, it is performative. It is cocreative, co-embodied, specially framed, contextually and intersubjectively contingent, sensuous, vital, artful in its achievement of narrative form, meaning, and ethics, and insistent on *doing through saying*: on investing the present and future with the past, re-marking history with previously excluded subjectivities, and challenging the conventional frameworks of historical knowledge with other ways of knowing. Each of the authors in this volume offers insights into the nature of oral history (as) performance, but all basically agree that the oral historian stages a conversation in the relatively artificial context of an interview.[5] The interview involves its participants in a heightened encounter with each other and with the past, even as each participant and the past seem to be called toward a future that suddenly seems open before them, a future to be made in talk, in the mutual embedding of one's vision of the world in the other's. The interviewer is her/himself a symbolic presence, standing in for other, unseen audiences and invoking a social compact: a tacit agreement that what is heard will be integrated into public memory and social knowledge in such a way that, directly or indirectly, it will make a material difference. The oral history interview lifts what might otherwise dissolve into the ephemera of everyday life onto the plane of ongoing exchange and meaning-making, infusing it with the power of shifting relationships among tellers and listeners (and listeners who become tellers to tellers who become listeners) near and far.

The oral history interview is a bounded event that asserts the "competency" of the primary teller to tell a particular history.[6] It is framed by interpretive codes (even insofar as the tape recorder is loaded with cultural expectations) that endow that history with special meaning and value, making the interview a private/public act that uniquely joins historical accounts already shaped by prior conditions, conversations, and rehearsals with the prospect of new meanings unfolding across a panorama of reception. Understood as performance, in these among other ways, the oral history interview is an ignition point, charged by and charging its historical moment, giving so many oral historians the sense that the occasion of the interview—no more and *so* much more than an ordinary conversation—is *momentous*.

What then does it mean to stage oral histories? To move them from the implicit to the explicit context of public performance? What happens to the critical, interpretive vitality of the primary exchange? How does the performative process of *remembering* amplify the uncertainties and contingencies—the narrative irresolution—in history? How might the peculiar relays of *remembering* in turn enhance the *poiesis* of history—the creation and re-creation of new histories that might be the answer to crumbling communities, forgotten lives, and generations of young people lost to the presentism of tv/video/digital mediation? How might in turn *poiesis* become *kinesis*—the embodiment of symbolic knowledge in social action?[7]

Staged performance or "re-performance" appreciates the magnitude of the primary interview encounter by expanding it to include other listeners; rallying its pedagogical force; and trying—in some small measure—to convey the particular beauty of two people meeting over history. It moreover does so live, not only mirroring the primary telling but actively favoring oral history as a mode of *embodied knowing*—as an epistemology that lives, in Annette Kuhn's provocative words, "on the pulse" (101): precarious, contingent, sensuous, felt. Emphasizing that oral history is a performance in itself, the performance of oral history insists on the distinctive value of knowing by listening to words passed "mouth to ear . . . body to body" (Trinh, 136), words entered into viscerally charged debates about both *what* and *how* to know, and words shimmering with what may be unsaid, felt, withheld, stammered, introduced in a pause, caught up in a breath, a sigh, an expressive rhythm, a physical or tonal gesture (see, e.g. Eisner's conversations with her interview partner, Chị Tôi, in the sixth chapter of this volume, or Fousekis' conversation with Carol Watts in the last).[8] In so doing, oral history performance challenges the textual drive toward narrative resolution and the conventional authority of more objective or objectifying modes of knowledge and representation with the power of open telling. At its best, it democratizes tellers and listeners by easing the monologic power of *what is said* into the collaborative, cogenerative, and yet potentially discordant *act of saying and hearing* it.

In so doing, oral history performance cultivates what Gloria Anzaldua and Cherrie Moraga have called "theories of the flesh": the root metaphors and ideas about the world that both emerge from and "bridge the contradictions" of experience (Anzaldua and Moraga, 23). Oral history performance refuses easy and all too conventional distinctions between experience and explanation, or body and mind—distinctions by which, for instance, scientific discourses have consistently dismissed the concrete, partial life of the "anecdote." It insists instead on the complexities of indigenous or vernacular conceptualizations of experience; the intersection of vernacular and "specialized knowledges";[9] and the possibility of mobilizing both through the interactive dynamics of restaging histories told and heard in interview settings.

The essays in this volume comprise something of a polemic. More or less explicitly, each author characterizes performance as central to the nature and aims of oral history. Collectively and individually, these essays suggest that performance is not so much an interesting or entertaining option as an obligation. At the most basic level, re-performance is an expression of devoted reception. It is one attempt to fulfill the promise—the sense of contractual responsibility and enormous possibility—of historical talk. Beyond the particularities of interview practice or historical method, it enacts what Kelly Oliver calls "the response-ability in subjectivity" (139): the sense that the ability to respond (response-ability) that inheres in the obligation (responsibility) to do so defines what it means to be a human self. As many of the authors in this volume suggest, beyond storytellers, we are witnesses.[10] We see each other and we (must) see to each other through the performance of witnessing. For Oliver, any one self is thus ontologically and ethically inextricable from "others." The self-subject as witness does not subsume or speak *for* others any more than it bespeaks an inalienable distinction between one's self and presumed other.[11] Rather, it gains resonance in vibrant relation to others. Accordingly, for Oliver, "the other is no longer *the* other. There is no the other, but a multitude of differences and other people on whom my sense of myself as a subject and an agent depends" (223). Oral history performance as a form of witnessing is one way of practicing the interdependence of human selves and of seeing through the past into an as-yet unspoken (much less written) future—for Oliver, one that will be, if indeed we recognize our defining role as witnesses, more just and loving.[12]

Remembering focuses specifically on *oral history-based performance*: performances that take their impetus from formal or informal oral history interviews when oral history is understood as the re-creation of storied experience for the primary purpose of gaining social-historical perspective. It does not pretend to encompass all of the wide-ranging, related work done under the rubric of "documentary theater" or the important and equally wide-ranging work of performing autobiography.[13] It recognizes essential kinship with but does not focus on: family and folk storytelling; heritage drama and historical reenactments; museum exhibition and performance; a broad definition of community-based theater;[14] and performances of historical witness and intervention not based on oral history interviews. It is particularly concerned with the "response-ability" of the person who hears oral histories and the corresponding strength of that person's agency as someone who acts on hearing if only by telling again.

One implication of Oliver's formulation is that history cannot be held privately. No one person "owns" a story. Any one story is embedded in layers of remembering and storying. Remembering is necessarily a public act whose politics are bound up with the refusal to be isolated, insulated, inoculated against both complicity with and contest over claims to ownership. That's her story, we might say, ostensibly valorizing the teller by remaining at arm's length and failing to recognize, much less reckon with, our place in the network of social relations her story invokes. In this way, we may neutralize by privatizing a given history. As Sam Schrager has observed, oral histories are cultivated in narrative environments; they bear the dialogical imprint of many voices and perspectives.[15] Each is already a communal text, documenting above all the "multitude of differences and other people" that converge on any one "memory act."[16] Oral history performance aims to distribute the great wealth of any one or anyone's story/history: enriching each teller along the way.

Accordingly, Anna Deavere Smith's revolutionary production of *Fires in the Mirror*, followed by *Twilight: Los Angeles, 1992*, featured what seemed an almost endless range of perspectives on the Crown Heights Riots in 1991.[17] Acclaimed for Smith's virtuosic replay of twenty-seven characters, *Fires in the Mirror* is as much about the poetics of historical narrative as it is about the histories those poetics uniquely engage. Concerned with the complexities of race relations in the contemporary United States, Smith looks for American "character" in vernacular rhythms and images:

> Speaking teaches us what our natural "literature" is. In fact, everyone, in a given amount of time, will say something that is like poetry. The process of getting to that moment is where "character" lives. (xxxi)

Character, Smith finds, emerges "in the gaps," in those places where language fails, at those moments when it proves next to impossible to tell a whole or neat story, when the poetry of human history both rises from the rubble and falters:

> My sense is that American character lives not in one place or the other, but in the gaps between the places, and in our struggle to be together in our differences.

> It lives not in what has been fully articulated, but in what is in the process of being articulated, not in the smooth-sounding words, but in the very moment that the smooth-sounding words fail us. We might not like what we see, but in order to change it, we have to see it clearly. (xli)

Smith projects a cacophony of voices that, in their friction and failures, reveal the inequities that listening only for the coherence of a given narrative might otherwise obscure.

Julie Salverson complements Smith by hailing another set of gaps: those between the audience member and the lives represented on stage. Challenging what she calls an "erotics of injury"—the melancholic, often pleasurable identification with performance of/by the alleged victims or survivors of social trauma, Salverson warns against the potentially mystifying and reiterative effects of conventional empathy. She calls instead for an aesthetic of "detachment and contact":

> It is no longer enough—if it ever was—to assume that theater is by its very nature about connection; now those of us who practice theater that engages with people's accounts of violent events must articulate the nature of that contact. I want to explore how theater operates as an ethical space in which a relationship between detachment and contact occurs. When, I wonder, is the meeting of lives (the narratives we construct, intuit, and perform about ourselves) about a contact that consumes the other person and reduces them to our terms? When, on the other hand, is it a contact that lets us come together differently and binds me deeply to another without collapsing either the "I" or the "other" into a totalizing "we"? (Salverson 2001, 119)[18]

Salverson and Smith insist on a testimonial theater filled with uncertainties and marked differences—even insofar as, for example, Moisés Kaufman and the Tectonic Theater's *The Laramie Project* is flush with questions. Placing center stage the interactions among the actor/interviewers and the residents of Laramie, Wyoming, where Matthew Shepard was brutally murdered, the play dramatizes the search for an ever-elusive complete or total(izing) story. *The Laramie Project* has perhaps done more than any other work to popularize oral history performance.[19] At the same time, it has been duly criticized for smoothing over narrative disjunctions and the raw edge of homophobia that was ultimately responsible for Shepard's death, presenting a kind of *Our Town* version of contemporary, horrific violence. This has been in part the effect of repeat productions in communities across the United States in which the original actor/interviewees are re/displaced by actors playing interviewer/actors, putting the representation of Laramie and the interaction between the interviewers and residents at one further remove from the reality of audience members who might otherwise identify with the members of the Tectonic Theater company as "people-like-themselves," leading them to feel—as such—that they too might take up this response-ability, that they might perform the role of asker/interviewer, that they might wonder harder about histories already smoothed over by time and repetition.

While this critique bears considerable weight, it also points to the (im)balance between representation and reality in all oral history performance. In addition to the gaps within and between stories (following Smith), and the gap between the lives of audience members and the lives represented on stage (following Salverson), is another crucial gap in oral history performance: that between representation and the "actual" events and tellers to which that representation refers. It would be unnecessary to pursue performance if its representational status were something to bury, hide, or escape; if its failure to provide an "authentic" experience did not in some essential way add to the understanding of history oral history promotes. While "living history" may try to collapse reality and representation to give the impression that "you were there!," all of the essays in this volume recognize the gap in re-presentation and struggle to articulate its particular value to knowing and making history.

Oral history performance is strung between reference to real events and real listener/witnesses, between recollection and anticipation of historical change. It has the peculiar temporality of the *representational real*: an engine embedded in historical time, it invokes the *beyond time* of possibility, making possibility real or at least staking the grounds of real possibilities.[20] In most of the projects described in this volume, the performance of reality is paradoxically a performance of possibility.[21] Accordingly, oral history performance becomes the ethical space Salverson demands and Bruce McConachie defines in his important essay, "Approaching the 'Structure of Feeling' in Grassroots Theatre." McConachie describes a collaboration between the Williamsburg Grassroots Theatre Project and the Roadside Theatre Company in 1995–1996 based on interviews concerned with the gradual shift from segregation to desegregation in a small southern town. The project, for McConachie, exemplifies the dialectical draw forward and then back again that makes up the affective dynamics of "community-based theatre":

> Community-based theatre . . . is less about representing the realities of actual or historic communities—although markers of these realities need to be present to "authenticate" the experience—and more about imagining and constructing the relationships of an ethical community for the future. The images generated in a grassroots show provide a structure of feeling that induces the audience to divide an ethical "us" from an immoral "them" and then to examine who "we" are. (42)

In all of its gaps, "betweenesses," or liminality, oral history-based performance offers less an alternative recording of the past than an ethical imaginary of a future—a future that now feels so close "we" find ourselves almost at home in it, except that we must "examine who 'we' are" before we can cross its threshold.

In this light, I am particularly moved by Natalie Fousekis' discovery, recounted in her essay here, "Experiencing History: A Journey from Oral History to Performance," that when she and her student-colleagues finally started literally cutting up tape logs and splicing interview transcripts—when they started playing with the gaps and messing with the isolation, insularity, and linearity of interview materials—they also finally started "acting like historians."[22] Their historical investigation began with what seemed an irreverent plunge into (re)creativity. They ironically started performing their scholarly roles as historians when they stopped trying to save their interviewees' histories not only from mortal ruin (as preservationists might) but from theatrical disrepute (as moralists after Plato's injunctions against the unruly poet-performer undoubtedly would). The result was, as Fousekis so beautifully describes, a reluctant but steady shift in her understanding of resilient themes in the history of women's leadership and grassroots activism, as well as of herself as a daughter, scholar, and teacher. Her own transformation is now echoed in her classrooms, where her students' performances bring them into equally dangerous close proximity to history.

The politics of oral history performance are critical, intimate, and felt, what Madison calls a "politics of the near." Madison began her work as a Fulbright scholar in Ghana teaching literature through performance. Her students' performances spiraled outwards into what eventually became a public performance enacting contested perspectives on the Ghanaian "Trokosi" ritual of secluding young females in temple-shrines in reparation for crimes committed by male members of their families. The arguments that surround the Trokosi ritual draw on international human rights agendae, problems in global economics, and long-standing religious and cultural traditions. Far-reaching in its implications, the students' work nonetheless began close to the bone of their own histories and commitments. The final performance, *Is it a Human Being or a Girl?*, grew out of the symbolic staging of literary texts that expanded concentrically to encompass urgent social issues. Moving betwixt-and-between literary texts, personal and interview narratives, local debates, and global critique, Madison found a legion of possibilities for political performance—and a politics of performed possibility:

> The performer, beyond bringing movement and sound to words and flesh to feeling, opens literature to the possibility of the hidden. And, within this possibility, lies the potential for political *investment*. This political investment is of a very particular kind. It is a politics of the *near*. It is intimate and close because it circles from the boundaries of the text into our inner world. It moreover brings into focus the regulating factors governing our day-to-day lives and our personal destinies. It also puts our lives and destinies into question. Performance opens the secrets of literature because it invites embodied comparisons between undercurrents that constitute operations of power in the literary imagination and undercurrents that constitute operations of power in our lived experience. The read but unnamed and the lived but unnamed are present in the text and in life, but are often only tenuously or too partially realized. Performance promises engagement with what is otherwise hidden, oblique, or secret. This is a political enterprise.

The final performance left open the question of whether the Trokosi ritual is ultimately right or wrong. It circulated around a central gap: the unanswerable question, the single question leading to more questions, embodied in the figure of the ethnographer/recorder who repeatedly states: "I need to ask more questions." The ethnographer's presence heightens the reflexivity of the performance as itself an inquiry into "the read but unnamed and the lived but unnamed" politics of the ritual. In the process of excavating the "unnamed," however, the convictions that have kept it buried become evident—and the performance becomes full of the evanescent beauty of contrary beliefs.

Laurie Lathem also struggled with the representational value of oral history performance. As a playwright teaching playwriting, Lathem confronted the ethical, political, and artistic difficulties of translating oral histories into compelling dramatic forms. While Fousekis makes the painful crossing from text to performance through scissors—and the sudden discoveries that could then be made through juxtaposition, Lathem encourages her playwrighting students to abandon their original interview narratives altogether in an effort, paradoxically, to respond to them more fully. Most of the students participating in Lathem's Interview Project at the Berkeley Repertory Theatre had never before talked with an old person at any length. Expecting a lesson in crafting plays, they found themselves cast in the strange adventure of soliciting tales from people they'd previously pass by without a second look—and then, in the interview process, seeing them become something like celebrities before their very eyes. Lathem conveys the students' excitement and enthusiasm, as well as their ready, resistant ethics (one student wonders: "who am I?" to mess with someone else's story?). While she draws them into writing plays that rely on distinguishing between the interview subject and the "main character," they struggle to remain faithful to their interviewees' worlds and words. Eventually, Lathem notes, "somewhere between the interviews and the monologues we were now watching, the line between listening and creating had been crossed. Could anyone say where that line existed? . . . Before any writing had officially begun, the question had already been raised: whose stories were these?" The stories were and were not the students' "own." Nor were they, by any measure of textual fidelity, the interviewees'. The students' final performances realized the gap between the interviewees' stories and their own re-creations, to some extent dispossessing either student or interviewee of exclusive rights and creating something more than either might privately "own." In the end, the students' plays dramatized the incorporation of another's perspective into each of their own and, in turn, the expansion of their own to reflect another's.

For the interviewees who then became witnesses to their stories transformed through the listening/writing process, the final performances were acts of powerful confirmation of their respective histories, alive now in the memories and imaginations of a younger generation. Both the older and younger people reveled in recognition across generations. As Lathem notes, the community-building she sought began—and could have stopped—the moment the students walked into the senior center. But as Lathem, and many of the other authors in this volume suggest, the politics of oral history performance are not unidirectional. Indeed, the most significant effects of this work may have occurred through the "doubling back" of the performance on the students whose worlds—and eyes—opened in ways beyond compare.[23]

Similarly, it is unclear in Rouverol's work who benefited most—the North Carolina Anson County prisoners who crafted their stories into the performance, "Leaves of Magnolia: The Brown Creek Life Review Project for Young People," or the "at-risk" youths brought in to see and hear the performance. Rouverol describes in reflection, fieldnotes, excerpts from the script, and various responses to the performance, a performance process fraught with risk for all involved—for the inmates who risked power-sharing through narrative exchange, honesty and trust otherwise barred from the defensive rituals of their everyday lives, and moral inquiry into the consequences of their actions; for the interviewers/workshop leaders whose relatively weak authority made them vulnerable to challenge from the inmates and to the power of a penal system that would unpredictably require changes in the project (by preventing inmate-performers from participating and barring the initial, intended audience from attending); and for the young audience members who not only could see themselves mirrored in the inmates' storied lives but who were also literally incorporated into the performance in an interactive section that put their bodies on the same line the inmates walked. Integrated into the performance rather than positioned as, for instance, a follow-up Q&A, this section allowed young audience members to perform questions of criminal consequence *with* the inmate-performers. In the heat of these few moments of exchange, their lives became/could become interchangeable with those of the incarcerated men. In "Leaves of Magnolia," performance pushed risk and reflexivity to their respective limits, generating *real possibilities* for change.

Both Eisner and Case are oral historian/performers trying to convey, at least in part, what it means to perform oral history. Both write "towards" loss, understanding loss as a defining link between oral history and performance. When I saw Case perform "Tic(k)"—the short, one-person performance she presents here—at the Oral History Association conference in Durham, North Carolina in 2000, I looked around and also saw audience members stunned with sudden, welling tears. A sometimes playful, pointed collage that joins recollection of her grandfather's death with that of three elderly male interviewees, "Tic(k)" not only brings to the surface the mortal stakes of oral history (catch them before they die, record those libraries before they burn) but deeper bans against not only mourning those who have died but *feeling* loss, *wanting* to mourn. In the fleeting passage of performance, Case underscores both the speed with which lives pass and the living intimacies of interview-performances generally "put away" with archival materials. These are not stored in file drawers, however, but in the bodies of interviewers who become, in the interview process, "like" granddaughters, sons and daughters, mothers, fathers, and friends who remember loss, whose work is testimony to those who have passed but who are, in the end, often left with profound desire and pain. Performance is always about to disappear. It is its peculiarly magical "now you see it, now you don't!" quality that draws us to it in the first place. But it is also its vital ephemerality that draws death close and, in this case, invites remembering not only lost lives but losing them.

Rivka Eisner and her interview-subject have worked together so intensively now that indeed they have become like sisters. A Vietnamese national living in the United States, "Chị Tôi" (or "big sister") performs with Eisner a familial connection from which she had been effectively barred by the Vietnamese–American war: on the eve of her birth, her father left their home in the South to fight and eventually die in the North; her mother was forced underground and then eventually to the North, leaving her infant daughter behind. Chị Tôi's story is a history of loss and separation; it is also a story of lost history—of a past that came to her in whispers, scraps, reported discourse, the remains of a charred diary, and a few family photographs. Her interview performances and Eisner's subsequent re-performances may be immediate but they are not unmediated. In this case, "liveness" means articulating the multiple layers of translation and craft that make up (for) memory.

Eisner's aesthetic becomes one of "doubling." At its most basic level, performance is a repetition. It is a *doing again of what was once done*, repeating past action in the time of acting. Because the repetition occurs in time, it differs from the original to the extent that any one moment differs from another. Judith Butler has theorized the powerful, social-disciplinary constraints on the everyday performance of gender as "performativity." But in the time of embodied performance, even the heteronormative compulsion to repeat the "corporeal style" of gendered identities can never be exact.[24] It is riddled with error and so, indeed, with cost. *Performativity* in the material act of *performance*, Elin Diamond argues, reveals performativity for what it is: the reiteration of gendered codes so practiced and rehearsed as to become, for all intents and purposes, invisible (Diamond, 5). Performing performativity makes the invisible—gender discourses and the disciplinary stratagems that secure their repetition—visible.[25] Eisner, among others, elaborates the twice-behavedness of performance, going beyond even repetition-with-a-difference toward the more radical stance of doing two, often disparate things at once, magnifying the differences performativity would quiet.

Eisner opens up the gap between the "original" and its repetitions, understanding each as differential repetitions that she stages simultaneously. Accordingly, each repetition differs not only from prior instantiations but from each other. Eisner and Chị Tôi's worlds ricochet and rebound off of each other. Eisner doubles Chị Tôi's story in her own words and original movement. She doubles Chị Tôi's father's story in Chị Tôi's recorded translation and then again in her own syncopated echo. Eisner effectively doubles up the force of Chị Tôi's story by putting her body behind it—corroborating it in the collaborative creation and presentation of a usable (if double also in the sense of torn in two) tale of a broken family in a broken nation.

Locked in narrative identification with Chị Tôi, Eisner doesn't pretend to "be" Chị Tôi in performance. She doesn't "double" her in the sense of providing a mirror image. On the contrary, she works the hinges of their relationship and in Chị Tôi's story, seeking a likeness that travels across and between bodies, histories, and cultures—breath to breath and bone to bone—without assimilating one to the other or, in Salverson's words, creating a "totalizing 'we.' " This is one version, as Eisner explains, of the work of the interviewer-performer as a witness. What finally distinguishes Eisner and Chị Tôi, and draws them even more closely together, is that while Chị Tôi performs as a witness to a war-torn history, Eisner performs as a witness to Chị Tôi's performance: she relays in stark movement, symbol, and a symphonic layering of her own voice with the many voices that make up Chị Tôi's, what it may mean to put flesh to ghosts.

Michael Gordon collaborated with the professional company Theatre X to develop what he explicitly calls a "labor play" based on the oral histories of members of the United Food and Commercial Workers Local P-40 who participated in the twenty-eight-month strike at the Patrick Cudahy meatpacking plant in Milwaukee in the late 1980s. Drawing on the long tradition of WPA theater projects and "newspaper theater," Gordon positions the play as a public forum for renewing and revising public knowledge. His specific aim is to stimulate "public discussion about such important issues as attacks on unions, plant closings, job loss, and declining living standards." Accordingly, the play, *The Line*, became a dramatic critique of the foreclosures of dominant ideology on local memory. Gordon's critical leverage importantly comes "from below," from the strikers' own sense of betrayal and broken faith. In the course of the interviews, the interviewees reflected on their class position and challenged the alleged benevolence of the free enterprise economy in which they and their families had invested lifetimes of labor and yet which, in the end, betrayed them. *The Line* is a counter-narrative. It contradicts prevailing cultural scripts in which workers exchange dedication for job security and just rewards and in which the Cudahy workers had initially, faithfully played their designated roles. Pressing an alternative against a dominant version of history, *The Line* indeed stimulated discussion of what went wrong and what should be righted. It also proceeded to right history, not only by elaborating the workers' points of view—often buried as they were under official representations—but by literally giving the workers the last, angry word.

Touchable Stories, the Boston-based community arts group Shannon Jackson explores, expands the terrain of oral history performance from the stage to the interactive spaces of installations and "living mazes" that focus on common ground issues of ethnic and class difference. Locating these installations in the heart of Boston communities in which interviewers may have spent as much as a year living and listening, *Touchable Stories* creates what Jackson calls "relational field[s]": spaces that manifest history in the interactions of community members around material artifacts/art objects that resemble as much as they diverge from the "real." Inviting the co-presence of community members, these events nonetheless expressly refuse to fetishize what might otherwise be presumed to be the special authenticity of preserved objects, places, and voices. As Jackson explains, "the anonymous hands, disembodied voices, shadowed bodies, miniatures, dolls, scrims, tapes, and videos" that make up *Touchable Stories'* installations:

> resist literality and testify to the multiple technologies available to enable a moment of human connection. If this is "presence," it is one that is explicitly aware of its own production and unafraid to present a sense of discontinuity in the act of remembering. Together, *TS*'s oral performances illustrate the indirect, roundabout work of tangible story-telling.

For Jackson, *Touchable Stories* positions speakers and listeners in environments that induce "infrastructural memory": awareness of a shared material relation and the operations of difference in a specific context that may, through the "indirect, round-about work of tangible story-telling," help to form partial collectivities.

Working his or her way through the radical contextuality of *Touchable Stories'* installations, the witness is the performer, acting in the most pedestrian ways to nego-tiate a corner, open secret drawers, wind up a toy, even trash or "write over" conven-tionally untouchable (in every sense of the word—for gazing only, sacrosanct) artworks. The tactility and motility of *Touchable Stories'* work makes it, above all, an occasion for *poiesis*: for *making* memory, history, meaning and community in response. It is a dispersed interpretive context, spatializing the need beyond dialogic exchange for installations of other kinds, for installing new memories or re-remembering a past that once was or could have been, and now defines ways of being and acting in communal relation. *Touchable Stories* says history begins *here*. Touch its resonant forms. Recognize your place in its felicitous shadows and shapes. Tell it what to do *now*. And begin.

Notes

1. All the essays in this volume are original contributions (Gordon's essay, "Memory and Performance in Staging *The Line*," is a revision of an earlier publication). Other impor-tant published work on oral history performance includes the special issue of *The Oral History Review* (1990) dedicated to oral history-based performance (essays by Della Pollock, Shaun S. Nethercott and Neil O. Leighton, and Chris Howard Bailey, and Pam Schweitzer on "Reminiscence Theatre" in Britain). On how performance is being engaged in other fields, see also Dwight Rogers, Paul Frellick, and Leslie Babinski's experimentation with performance in their efforts to improve the experiences of first-year teachers.

2. Other work that is more directive for practice and that has been critical to a variety of community-based projects includes Augusto Boal, *Theatre of the Oppressed* and *Games for Actors and Non-Actors*, and Michael Rohd, *Theatre for Community, Conflict, and Dialogue*.

3. Following, directly and indirectly, Dwight Conquergood's 2002 mandate for performance as activist research.

4. See Phelan on her powerful insight into the afterlife of performances that disappear into the processes of "reckoning."

5. See Schrager's fundamental insight: "What the oral historian does is to provide a new context for the telling of mainly preexistent narrative" (78–79).

6. See the definitional framework Bauman offers in the title essay in *Verbal Art as Performance* as well his complementary perspective in *Story, Performance, and Event*.

7. Conquergood charts a course in performance studies from *mimesis* to *poiesis* to *kinesis*. He celebrates "the restless energies and subversive powers of kinesis," taking up de Certeau and Renato Rosaldo's respective efforts to put "'culture into motion'" (Conquergood, 1998, 31; quoting Rosaldo, 91).

8. See Cvetkovich's powerful discussion of interviewing lesbian participants in the AIDS activist group, ACT UP. Intrigued by the radical potential of oral history to "help create the public culture that turns what seems like idiosyncratic feeling into historical experience," Cvetkovich is also troubled by the methodological power of the interviewer/ author to reveal intimacies as well as, in some cases, to maintain silence (166).

9. See Madison "That Was My Occupation."

10. In his foreword to Barbara Myerhoff's *Number Our Days*, Victor Turner describes Myerhoff's sense of "our species as *Homo narrans*, humankind as story-teller, implying that culture in general—specific cultures, and the fabric of meaning that constitutes any single human existence—is the 'story' we tell about ourselves" (xv). Myerhoff claims "The tale certifies the fact of being and gives sense at the same time. Perhaps these are the same, because people everywhere have always needed to narrative their lives and worlds, as surely as they have needed food, love, sex, and safety" (271). Turner extends this understanding in later work, defining humankind as *Homo performans*: "If man is a sapient animal, a toolmaking animal, a self-making animal, a symbol-using animal, he is, no less, a performing animal, *Homo performans*, not in the sense, perhaps, that a circus animal may be a performing animal, but in the sense that man is a self-performing animal—his performances are, in a way, *reflexive*, in performing he reveals himself to himself" (*The Anthropology of Performance*, 81).

11. Answering to some extent Alcoff's landmark essay, "The Problem of Speaking for Others."

12. I want to note but cannot begin to encompass in this brief introduction the vast literature on witnessing and memory that grounds, extends, and challenges Oliver.

13. For complementary work on the performance of autobiography see e.g., Lynn C. Miller, Jacqueline Taylor, and M. Heather Carver, eds., *Voices Made Flesh: Performing Women's Autobiography*; the special issue of *Women and Performance* 10.19–20 (1999) devoted to performing autobiography, and e.g., Anne Davis Basting, "'God is a Talking Horse': Dementia and the Performance of Self"; Rena Fraden on Rhodessa Jones' powerful Medea Project; Jonathon Kalb, "Documentary Solo Performance: The Politics of the Mirrored Self"; Chris Anne Strickling, "Actual Lives: Cripples in the House," and Rosemarie Garland Thomson, "Staring Back: Self-Representation of Disabled Performance Artists."

14. See e.g., Susan C. Haedicke and Tobin Nellhaus, eds., *Performing Democracy: International Perspectives on Urban Community-Based Performance*; Eugene van Erven, *Community Theatre: Global Perspectives*; and e.g., Linda Frye Burnham, "Reaching for

the Valley of the Sun: The American Festival Projects *Untold Stories*"; Sonja Kuftinec, "[Walking Through A] Ghost Town"; and Diana Taylor, " 'You are Here': The DNA of Performance."

15. See Schrager.

16. See Bal, Crew, and Spitzer, eds., *Acts of Memory*. This perspective is certainly influenced by the Bakhtinian "revolution" in thinking about voice as dialogically composed at the intersection of any number of often conflicting discursive contexts.

17. For important critique of Smith's work, see Kondo; for helpful elaboration, see Denzin, 89–105.

18. See also Salverson 1996, 2000.

19. Note the grassroots history of such work in companies like Tale Spinners in San Francisco (thanks to Mercilee Jenkins for this reference) and the Roadside Theatre out of Appalshop in Whitesburg, Kentucky. Note also the recent success of *The Exonerated*, by Jessica Blank and Erik Jensen, at The Culture Project in New York. The play, based on interviews with sixty people who had spent from two to twenty-two years on death row before being exonerated for crimes they did not commit, featured a rotating cast of celebrity actors in "readers' theatre" style. Studs Terkel's work has, of course, often been called into voice and production, perhaps most notably in Derek Goldman's adaptation of Terkel's *Will The Circle Be Unbroken?: Reflections on Death, Rebirth, and a Hunger for a Faith* at the Steppenwolf Theatre in Chicago, 2004.

20. Correlating to Richard Schechner's infamous assertion, following on Victor Turner's sense of the "subjunctive" nature of ritual, that "sometimes—especially in the theater—it is necessary to live as if 'as if' 'is' " (Schechner, xiii).

21. For a complementary perspective, see Madison on "Performance, Personal Narratives, and the Politics of Possibility."

22. As an interesting corollary, see Tim Raphael's alternative pedagogy for pursuing issues in the history of white supremacy. Based in part on Hayden White's sense of the analogous relation between writing history and writing a play, Raphael explains: "By underscoring the similarities of the tools and techniques employed by historians and writers of theatrical 'fiction,' students would, I hoped, begin to develop a critical stance toward the implied inevitability of the historical narratives they encountered. By situating historical writings within a field of multiple narrative possibilities, I hoped to stimulate students to imagine their writing as an installment in an ongoing dialogue out of which historical 'truth' emerges as a contingent product of a contestational process waged between competing discourses" (127–128).

23. For a complementary/alternative pedagogy, see Armstrong, 2000.

24. See Butler 1991 and 1993.

25. On "doubling," see also Pollock (1999), particularly ch. 4, "Secrets/Doubles."

Works Cited

Alcoff, Linda. "The Problem of Speaking for Others." *Cultural Critique* 20 (1991): 5–32.

Anzaldua, Gloria and Cherrie Moraga, eds. *This Bridge Called My Back: Writing by Radical Women of Color.* New York: Kitchen Table Press, 1983.

Armstrong, Ann Elizabeth. "Paradoxes in Community-Based Pedagogy: Decentering Students through Oral History Performance." *Theatre Topics* 10.2 (2000): 113–128.

Bal, Mieke, Jonathon Crewe, and Leo Spitzer, eds. *Acts of Memory: Cultural Recall in the Present.* Hanover, NH: Dartmouth College, 1999.

Basting, Anne Davis. " 'God is a Talking Horse': Dementia and the Performance of Self." *TDR: The Drama Review* 45.3 (2001): 78–94.

Bauman, Richard. *Story, Peformance, and Event: Contextual Studies of Oral Narrative.* Cambridge: Cambridge University Press, 1986.

———. *Verbal Art as Performance.* Prospect Heights, IL: Waveland Press, 1977.

Boal, Augusto. *Games for Actors and Non-Actors.* New York: Routledge, 1992.

———. *Theatre of the Oppressed.* New York: Theatre Communications Group, 1985.

Burnham, Linda Frye. "Reaching for the Valley of the Sun: The American Festival Project's Untold Stories." *TDR: The Drama Review* 44.3 (2000): 75–112.

Butler, Judith. *Gender Trouble: Feminism and the Subversion of Identity.* New York: Routledge, 1990.

———. *Bodies That Matter: On the Discursive Limits of "Sex."* New York: Routledge, 1993.

Conquergood, Dwight. "Performance Studies: Interventions and Radical Research." *TDR: The Drama Review* 46.2 (2002): 145–156.

———. "Beyond the Text: Toward a Performative Cultural Politics." *The Future of Performance Studies: Visions and Revisions.* Ed. Sheron J. Dailey. Annandale, VA: National Communication Association, 1998, pp. 25–36.

Cvetkovich, Ann. "AIDS Activism and Public Feelings: Documenting ACT UP's Lesbians." *An Archive of Feelings: Trauma, Sexuality, and Lesbian Public Cultures.* Durham, NC: Duke University Press, 2003, pp. 156–204.

Denzin, Norman K. *Performance Ethnography: Critical Pedagogy and the Politics of Culture.* Thousand Oaks, CA: Sage, 2003.

Diamond, Elin, ed. *Performance and Cultural Politics.* New York: Routledge, 1996.

Fraden, Rena with Angela Y. Davis. *Imagining Medea: Rhodessa Jones and Theatre for Incarcerated Women.* Chapel Hill, NC: University of North Carolina Press, 2001.

Frisch, Michael, ed. Special Issue: "Oral History Theatre and Performance." *The Oral History Review* 18.2 (1990).

Haedicke, Susan C. and Tobin Nellhaus, eds. *Performing Democracy: International Perspectives on Urban Community-Based Performance.* Ann Arbor: University of Michigan Press, 2001.

Jerome, Judith and Leslie Satin, eds. Special Issue: "Performing Autobiography." *Women and Performance* 10.19–20 (1999).

Kalb, Jonathon. "Documentary Solo Performance: The Politics of the Mirrored Self." *Theater* 31.3 (2001): 13–29.

Kaufman, Moisés and the Members of Tectonic Theater. *The Laramie Project.* New York: Random House, 2001.

Kondo, Dorinne. "(Re)Visions of Race: Contemporary Race Theory and the Cultural Politics of Racial Crossover in Documentary Theatre." *Theatre Journal* 52 (2000): 81–107.

Kuftinec, Sonja. "[Walking Through A] Ghost Town: Cultural Hauntologie in Mostar, Bosnia-Herzegovnia or Mostar: A Performance Review." *Text and Performance Quarterly* 18.2 (1998): 81–95.

Kuhn, Annette. *Family Secrets: Acts of Memory and Imagination.* London: Verso, 1995.

Madison, D. Soyini. "Performance, Personal Narratives, and the Politics of Possibility." *The Future of Performance Studies: Visions and Revisions.* Ed. Sheron J. Dailey. Annandale, VA: National Communication Association, 1998, pp. 276–286.

————. "'That Was My Occupation': Oral Narrative, Performance, and Black Feminist Thought." *Exceptional Spaces: Essays in Performance and History*. Ed. Della Pollock. Chapel Hill, NC: University of North Carolina at Chapel Hill Press, 1998, pp. 319–342.

Miller, Lynn C., Jacqueline Taylor, and M. Heather Carver, eds. *Voices Made Flesh: Performing Women's Autobiography*. Madison, WI: University of Wisconsin Press, 2003.

Myerhoff, Barbara. *Number Our Days*. New York: Simon and Schuster, 1978.

Oliver, Kelly. *Witnessing: Beyond Recognition*. Minneapolis: University of Minnesota Press, 2001.

Phelan, Peggy. *Unmarked: The Politics of Performance*. New York: Routledge, 1993.

Pollock, Della. *Telling Bodies Performing Birth*. New York: Columbia University Press, 1999.

Raphael, Tim. "Staging the Real: Breaking the 'Naturalist Habit' in the Representation of History." *Theatre Topics* 9.2 (1999): 127–139.

Rogers, Dwight, Paul Frellick, and Leslie Babinski. "Staging a Study: Performing the Personal and Professional Struggles of Beginning Teachers." *Dancing the Data*. Ed. Carl Bagley and Mary Beth Cancienne. New York: Peter Lang, 2002, pp. 53–69.

Rohd, Michael. *Theatre for Community, Conflict, and Dialogue*. Portsmouth, NH: Heineman, 1998.

Salverson, Julie. "Change on Whose Terms? Testimony and an Erotics of Injury." *Theater* 31.3 (2001): 119–125.

————. "Anxiety and Contact in Attending a Play about Land Mines." *Between Hope and Despair: Pedagogy and the Remembrance of Historical Trauma*. Ed. Roger J. Simon, Sharon Rosenberg, and Claudia Eppert. New York: Rowman and Littlefield, 2000, pp. 59–74.

————. "Performing Emergency: Witnessing, Popular Theatre, and the Lie of the Literal." *Theatre Topics* 6.2 (1996): 181–191.

Schechner, Richard. *Performance Theory* (New York: Routledge, 1977, 1988).

Schrager, Samuel. "What is Social in Oral History?" *International Journal of Oral History* 4.2 (1983): 76–98.

Schweitzer, Pam. "Many Happy Retirements." *Playing Boal: Theatre, Therapy, Activism*. Ed. Mady Schutzman and Jan Cohen-Cruz. New York: Routledge, 1994, pp. 64–80.

Slim, Hugo and Paul Thompson. *Listening for a Change: Oral History and Community Development*. Philadelphia: New Society Publishers, 1995.

Smith, Anna Deavere. *Twilight Los Angeles, 1992: On the Road: A Search for American Character*. New York: Anchor, 1994.

————. *Fires in the Mirror: Crown Heights, Brooklyn and Other Identities*. New York: Anchor, 1993.

Strickling, Chris Anne. "Actual Lives: Cripples in the House." *Theatre Topics* 12.2 (2002): 143–162.

Taylor, Diana. "'You are Here': The DNA of Performance." *TDR: The Drama Review* 46.1 (2002): 149–169.

Thomson, Rosemarie Garland. "Staring Back: Self-Representations of Disabled Performance Artists." *American Quarterly* 52.2 (2000): 334–338.

Trinh, Minh-ha T. *Woman, Native, Other: Writing Postcoloniality and Feminism*. Bloomington, IN: Indiana University Press, 1989.

Turner, Victor. *The Anthropology of Performance*. New York: PAJ Publications, 1986.

Van Erven, Eugene. *Community Theatre: Global Perspectives*. New York: Routledge, 2001.

TWO

Trying To Be Good: Lessons in Oral History and Performance

Alicia J. Rouverol

Alicia Rouverol discusses the development of a performance event based on life review inter-views she conducted within the complex context of a medium-security prison. The Brown Creek Life Review Performance Project she describes layers the model of "shared authority" that has become commonplace among oral historians with scenes of brokering power with and among inmates; the very high stakes involved as inmates not only tell their stories but face the responsibility for incarceration that those stories reveal; and the intergenerational hope and risk involved in passing on those stories to young people on the edge of prison life. The Brown Creek Project documents a variety of small and large changes wrought by per-formance, changes that may not be guaranteed or exactly repeatable but that may unfold in the exchange of stories across generations and the prison threshold.

Since 1998, I have been at work on the Brown Creek Life Review Project at Brown Creek Correctional Institution, an all-male, medium-security facility that houses more than 800 inmates in Anson County, North Carolina. The project involved groups of inmates in "life review" storytelling sessions; formal interviews with me; and a performance project based on the stories of their lives for audiences of at-risk youth. More than twenty men participated in the project—Anglo, African American, and Hispanic—ranging in age from mid-20s to early-70s. I recorded their stories and collaborated with them on a script, titled "Leaves of Magnolia," that eight men performed at the prison in the spring of 1999 and again in 2001. The results were electrifying. The inmates had struggled to understand the events that had shaped their lives and led them to Brown Creek. They wrote letters home to address issues of abuse, which we later incorporated into the performance; some came forward wanting to make restitution for their crimes. At-risk youth from rural and urban settings in North Carolina who witnessed the performances were similarly affected. The youth wrote letters to the inmates, and spoke out to judges and program coordinators in the juvenile system about the lessons they had learned at the prison. In a taped session held a few weeks after the performance, these young people acknowledged their own life circumstances and challenged themselves and one another to steer clear of a place like Brown Creek.

In this essay, I examine the Brown Creek Life Review Project as what Linda Shopes calls an "ethnography of practice," as a kind of field study of performance that blurs distinctions between social and aesthetic practices. I explore these practices by recounting the development of the performance through various narrative strategies. The essay includes a brief history of the project and discussion of the theoretical frame of life review and performance; but primarily the work we pursued and accomplished will be illustrated through fieldnotes, interview excerpts and narrative, documentary accounts of key moments during the script development, rehearsals, and performances. By using this mix of narrative approaches—from theoretical analysis to edited interviews to ethnographic and narrative nonfiction writing—I attempt to show the multiple levels in which oral history and performance can be used in a life review performance project and what we can learn about doing ethnography in the process.

History of the Brown Creek Life Review Project

I first went to Brown Creek Correctional Institution in 1996 to conduct an oral history workshop for a group of prisoners enrolled in Brown Creek's education program. Kathy Walbert, my colleague at the Southern Oral History Program at the University of North Carolina at Chapel Hill, and I were invited to conduct the workshop by Winnie Bennett, a social worker and faculty member at Anson Community College (ACC), as part of a North Carolina Humanities Council-funded project titled "Building Community Through Art, Poetry, and the Humanities." Mark-Anthony Hines, a faculty member at ACC and an instructor at the prison, agreed to facilitate our presentation.[1] On a cold March day, with a high wind whipping across the yard, I arrived at Brown Creek with Kathy. Joe Madaras, the head of corrections education at Anson Community College, took us down to the Chapel, where about twenty men, mostly white and African American, were waiting for us. Everyone was dressed in the same light brown uniform, long pants and short-sleeved shirts, with only their work boots or Nikes to claim a distinct identity. They sat facing us in school-style desks. Some had spiral notebooks and number two yellow pencils and scribbled furiously as we spoke. Others sat staring out of the window onto the yard.

The white cinder block walls pressed in on me when I stood up to talk. How to reach people who have good reason to not want to be reached? I talked about what inspired me most in oral history: life review, the process of reviewing our lives to make sense of our lives. I talked about how telling our stories can connect us to those who hear our stories. I spoke about a project by anthropologist Barbara Myerhoff, how the elderly people she interviewed in a Jewish American community in Venice, California, felt cut off from their past and disconnected from the future—and how reviewing their lives had helped them find some actual and symbolic continuity between them.[2] I suggested the men tape-record their stories and send them home to their families, to their children. I closed by reiterating a point Mark-Anthony Hines, our facilitator that day, had made at Brown Creek's commencement ceremony the previous term: "The mind cannot be imprisoned. The mind is free." I told them that our stories at least cannot be confined. A number of the men shifted uncomfortably in the hard chairs; one of the inmates, sitting directly opposite me at the back of the room, turned away, choking up.

Slowly the students began to raise their hands. "Not just our families," one inmate said, "but young people, so they don't land here at Brown Creek." The men kept raising their hands with new questions, ideas, and suggestions. "How would we handle equipment?" I asked Joe. When he described the inmates' limited access to the necessary tapes and tape recorders, I mentioned another project in the works: a collaboration with the Southern Oral History Program to develop a series of oral history performances based on archived interviews with grassroots women activists and leaders.[3] This led me to suggest that the inmates could write down their stories, then edit them to create a script. Mark-Anthony leapt at the idea. "Now you just set off a spark for me," he said, and everyone in the room laughed. More hands shot up: one man asked if we could send them materials, another asked if we could help them do a project there. Another man said, with a twisted grin: "I want to know how do you keep a project like that going on the inside, where every day they're trying to grind you down . . ." And then, as if to prove the point, Joe announced we were out of time, and that the yard would be closing soon.

As we walked out, the men flanked us on either side, barely enough room for us all on the narrow stretch of sidewalk leading out of Education. It was bitterly cold; I pulled my coat around me for warmth. The men walked with us the entire way out. It was clear they wanted to keep contact.

Over the next year, I went on to conceive the Brown Creek Life Review Project, working with Winnie Bennett and Mark-Anthony Hines to secure grant support from the North Carolina Humanities Council, all of us working with Joe Madaras to secure preliminary approval from the prison. Nearly two years later, in January 1998, I returned to Brown Creek to initiate the project. Returning to Brown Creek marked the continuation of a journey that took five years and three different groups of inmates to complete.[4] The play we developed, *Leaves of Magnolia: The Brown Creek Life Review Performance Project*, focused on the men's lives prior to Brown Creek, the experiences that led to their incarceration, as well as the experience of incarceration itself. We used the central metaphor of a tree, a magnolia, which never loses its leaves, as a reminder to the inmates that their identities—even in incarceration—could never be fully stripped away.

The project began under the auspices of Mark-Anthony Hines' public speaking course at the prison, which Mark-Anthony and I co-taught in the spring of 1998. The course included instruction in public speaking, but focused primarily on taped group storytelling sessions. The following fall and spring semesters, I teamed up with Marlene Richardson, a community theater director, who also taught in the Anson County schools, and Joe Madaras, on the days when Marlene couldn't make it.[5] For months Marlene, the men, and I slogged through the process of creating the performance in a class we held weekly at Brown Creek. I combed the transcripts from the previous semester that had been prepared by an SOHP transcriber, pulled out what seemed to me the strongest, most compelling narratives, and created the bare bones of a script. The men wrote additional narratives, and drafted letters and poetry for inclusion. Some of the students improvised new scenes, which I taped, transcribed, and brought back to the classroom in the form of a revised script. Two years later, in the spring of 2001, working with Marlene and another group of inmate-students, I would resurrect the script, altering it to meet the demands of a younger audience (see figure 2.1).

In March and again in May 2001, at-risk youth from rural and urban settings in North Carolina were granted permission to witness the final performances of "Leaves

Figure 2.1 Rehearsal with inmates at Brown Creek Correctional Institution, March 2001. Photo by Cedric N. Chatterley.

of Magnolia: The Brown Creek Life Review Performance Project for Young People." Marcia Morey, 14th District Court Judge, took Durham youth twice into the prison to see "Leaves of Magnolia." She commented, months later: "The inmates' performance sparked a revolution in the souls of all of us who experienced it . . . To hear, see and feel [eight] inmates talk about abuse in their childhood, their search for love and belonging, their first encounters with the law, to life in prison facing 'roguing,' shanks [knives], and loneliness, had more of an impact on our youth than any judge in any courtroom could ever dream of." Clearly life review was critical to this "revolution," but it was performance that carried the spark.

Life Review, Oral History, and Performance

People often ask me—as did the inmates at Brown Creek—what life review is and how it differs from oral history. A term coined by gerontologist Robert N. Butler in the early 1960s, "life review" is the process by which individuals assess and make meaning of their lives through the kind of retrospective reflection enabled by story: by searching for a sequence and momentum from which one might derive driving values and pivotal experiences. A decade later, anthropologist Barbara Myerhoff picked up on Butler's work and undertook a study that broke open the field. In her classic work, *Number Our Days*, she explored the lives of elderly Jewish-Americans in Venice, California. Her narrators—pre-World War II immigrants from Eastern Europe—saw themselves as heirs to a culture that had been extinguished by the Holocaust. Yet they also felt culturally and socially separated from the next generation, since their own children had moved solidly into mainstream American life.

In 1996, when I first went to Brown Creek, I found a population not dissimilar in key ways. The men were cut-off from their previous lives, isolated from family and community, and faced a future they could not envision. Most commonly used with the elderly, life review has rarely been used as an intervention with younger individuals facing life crises.[6] Yet, to the extent that reviewing one's life implies change based on new understanding, it seems particularly well-suited even to young lives in crisis.[7] I began to wonder: why couldn't life review be used to help these men constructively address their life circumstances? And why couldn't their stories be a vehicle to help young people do the same? In taking on this project, I wanted to understand how narrative shapes our understanding of our experience, and how "story-ing" our lives can help us to reshape the direction of our lives, as psychologists George Rosenwald and Richard Ochberg have claimed.[8]

Life review posits that talking about one's life can change one's life. It assumes that, as a dialogic process often conducted in a public setting, it will have an impact on both the teller and the listener. But change does not come readily. Some individuals resist the necessary extent of reflection, some are simply not ready to address or process difficult life experiences.[9] Yet even those inmates on the project who did not claim that their lives had been significantly changed by our sessions found the process "therapeutic." The therapeutic dimensions of life review make some people in the field of oral history very nervous; "we're not therapists," as least one oral historian has been heard to exclaim.[10] And we are not (which is why I often team up with social workers, as I did on this project). In some cases, we don't know, and perhaps never will know, the full impact of the deep listening to which we typically aspire; and this may be just as true for the Brown Creek Life Review Project as other such endeavors.[11]

Oral history, on the other hand, involves the more general process of gathering, by taped-recorded means, reminiscences, interpretations, and accounts of the recent past. Its aim is historical in nature.[12] My colleagues at the Southern Oral History Program frequently asked me what "historical question" I was addressing in my work at Brown Creek. I responded by saying that I was documenting the experience of incarceration in an all-male, medium-security facility in rural North Carolina at the close of the twentieth century. The one-on-one interviews I conducted with the men— what might be considered standard oral history interviews—helped me to fill in the inmates' life histories. These taped sessions also became a forum for broader discussion of the prison experience—everything from homosexuality to race and the role of religion in the prison system. I often asked about prison reform, rehabilitation, and restitution. In this project, then, I relied on life review (taped group sessions in which the inmates reflected on key life events, from childhood through young adulthood, including turning points that led them to Brown Creek), as well as oral history (taped one-on-one interviews, in which the inmates offered more detailed life history information and answered specific questions about the experience of incarceration).

Some details about this particular interviewing process might prove useful.[13] Undertaking interviews in a prison setting differs from institution to institution. At Brown Creek, I had relative freedom. We conducted group sessions in our classroom in "Education," the area of Brown Creek designated for school courses. I conducted one-on-one interviews in any open classroom I could find—frequently without a guard in sight, though usually close by. I worried initially that the administration would want to screen the interviews, but they never did. Their primary concern was that I not address the inmates' crimes on tape, so that the prisoners would avoid self-incrimination. Yet the inmates often pursued the topic on their own, especially in the one-on-one interviews, talking in greater or lesser detail depending on their status. (Those not appealing their sentences, for instance, felt at liberty to speak much more openly about their crime.)

The taped group sessions, by contrast, developed a very different dynamic: I spoke far less on tape; Marlene—as co-facilitator—spoke much more, and she often challenged the men to address hard topics that I might not have addressed so easily, such as race and education in rural communities, or race in the judicial system. These sessions were not "life review" per se, as much as group storytelling sessions. They began on the topic at hand: one inmate's account of his early life or how he landed at Brown Creek; but they quickly led to heated, charged discussions—especially in the last semester, when the inmates knew they would be speaking to young people. The stakes were high. The men pressed one another on issues of guilt and innocence, or the moral question of prison rings (black markets and the alliances and disagreements that evolve between inmates in the process). These taped sessions, many of them held just weeks before our final performance, offer some of the richest material of all. One inmate—Truman—was a kingpin in these discussions. He asked questions of his cohorts that neither Marlene nor I could ask, and they delivered for him.

Truman's story is one of the more remarkable tales I recorded. Now in his fifties, Truman was a self-acknowledged career criminal, in reform school by age six or seven, after his father left. He defines his life not by the time he's been outside, but by the years he's been inside. "I wanted to be exactly what I turned out to be," he says, "a criminal, a crook." Born into a "liquor house" and a family of church-goers, Truman criticized religious dogma in any shape or form. In fact, he opted not to participate in the final performance because he didn't see eye-to-eye with many of the others in the group for whom religion had been part of the answer to their struggles, not part of the problem. Nonetheless, he acted as a lightning rod for the entire crew, asking hard questions of his fellow inmates and holding them accountable for their actions. These kinds of exchanges, I think, simply would not have happened without life review as the frame for this project.[14]

From the start, I wanted to do this project as a collaboration with the student-inmates. With virtually all my oral history work, I team up with my interviewees to co-create the final products (exhibits, performances, books, etc.) based on the interviews we conducted together.[15] Collaborative oral history is based on the idea that power should and essentially does not reside solely in the hands of the interviewer, but is instead shared—a "shared authority." Oral historian Michael Frisch specifies his understanding of "shared authority" to the shared nature of an oral history interview. Folklorist Elaine Lawless advocates involving one's interviewees in the subsequent analysis of the interviews, arguing that authority should be shared beyond the interview itself. Ultimately, by my thinking, this sharing of authority should continue through all phases of our work with our interviewees.[16] Putting these concepts into practice meant treating the inmates as colleagues, using the same strategies I would use in any community in which I conducted fieldwork. Collaboration in a correctional setting is especially challenging, however, for any number of reasons, not the least of which is that the prison setting is all about power—who has it, who wields it, and what that means on a daily basis for all who live or work at the prison.[17] While I recognized that I was working in a setting in many ways defined by competition over power and control, I insisted on a peculiar kind of power not generally visible in prison power-bartering: the powerful right of each inmate to own their own stories, to determine how they would be seen and heard (especially against the grain of stereotypes and prison protocols), and to be the authority in and on their respective stories.[18]

I tried to share my own authority by soliciting their input on the script and the development of the performance; but in myriad ways the inmates often took authority. They began asserting control early on in the scriptwriting process. Once, when we were reviewing transcripts for possible inclusion, we began discussing something not addressed in the taped sessions (and therefore not included in the transcripts): the issue of prison visits by family, a painful topic for many. One of the inmates, Perez, stood up abruptly, left the room, then stepped back in. He cleared his throat, pulled at his belted pants as if to straighten himself, and then launched into a brilliant improvisation about "visitation" in a prison setting. He fumbled through a few lines about his experience of waiting for a family visit, then spoke poignantly about how difficult it is when your family leaves. Perez seized authority by moving beyond a textual approach—my approach, initially—to creating the performance. And improvisation, from then onward, became a strategy for the inmates to insert their own material into the script. One inmate, Fenton, claimed a different kind of power and control at each rehearsal by not bothering to learn his lines. He paraphrased them instead, which drove our director mad and both irked and entertained the rest of us. Yet another inmate, McCarl, ended up nearly dropping out during the rehearsal process, because, as he later put it, "I'm not gettin' my say. I need my story in here, in this play."[19]

As we moved from interviewing through analysis of the transcripts to creation of the script, the inmates increasingly began to take ownership of the project. In the classroom, and later before their audience, they asserted their authority as experts of their own stories and "assum[ed] responsibility for inventing themselves"—or in this case, re-inventing themselves.[20] In a taped evaluative session after the 1999 performance, one of the inmates acknowledged that he had never really taken responsibility for his crime until he had to read the lines of his own "script" week after week:

Ross: The most thing I liked about developing the script was the responsibility . . . Because at first I thought, "I just got caught. I wasn't wrong. I was just someone who got caught." Now as we started developing the script, I see where I messed up . . . No, I was wrong, I have to take responsibility for what I did. And maybe that's the most thing I liked about the script and telling my story. Not only telling it, but reading it—studying it over and over. I made a mistake here. Now I see where the ripple effect and things started to go wrong for me. And now, when you start reading that script: Now I can change, now I know where the problem was. I know what the problem is. Now I've got to go about solving it.[21]

Performance as a medium gave the inmates a degree of control they often found lacking in their everyday lives within the prison walls. In another sense, it also formalized a performative mode that many engaged in daily, on the yard or in the bunk areas, as a form of self-preservation. The inmates often talked about this off-tape; in a discussion about collaboration, held during that same taped evaluative session, one inmate, McCarl, recognized the degree to which "fabrication" in their daily lives had been a survival strategy. I include here the surrounding discussion to provide context for McCarl's comment and to raise broader points about a collaborative approach to life review and performance:

ROUVEROL: So the collaboration among yourselves. What about the part of collaborating with Mr. Madaras, Ms. Richardson, and myself? Because remember how we talked in class about how we were going to shape this project together?

McCARL: Well, I guess for one, I'd like to say the word, I guess you could say "trust" came in. Because really, all in all, there was certainly things that I was kind of doubtful. How would I say certain things toward you all, how would you all take it . . . ? But it went fairly well. You all okay with me.

DEU: Understanding goes a long, long way. When you understand more about somebody what they've been through, like in their life, you understand that person a whole lot better. Whether it be us, an inmate, or those who are incarcerated. How we relate to each other, and how you relate to others. And how you may relate to us, too. Because I had no idea of what conceptions you had of us before you came, or maybe even the first few times that you came.

ROUVEROL: So that knowing that I'd heard your stories, then, and maybe accepted your stories, or accepted you all?

DEU: Or maybe it brought some understanding—of us. Maybe it helped you see a different light, a different side. Where a lot of people who don't have contact unless they're family members, they just don't know that they have, and then they accept, stereotypes.

McCARL: With this [project] came opportunity to open up. You know what I'm saying? Because you can't just talk to anybody just like you want to, really. You've got to fabricate certain things. But you know, this gave me a chance to ask to say what was on my mind. People was actually listening to it.

ROUVEROL: To be heard.[22]

In this excerpt, the inmates describe outcomes of collaborative life review and performance I had not been aware of previously, but that were especially significant to them. To not have to fabricate in the classroom was key for many of the inmates, for whom surviving in a prison can require posturing among their cohorts. The inmates often commented that "if you weren't above, then you were below," literally and figuratively, in a prison environment. Increased trust, in a setting in which information is frequently used and abused, was another outcome of performing their stories for one another. Finally, "having their say" through performance enabled the inmates to feel understood or to be heard, or for McCarl, to "say what was on [his] mind." This comment takes on new meaning when we consider the events linked to his incarceration: "As far as my turning point, I guess I was the age of twelve, when I sort of felt didn't nobody love me no more." Later, he said, "I had a lot of stuff. By me holding back a lot of things it caused me to explode . . ."[23]

But the context of greater freedom and authority on a collaborative performance project of this kind also challenged the men. Questions of authority became increasingly tricky as we began rehearsals for the performance. Marlene, our performance director, had a tendency to bark directions at the inmates, which rankled them. I felt as though our collaboration was breaking down, and addressed the issue in a class session that proved to be a turning point. I explained that collaboration and reciprocity meant no one was on top here, that the process was lateral, and it required mutual respect and a measure of responsibility on all our parts. The complex web of power and authority in this performance project—the inmates' attempts at taking ownership during the scriptwriting process, as well as my own, occasional resistance to the demands collaboration made on me—are best explored through an edited excerpt from my fieldnotes. In the following excerpts, I address incidents that came up daily in the classroom as we set about creating the performance. As ethnographic accounts, they might also be considered illustrations of "ethnographies of practice."

Edited Fieldnotes:

Fenton's eyes were steel-blue. He had a way of sizing you up, his square jaw set until his face broke into a smile, then he'd throw back his head in laughter. When he spoke, he spoke deliberately. He often called inmates on their behavior when they didn't measure up. And he often called us on ours. You're on trial with these guys daily, and Fenton tried us most.

Our classroom was the site of those daily trials. And that site changed weekly, depending on the space available in Education. Education consisted of a series of low, red brick buildings, fenced off from the West Yard, where inmates congregated near their "blocks," or housing. Later we held rehearsal in Visitation, which was located closest to Master Control, so that visitors could enter the prison without passing through either the West or the East Yards. Everyone entering Brown Creek passed through security at Master Control. As you stepped inside the prison, the steel door clanged shut behind you with a resounding thud that Marlene and I never quite got used to.

One day we were in Visitation, closing in on our March 1999 performances. I was on the phone with Marlene, who was ill and wasn't sure she could make rehearsal. I grimaced, but didn't say anything at first. I knew Marlene had high demands on her teaching job, but it was hard for me when she couldn't make it and I had to go it solo in our classroom at Brown Creek. I tried to talk her into skipping school, suggesting she join us at the end of the day. She said she couldn't do that because her principal would be really upset if he learned about it. I set down the phone, returned to the circle of chairs where the inmates were running their lines. "I can't believe you suggested that," Fenton said. He shook his head in a kind of *tsk-tsk* motion. The men held me up to a high moral standard, and if I ever strayed, it bothered them—especially Fenton.

And then there was the time a few months earlier, when we struggled through rehearsal in the Electrical Room, with its exposed beams and wires—an especially uninspired setting, but the only classroom open that day. We'd begun the project in that room the year before, a painful reminder of how slowly we'd progressed. The men were tired, we were tired. Rehearsal was dragging. Ross sat hunched over the desk as he read his part, his dark broad hand draped over his shoulder. He was tapping his foot, shod in the bright high-top sneakers he often wore, distinguishing his family's relative wealth. He stumbled over one of his monologues, and Marlene said to him, "We've already got that bit about your family's farm and the hogs, can't we cut that?"

He turned to me, and said, "I *told* you to cut that out."

I tensed up. This wasn't the first time Ross had been sharp with me in class.

Everyone in class was silent.

Fenton looked over at me and said, "Are you going to let him say that?"

I took a stand with Ross that day—a turning point in our relationship—but only because Fenton had pushed me to do so.

I turned to Ross. "This was a lot of work. It took a lot to get this done, and we're not out of the woods yet."

"But are you going to make more of these changes?"

"Yes, but not until we're really done with all the tinkering," I said. And then I paused, exasperated, "You know, I'm not the slave here."

I was appalled after I said the words. This was the South after all, and the term isn't used lightly here, and for good reason. But there is this authority, chain-of-command concept in the prison that they all buy into. If someone isn't above (as I was trying not to be through collaboration), then that means you're below. Collaboration for some meant license to challenge authority, which for some meant license to disrespect.

Afterwards, as Marlene and I mounted the long flight of steps from Master Control to the parking lot, we talked about what transpired in class. The sun was low and long, a warm breeze swept between us. The prison yard below us was deserted at this hour; it was time for "the count," when every inmate must be accounted for. I felt depressed. I couldn't believe what I'd said to Ross, even if I hadn't intended to.

Marlene was saying what a good job McCarl had done, how he'd made a turn-around. McCarl was young, in his mid-twenties, of small build and dark-skinned. When he looked at you, his gaze pierced right through you. Bright but temperamental, he and Marlene often came to loggerheads. He had nearly dropped out months before. "*Why?*" he said to me in the hallway, the day we talked things out, "Why? Because I'm not gettin' my say. I need my story in here, in this play," he said, tapping his chest.

McCarl getting on board was good news indeed. Marlene brushed back a strand of hair as she spoke. She always wore fine pantsuits and colorful lipstick, refusing to let Brown Creek "institutionalize" her. "He's a good actor, really good, and I told him so this afternoon."

"Yeah," I said, "He used to get under your skin. The way Ross now gets under mine."

"Ross has too big a part," she said, and then went on to acknowledge that she too was feeling frustration toward him (a comment that reassured me somewhat). She said she liked McCarl a lot. "He's real straight. And Coulter." Coulter was one of the more quiet and sensitive young men.

"And Tabor," I added. He was the poet on our project.

She agreed. "And also that fellow—what's his name, in the chair beside Tabor?"

"Fenton?"

"Yeah," she said. "He's honest; he tells it straight."[24]

As I write this essay, I reflect again on the uncomfortable moments of this project.[25] How to share authority in ways that would honor the inmates, but how not to buy into the dynamic of prison authority that so defined their lives and often hampered the development of our performance project? I often struggled to engage with the men in ways that respected who they were as individuals, while remembering that as an instructor in that setting I was functioning as a teacher—someone who urges, supports, and demands the most of her students. I was scrupulous in my boundaries, which seemed essential to my relationship with the men. On days when I felt I "lost my cool," as I felt I did that day with Ross, I castigated myself for not handling the situation properly. (I eventually spoke individually with Ross, as Marlene later urged me, which helped us move toward a better working relationship.) Yet challenging moments like this would be faced by any instructor undertaking performance with a group of students whether they were inmates are not. The prison environment simply complicated the dynamics, requiring us to make authority a central topic of discussion, study, and constant negotiation.

Undertaking a performance project in a prison, though, *does* have particular constraints. The hurdles we faced—securing prison permissions for the 1999 performance, securing approval to bring in the at-risk youth, the bureaucratic realities of the prison setting—could not be ignored. Keeping the inmates engaged in a project this demanding took focused energy on our part, Marlene's and mine especially. In March 1999, just weeks before our first schedule performance, we faced our ultimate hurdle: securing permissions for a public performance of Leaves of Magnolia (see figure 2.2) and the participation of the youth. The prison superintendent insisted we hold our first performance as a screening for the administrations of both Brown Creek and Anson Community College, to determine the play's "suitability for young people." Apparently it proved safe enough and we were given approval to proceed with a second, more "public" performance. But several days prior to that second performance, we learned that neither the inmates' families nor the young

Figure 2.2 Question-and-answer period after *Leaves of Magnolia* performance at Brown Creek Correctional Institution, March 2001. Photo by Cedric N. Chatterley.

people could attend. (The superintendent claimed safety concerns as the primary reasons for denying the former; for the latter, he insisted the group selected was too young.) We were all devastated. I came away realizing that I had focused almost exclusively on my creative collaboration with the inmates, and not on my political collaboration with the administration.[26]

In the spring of 1999, after our two performances, I took a hiatus from the project. I felt burnt-out from working at the prison, and professional and personal demands called me away. I had mixed feelings about the prospects of our proceeding, and yet knew this experiment in life review and performance had not reached its full potential. True, we had had some real victories: two men came forward to address issues of sexual abuse from childhood and shared these experiences not only with their cohorts in the classroom but with family members at home. And two men came forward to make restitution for their crimes. Neither of these were outcomes I had anticipated. Transformations *had* occurred in this first phase of life review and performance for the "tellers," but what of the "told"? I felt we had to reach our intended audience or our project goal—change for the inmates, change for the youth—would not fully be achieved. Intuitively I sensed that, for the inmates, performance before their intended audience offered a key strategy for change, though I could not articulate the precise reason at the time. Barbara Myerhoff's work—the degree to which her narrators strengthened their sense of identity at a critical life juncture by, as she says, representing themselves to themselves—kept me going at this low point. And I knew, too, from working with Della Pollock, that the interactive, reflexive mix of perform- ance and audience engendered a certain synergy that would have an impact, even if I did not know precisely what those effects would be. Performing their stories for the young people, I sensed, would be the turning point.

By the fall of 2000, I took steps to resurrect the project. We had won some allies within the prison administration from the 1999 performance, and I hoped that with enough advance notice this time we might secure approval to bring in the youth. Joe Madaras seemed confident that we could, especially with more focused interac- tion with the administration. He was right. This time, I met with members of the administration several times before even setting foot in the classroom, securing their support far in advance of any potential performance. Marlene and I resumed work with a group of new and not-so-new students, and within three months—after inten- sive taped sessions—we had revised the script, moved directly into rehearsal, and the inmates were ready to perform. This final phase proved the most rewarding; this new group of students, combined with several "veterans" from the first phase, took their charge seriously. The veterans mentored their cohorts; new voices brought fresh energy and enthusiasm. Marlene joined me in many of the script development sessions as the inmates fought, literally, over how best to reach the young people. We lost some students to "the hole" once again ("the hole" is segregation where inmates are isolated from the rest of the population); some inmates were transferred. And the group sifted down to eight men in total. By March 2001, we had secured all the necessary permissions; we had prepared and solicited support from at-risk youth coordinators and prison administrators; we were ready to launch our final perform- ances of *Leaves of Magnolia: The Brown Creek Life Review Performance Project for Young People.*

What took place that March and again in May, when we did our final, command performance at the request of Thadis Beck, NC Secretary of Corrections, is best explored through another fieldnote excerpt, this one less fully edited or re-crafted for narrative coherence.[27] This excerpt is from "day one" of the March perform- ances; on each day, the inmates performed twice, to two different groups of young people.

Fieldnotes:

Wednesday, March 28. First day of performances. The night before was a late one for me. Still making phone calls. Talking with Cedric Chatterley, our photographer, and Kenny Dalsheimer, the videographer. Revising release forms, and making last minute arrangements with Joe Madaras and some of our at-risk youth coordinators, Larry Wallace and Jackie Wagstaff. Larry had gotten the letter from Judge Marcia Morey, requesting permission of Brown Creek's superintendent to bring in at-risk youth under the age of sixteen, and would be faxing it the next morning. Hallelujah!

We didn't know what would come of it, but it was still worth a shot. Jackie Wagstaff would be bringing kids with Martina Dunford on Wednesday. I was thrilled. It meant we'd have a decent audience. I heard from Larry Wallace that Jerome Allen would be bringing kids on Friday with him and Amy Elliott. It was looking good.

The next morning, on the 28th, Cedric picked me up and then we stopped at Kenny D.'s studio off E. Pettigrew Street. Nice weather at last. Clear, sharp. We drove down with Kenny in the back seat, Cedric driving, and me in the passenger's seat, trying to deal with the physical discomfort of pants that didn't fit. Cedric had no idea I was pregnant—God knows no one else on the project knew. I had to chat a bit to Kenny, which was wearing me out. The night before I'd had to get my comments together, finish the release forms, and have my husband make the last change on the music tape. Plus I was still trying to determine who was coming—still hadn't heard back from either *The Independent* or the Raleigh *News & Observer*. Both seemed unlikely. In any event, I was—as usual—pretty damn tired. But I rallied as we drove down. At Ellerbee, we stopped at a diner for Kenny to pick up a ham biscuit.

We arrived at Brown Creek and found no Marlene in the parking lot. Waited for a bit, then decided we should head on down. The day—the light—was brilliant. I tried to help carry the camera and video gear, but nothing too heavy. We went to Master Control. They spent probably ten minutes going through both Cedric's and Kenny's stuff, while I milled about. Marlene hadn't checked in yet, according to the officer. I squatted down to pick up some of the gear. "You okay?" one of the officers asked. My look of discomfort must have been severe.

In Visitation, the men were really pumped up. They had set up the chairs, and I worked with Bradley and Huff to create an aisle, some way to bring the boom box to my seat up front. They'd taped everything down, and without complaint re-taped everything so that I could have the box right beside me. People were running lines to themselves like "real actors." McCarl was standing alone a lot—it was his way, it seemed, to handle the pre-performance stress. Cedric was having a hey-day photographing in the back room. Marlene was running late, which was stressing me out a bit. We'd already gotten there late ourselves, due to my schedule plus the long check-in at Master Control. Joe was there, looking more than a little angst-ridden.

"How's it going?" I asked.

"Okay," he said, "though I've just called in one of my last cards, I think. The letter arrived, and I've learned that Jackie and Martina are definitely bringing kids under age 16. I just had to have a chat with the superintendent, and boy, did he chew me out. He said it was okay for today, but that he hadn't really given permission . . ."

Joe doesn't often look this stressed. He said the superintendent said that *he* wouldn't want *his* kids to see this. "But they're seeing worse on t.v. every day," Joe said. "This is not that bad." He just couldn't get the superintendent's frame of mind.

But, because of the judge's letter, and because Martina and Jackie were en route, there was nothing to be done.

"Could he still stop them at the gate?" I asked.

"If he wants to, he could stop them."

As it turned out Jackie and Martina were more than an hour late. I was climbing the walls. Marlene was in the back room by this time, keeping the men in tow, reassuring them mostly. Coleman and Chase, especially, and Ross. They were really pumped. Harlan Gradin, our program director from the Humanities Council, was already in the audience; and given his support of this project, and his expectations, I felt a lot of pressure.

I went in the back room, and ended up chatting with Marlene briefly. She told me not to worry; the performance would come off okay.

Martina and Jackie did at last arrive; we got them settled in. I went up to Master Control; and my first glance at the kids was almost as unnerving as my first glance at the inmates, the very first time I came to Brown Creek. You know when you're a little out of your league, when it's going to take time to find your way into a community. And we had a little more than an hour with these kids—not enough time, I was already feeling.

I greeted Martina, Jackie, and their colleague, Mohammed. The prison had set up some kind of screening device, or moved it away from the door, so that the kids could walk through it. I just wish Cedric could have shot that scene. I'll never quite forget it: the quintessential awkward youth, kids with jeans hanging down, tall kids, smaller kids, but every face avoided eye contact.

I spoke with Martina and Jackie about the photography and permissions to photograph the youth. They placed their court kids on the other side, away from the door, to avoid their being photographed. Jackie and Martina sat in the front row, just down from Marlene and me. But before we started up, I went out back and said to the men, "These kids don't make eye contact. Okay? You're going to have to really reach out."

Prior to this—prior to the young people's arrival—we had said grace, which Cedric photographed. I think Coleman said grace that day; I was holding Joe's hand and Coleman's too. It was lovely, very moving. My favorite moments are those, because it's when—really the only time—we all make physical contact. And even when we break, as we did afterwards, and there's a shift back into pre-performance jitters, there's still some kind of connection that has happened.

After my brief chat, I went out front; Joe and I agreed I should start. Did an okay first delivery welcoming folks. But it felt a bit strained; difficult to reach these kids, so I tried to change my language. Now, in retrospect, I wish I'd said more about the leaves of magnolia theme. But I hadn't wanted to get too heavy-handed about them needing to change their lives . . . I had to call Marlene from the back, practically. She spoke up eloquently, and the kids all listened. That's where speaking the same language makes a real difference. Joe said a few words, but not much at this juncture.

The performance went forward, and I felt this chill up my spine as the men came out. Heads down, serious; each of them really committed in his own way. That first performance was fantastic, almost flawless. Ross tended to repeat one line: "That's prison," which drove both Marlene and myself mad. And there was that flat moment between the two scenes in the last Act. But short of that it was strong. I watched the kids' faces: some of them sang along to the soundtrack, "Life" and "Ride or Die," especially. Smiles began to emerge. Faces that were closed began to open, paying closer attention.

Even the Q & A went well. These were the Durham kids. Jackie later described them to us when we were outside of Visitation: "One of these kids tried to light his parents on fire. Another one, his grandma is so scared of him, she locks her bedroom door every night." They weren't an easy group. But in comparison to the 3:00 p.m. group, they were peaches and cream, as we were to find out.

The performance ran just over an hour. Joe got up immediately afterwards and launched into a rap about how we could all leave now, but these inmates have to stay. I wanted to see the men come back and out, take a curtain call. Which they did, saying their names and the lengths of their sentences. It was quite powerful. The kids were freaked to learn how long their sentences were, especially, as we learned later, Huff's. We had some further discussion, the kids chatted with the inmates afterwards, and then the group had to be hustled out; the Anson Challenge Academy kids were headed in . . .

Initially, boredom, resistance, and fear marked the expressions of the young men and women who came to Brown Creek over five performances to watch *Leaves of Magnolia: The Brown Creek Life Review Performance Project For Young People*. We had, however, built in an interactive segment that began in this way:

Act Three

Turning the Corner: Making Meaning, Making Choices, Finding Alternatives

Narrator moves centerstage, right in front of the audience. Performers go to their seats, facing young people.

NARRATOR: Okay. All of these things we been saying are true. But they don't have to be true for you. We've got a thing or two to say about what we have learned here at Brown Creek—and then we want to hear from you. We been reviewing our lives, now we want you to review yours. Because you don't got to come to Brown Creek to learn what we learned. You can learn it on the other side of these walls.

Choices, it's all a matter of choices . . .

CHASE: One of the most important things coming up is your surroundings, your friends.

VICTOR: A seed can get planted regardless of what age you are. You don't have to be a child. And once that seed is planted . . .

DEU: It can be too late to turn back. I had pushed all my help away and I was just stuck out there.

DUSTY: And once you get stuck out there, you've got to find someone to throw a line to you.

Music ["Change is Gonna Come"] as Performers take their seats.

DUSTY: You know, I actually sit back here and think about these things now and know that it really didn't teach me nothing. I wanted to get that quick money, you know, quick schemes. I figured I'd get it and then go and finish school. Just let me get the money first . . . That's not really being a man. I see now that being a man is just doing the right things. Freedom is not doing what you want to do but making a choice to do the right thing.

Choices . . .

ALL PERFORMERS: It's all a matter of choices.

FENTON: It seems like a lot of us here at Brown Creek are here because we either: one, ran from manhood and just didn't want to confront it head on like we should have; or two, we had some gross misconceptions about what manhood actually was.

DEU: One thing to keep in mind, there is all sorts of barriers that seem to prevent some of us from being the man we want to be, especially African Americans and working class people. There are things out there that make us, force us, to run from manhood and do things contrary to what being a man is all about.

TRUMAN: One of the most formative experiences for me was when I realized there was a black person, there was a white person, and there was supposed to be a difference. There was none to me. Until I was caught up town in a certain section of town I wasn't supposed to be in. At that point, it became a challenge. You know, a game. Beating them by being up there and not being caught. And from that, I got a false sense of confidence of beating people and beating the system.

FENTON: But you know, this country that we live in if you are part of a certain socioeconomic spectrum the chances of you getting locked up sky rockets.

ROSS/RUDY: It's structured the same way with the crack cocaine and the powder cocaine. The white man uses a lot of cocaine—not to get into the race thing—but the black people, they're dealing and selling crack. You got these white cats over here, dealing and getting busted with the powder and they aren't getting hardly no time—that's how the government structures it. But you got these other cats over here getting busted for crack, doing serious time.

TRUMAN: That's a fact, that's a fact.

FENTON: And you know, you can't put it behind you. I don't care where you apply for a job, even at McDonald's, they're going to check your record. And I don't care how much education you have got—it helps and I am a champion of this Education program down here—but the truth be known we are all going to be convicts when we get out of here. Okay? We are going to be paying for this the rest of our life, just for that one mistake we made.

Choices . . .

ALL PERFORMERS: It's all a matter of choices.

FENTON [turning to a young person near him]: What are some of the choices—or situations—you're facing?

Bit by bit, hands shot up, a young man here, a young woman there. They asked the inmates about their experiences with gangs, their encounters with drugs and alcohol, about the role models they didn't have, and about what prison is really like:

> "What's wrong with reefer? You only get ten days . . ."

> "Sometimes it's rough, sometimes you can't choose the right way all the time, because you got to make ends meet . . . I mean, you ought to think about the consequences, but at the time you don't . . ."

> "How many of you all, when you all pulled it down, did you stand by yourself?"

> "When you all first came into the system, did anyone try to rape you?"

> "Are you scared to go to sleep at night?"

> "How do you feel when you eat the food sometimes?"

> "How do you all hide your feelings when you want to cry or are worried about something?"

> "You been doing education in here. Do you think it's working? Are you all rehabilitating yourselves?"

> "Did any of you all have kids? Did you think about those kids before you all did the crime that you did?"

Performance worked on multiple levels in *Leaves of Magnolia*. The interactive portion of the script uniquely engaged the young people with the inmate-performers. In so doing, they became a part of this production. The inmates, in this scene and throughout the play, performed not only their own stories but also those of their cohorts who had been transferred during the project's earlier phase. The experience of retelling their cohorts' narratives, I think, had its own transformative effect.[28] They not only had to address their own "script," as Ross put it, but that of their fellow inmates, whose issues and experiences of growing up often resonated with their own. In the 2001 performances, the inmate-performers addressed the young people in the audience with a different kind of authority than they had previously—that of their own experience and the learned or assimilated experience of their colleagues. They knew one another's stories intimately by the close of the project; they knew also that their fellow inmates' missteps that led them to Brown Creek were not so different from their own. Owning their stories meant seeing themselves as protagonists in them and thereby taking responsibility for the actions they described. Taking responsibility for those actions—their own as well as their cohorts'—meant they could be all the more authoritative with the young people. (It paid off in power.) And they could call the at-risk youth on *their* behavior, as they did in the midst of the performance, because they had called themselves on their own, much as Ross had acknowledged his responsibility in the 1999 taped evaluative session. Performing their stories for the young people was the *tour de force* for the inmates; in our 2001 taped evaluative session, they shared feelings of triumph and a sense of completion. They had achieved their goal. Judge Morey's description of the young people's responses in drug court gave the inmate-performers a sense of confidence and true victory.[29] For someone like Ross, who hung in with the project for more than three years, this was perhaps the ultimate meaning of the life review work with which we began.

The inmates also felt moved, as we did, by the letters written by the youth who attended the performances. I tracked a set of these down from Martina Dunford, one of our at-risk youth coordinators from New Horizons, in Durham, North Carolina, an alternative school for 365-day or end-of-year suspended kids. I read them aloud to the inmates before the final performance in May 2001 and a few to the audience as well:

> "Now that I have looked over my life, I have noticed that I am in prison. Getting out of prison to me means doing the right thing. I have now decided that I'm gonna do the right things so I can get out of prison. Keep your head up no matter what and always know that you got through . . ."

> "My visit to Brown Creek was a great experience, because it helped me realize what path I was headed toward, and I now know how smoking wasn't doing anything to help me, it was just slowing me down. And the way the prisoners presented the way they got locked up made me not want to do anything to get locked up or get involved with the law."

The Brown Creek Life Review Project helped inmate-actors take on new levels of authority in their lives, in a setting in which they struggle with authority daily even to the extent that they hold onto their sense of themselves by threads of power. The inmate-performers became "actors" in their own lives, symbolically addressing key problems areas from their past, while attempting to chart new, practical directions for themselves as they approached the prospect of eventual release. The young people in the audience (the "told") witnessed the inmates' stories (those of the "tellers"), and began to question their own life circumstances and to challenge one another to stay away from Brown Creek—as they did in a taped session I conducted with them several weeks after the performance.[30] Life review as a tool urged the inmates to reflect; performance as a medium, and one of the few venues for creative expression available to the inmates, enabled them to take action on those reflections.[31] Though an extraordinarily difficult setting in which to undertake a life review performance project, the prison environment grounded this performance in key ways. The young people could not ignore the "stage" on which the inmates performed, the "stage" of the inmates' daily lives in incarceration and a stage they might (and did) easily share.

The inmate-performers not only grasped the significance of their own stories, but also the degree to which they are social/symbolic "actors" in a broader sense, in their respective lives and in the social worlds they shared with each other and with the youth for whom they performed. The inmates' life review process involved the men in looking back, and the young people in looking forward, while urging them both to "act" differently next time. This performance helped youth and inmates both to change the script of their own lives at a critical juncture, when each was "at risk" of repeating behaviors that might land or keep them, respectively, at Brown Creek. In the Brown Creek Life Review Project, oral history and life review combined in performance to produce a way of rethinking history that not only gave new meaning to the past but reshaped the present and literally, I can't help but believe, changed some futures.[32]

Notes

1. The Southern Oral History Program (SOHP)—where I worked as Projects Director, then Assistant Director, and finally as Research Associate, to undertake my own research and writing—served as the initial platform for the project and one of its key sponsors. Others included Anson Community College and the Durham Arts Council (DAC). DAC served as the project's final sponsor, and also hosted a series of training sessions for artists working with at-risk youth that helped prepare me for the young people's participation. Funders included the North Carolina Humanities Council and the Z. Smith Reynolds Foundation.

2. Barbara Myerhoff, *Number Our Days* (New York: Simon & Schuster, 1978).

3. The performance project, *In a House of Open Passage*, was developed by Della Pollock and her students in the spring of 1997. It was based on the SOHP's Women's Leadership and Grassroots Activism Project, an oral history initiative codirected by SOHP Director Jacquelyn Hall and myself. Della and I coordinated the series of public performances that took place in four different locations in the greater Triangle area. Participating in Della's project and witnessing audience response to students telling the lives of regional activists and leaders in a montage style designed to provoke conversation with audience members inspired my work on the Brown Creek Life Review Project. Della went on to serve as a consultant on my project, reviewing early drafts of the script and urging me to take ownership of performance as a vehicle for the inmates' stories. I am indebted to her for her support and encouragement throughout the project. My work at Brown Creek was also inspired by folklorist Bruce Jackson and theatre activist Augusto Boal. See Bruce Jackson, *In the Life: Versions of the Criminal Experience* (New York: Holt, Rinehart and Wilson, 1972); Bruce Jackson and Diane Christian, *Death Row* (Boston: Beacon Press, 1980); and Augusto Boal, *Theatre of the Oppressed* (New York: Theatre Communications Group, 1985).

4. A total of twenty-one men were involved in the project over four semesters. Because of the transience of the prison population, and because some men were more comfortable performing than others, the group sifted down to eight members each time, for both sets of performances, in 1999 and again in 2001. Two members from the original workshop joined the first group in January 1998; but only four of those students could participate the following fall. When we resumed two years later in 2001, we had only three of the men who had performed in the original *Leaves of Magnolia*.

5. As an end-of-year specialist tutoring children in the Anson County school system, Marlene Richardson taught many of the kids who might later be considered at-risk.

6. While Butler and others acknowledge that life review occurs among people of all ages, sometimes triggered by crisis events, a review of the literature points to few studies of the use of life review with younger individuals. See Barbara K. Haight and Shirley Hendrix, "An Integrated Review of Reminiscence," *The Art and Science of Reminiscing: Theory, Research, Methods, and Applications*, eds. Barbara K. Haight and Jeffrey D. Webster (London: Taylor & Francis, 1995), pp. 3–21. Of the examples located, studies involving younger people seem to do so only as a consequence of a broader research agenda; e.g., Lynn D. Woodhouse, "Women With Jagged Edges: Voices From a Culture of Substance Abuse," *Qualitative Health Research* 2.3 (1992): 262–281. This has been equally true of my own life review research; my aim initially was not the use of life review among younger people, but rather the use of life review among an inmate population. The Brown Creek Life Review Project, as it turned out, involved men ranging in age from mid-20s to early-70s. A subsequent project of mine, the Durham HIV Life Review Project, involved men ranging in age from their 30s to 70s. Both projects have spurred my increasing interest in the use of life review with those in their younger and mid-life years, and not just the elderly.

7. Butler argues that life review is "characterized by the progressive return to consciousness of past experiences, particularly the resurgence of unresolved conflicts. These conflicts may be reviewed again and reintegrated. If the reintegration is successful, it may give new significance to the older person's life and prepare him or her for death by mitigating fear and anxiety" ("Foreword: The Life Review," *The Art and Science of Reminiscing*, p. xvii). Canadian psychologist Paul T. P. Wong posits the value of integrative reminiscence, in which "accepting negative past experiences and integrating them with the present" can lead to ego integrity. (See Wong, "The Process of Adaptive Reminiscence," *The Art and Science of Reminiscing*, p. 29.)

8. George C. Rosenwald and Richard L. Ochberg, "Introduction: Life Stories, Cultural Politics, and Self-Understanding," *Storied Lives: The Cultural Politics of Self-Understanding*, ed. Rosenwald and Ochberg (New Haven: Yale University Press, 1992), pp. 1–18. Rosenwald and Ochberg explore the use of narrative in various fields, drawing on articles in sociology, anthropology, oral history, and psychology, and its effects on the "teller" especially. The publication points to a parallel development in narrative studies, in which individuals narrate their lives in counseling settings. See also Gary M. Kenyon and William L. Randall, in *Restorying Our Lives: Personal Growth Through Autobiographical Reflection* (Westport, CT: Praeger, 1997).

9. In the case of the elderly especially, life review among less well-adjusted people can sometimes result in obsessive reminiscence, in which the interviewee fixates on events from the past without gaining understanding or closure from the process of recollection. See Peter Coleman, "Reminiscence Within the Study of Ageing: The Social Significance of Story," *Reminiscence Reviewed: Evaluations, Achievements, Perspectives*, ed. Joanna Bornat (Buckingham, England: Open University Press, 1994), p. 16; see also Butler, "The Life Review: An Interpretation of Reminiscence in the Aged," *New Thoughts on Old Age*, ed. Robert Kastenbaum (New York: Springer Publishing Company, Inc., 1964), pp. 271–272. One presumes that younger interviewees likewise can cycle back through reminiscences without successfully breaking through to a greater level of understanding or self-awareness. For a definition of reminiscence and how it differs from life review, see Ursula M. Staudinger, *The Study of Life Review:*

An Approach to the Investigation of Intellectual Development Across the Life Span (Berlin: Max-Planck-Institut fur Bildungsforschung, 1989), pp. 70–72.

10. At the 1996 Oral History Association annual meeting held in Philadelphia, during the heated discussion that followed a presentation on life review, one audience member— a veteran to the field of oral history—made this very point. Although life review as a subset of oral history has not been explored extensively here in the United States, for the past few decades it has been a significant field of study among oral historians in the United Kingdom. See Joanna Bornat, "Oral History as a Social Movement: Reminiscence and Older People," *The Oral History Reader*, ed. Robert Perks and Alistair Thomson (London: Routledge, 1998), pp. 189–205. For a compilation of work in life review by British researchers, see *Reminscence Reviewed*, ed. Joanna Bornat. For a discussion of the differences between life review and therapy, see Mike Bender, "An Interesting Confusion: What Can We Do with Reminiscence Groupwork," *Reminiscence Reviewed*, pp. 32–45.

11. An assessment of long-term impact would only be possible through longitudinal studies. It should be noted that, according to some researchers, six weeks constitutes a longer-term life review project. Most of my work in life review has been conducted over several years. On the Durham HIV Life Review Project, interviews with many of our participants took place over two years. On the Brown Creek Life Review Project, interviews spanned a year or more; in some cases, three years; and, after additional follow-up interviewing, may span upward of five years. The longer time-span in which I am working should offer more conclusive evidence on the effects of life review and performance among a select group of inmates.

12. Alice Hoffman, "Reliability and Validity in Oral History," *Oral History: An Interdisciplinary Anthology* (Nashville: American Association for State and Local History, 1984), p. 68. See also Donald A. Ritchie, *Doing Oral History* (New York: Twayne Publishers, 1995), esp. pp. 1–10.

13. Participants on the project were selected initially by my first collaborator, Mark-Anthony Hines, and later by Joe Madaras, both of whom knew the inmates well. There is no question that we worked with a select group of prisoners; many had been in the Education program for years. Mark-Anthony and later Joe "weeded out" some of the more problematic individuals, i.e., those who might prove disruptive in the classroom or who would not be trusted by fellow inmates. As the project progressed, though, we drew in more complex participants; e.g., Truman, who did not remain in the performance project because of differences with his fellow inmates, but nonetheless contributed essential pieces to the final production as well as to the group taped sessions.

14. I will be developing a book on the Brown Creek Project, in which I offer more details about this valuable technique, describing specifically how we set up the project, so that others aiming to do similar work might use it as a model. No project, just as no facility, is quite the same. But the principles I've used here—what 14th District Court Judge Marcia Morey says, "sparked a revolution in the souls of all of us who experienced it"—could certainly be replicated elsewhere.

15. The same year I launched the Brown Creek Life Review Project I developed another life review initiative, the Durham HIV Life Review Project, with folklorist Lisa Yarger and social worker Jennifer Sosenksy. The project involved a similar format of group storytelling sessions and one-on-one interviews, but culminated instead in a slide/image presentation, publication, and videotape, titled "Whole Lives: Reflections on Living with HIV"—not a performance aimed at young people. Like the Brown Creek

Life Review Project, we involved the interviewees in the development of the programs resulting from the interviews. Collaboration with the interviewees and community members was also central to the Northeast Central Durham New Immigrants Project (1999–2001), codirected by folklorist Jill Hemming and myself. That project resulted in a bilingual booklet, a dance performance by young people, a community mural, a videotape on housing, and a CD-ROM. My collaborative approach to oral history, though, first took root in my previous book project (see note 17).

16. See Michael Frisch, *A Shared Authority: Essays on the Craft and Meaning of Oral and Public History* (Albany: SUNY Press, 1991) and Elaine J. Lawless, *Holy Women, Wholly Women: Sharing Ministries of Wholeness Through Life Stories and Reciprocal Ethnography* (Philadelphia: University of Pennsylvania Press, 1993). In her study, Lawless engaged the women she interviewed in her process of analysis and called this technique "reciprocal ethnography." For a discussion of what I call collaborative oral history, see Cedric N. Chatterley and Alicia J. Rouverol, with Stephen A. Cole, *"I Was Content and Not Content": The Story of Linda Lord and the Closing of Penobscot Poultry* (Carbondale: Southern Illinois University Press, 2000). See also Rouverol, "The Closing of Penobscot Poultry and the Story of Linda Lord: One Woman's Experience of Deindustrialization," *Journal of Applied Folklore* 4 (1998): 5–21. For a discussion of the book's collaboration with our chief interviewee, see Rouverol, " 'I Was Content and Not Content': Oral History and the Collaborative Process," *Oral History* 28.2 (2000): 66–78.

17. See Michael Frisch, "Sharing Authority: Oral History and the Collaborative Process," *Oral History Review* 30.1 (2003): 111–113. This issue features a special section on "shared authority," a series of articles that grew out of a panel on the problems of collaborative oral history research that I organized for the XIth International Oral History Conference in Istanbul in 2000. In my article, I explore the challenge of collaboration in a prison setting, as well as the particular dynamics of power and authority within the corrections system, and how that played out in our classroom. See Rouverol, "Collaborative Oral History in a Correctional Setting: Promise and Pitfalls," *Oral History Review* 30.1 (2003): 61–85.

18. The book, like the performance project, will be developed in collaboration with the inmates. As the manuscript nears completion, photographer Cedric Chatterley and I will return to Brown Creek to solicit the inmates' reactions to the edited interviews and selected photographs, to determine what has been left out, or misconstrued, and to identify where compromises in perspective need to be reached. Our hope is that, as a result, the end product will speak more effectively to readers, especially at-risk youth.

19. Fieldnotes, February 22, 1999. Note: For publication, pseudonyms have been used for all inmates involved in the project.

20. Barbara Myerhoff, "Telling One's Story," *Center Magazine* 8.2 (1980): 22.

21. Ross, group interview with author, April 19, 1999.

22. Group interview with author, April 19, 1999.

23. Group interview with author, October 8, 1998. It should be noted that McCarl was incarcerated for a shooting.

24. As a sidenote, Fenton was supposed to have gone on to Honor Grade (minimum security) the summer before our first performance. This was meant to be good news; it meant he was on his way out of the system. But by fall of 1998, when we resumed our project, he'd been shipped back.

"Why?" Joe Madaras asked him, the day we all gathered for the start of our semester. He blinked, fingering his tie as he spoke, the way he often did when he was agitated. Joe was head of prison education; he had a vested interest in these men not coming back.

"I tested positive for marijuana."

Fenton said he didn't like the other facility, but didn't say why. I wondered at the time if he had tried to get back to Brown Creek, if this camp was the lesser of the evils. I thought maybe he'd come back on purpose, because he wanted to stick with the project, because the spring before he had seemed so engaged. But now he seemed remote. He was on work crew through the fall—punishment for having failed the drug test—and he often came to class tired. He sat quietly, too quietly, for him. We were pretty sure he was stoned much of the time.

25. See Rouverol, "Collaborative Oral History in a Correctional Setting," esp. pp. 75–76, for a different reflection on this fieldnote excerpt. In that article, I used a tighter version of this account, emphasizing the power dynamics, given that article's focus on sharing authority and problems in collaboration. I felt that article required a sharper focus and would not enable me to fully explicate the exchange between Ross and myself, and later Marlene and myself—in short, that I could not do the incident justice.

26. For more discussion on the turning points of my collaboration with the administration, see Rouverol, "Collaborative Oral History in a Correctional Setting," pp. 79–82.

27. It turned out Mr. Beck was unable to attend that final performance due to family illness. But he did insist that the performance take place and that the press be allowed in (major media, especially television crews, had previously been denied access by the prison superintendent). We felt we had finally won over the NC Department of Corrections.

28. See Della Pollock, "Telling the Told: Performing *Like a Family*," *Oral History Review* 18.2 (1990): 18.

29. For the book, I aim to do some additional interviewing with the young people to be able to provide a more longitudinal perspective on the impact of this project on them.

30. Group interview with author, May 9, 2001. Note: my use here of the "teller" and the "told" is not precisely the same as Della Pollock's usage in her article, "Telling the Told."

31. Because of limited access to equipment, and because Brown Creek Correctional Institution is medium-security, the inmates had few venues available to them. On other performance projects involving minimum-security inmates—such as Rhodessa Jones' work in the San Francisco jails, and a recent performance project in the correctional facility for women in Raleigh, NC, involving women prisoners in writing and performance—inmates could travel outside the facility. With the Brown Creek Life Review Project, we could not take the inmates out; the young people had to be brought in.

32. Paul T. Wong notes that "remembering the past not only empowers individuals for the present, but also prepares them for the future" (*The Art and Science of Reminiscing*, p. 24). In the book, I will include updates on both inmates and youth who I am currently interviewing, to give the reader a sense of the prospects and promise, or conversely the limitations, of this kind of performance project.

THREE

Touchable Stories and the Performance of Infrastructural Memory

Shannon Jackson

Shannon Jackson, a leading historian of performance and scholar of performance in every-day life, presents the work of Shannon Flattery and the Boston-based Touchable Stories project, locating it within the context of various forms of twentieth-century experimental theater and recent debates about the status of memory in language. In the work of Touchable Stories, performance takes the form of large-scale installations based on extensive fieldwork among residents of working-class neighborhoods ultimately embedded in the legacy of a community arts organization. Touchable Stories is a material practice: it is about moving through and, in every sense, feeling a sometimes labyrinthine combination of local place, local voices, and local objects, with the aim of drawing residents into new and renewed understanding of common networks of material history and imagination—or what Jackson calls "infrastructural memory." Jackson moves between sensuous details and theoretical frames, weaving a ruddy vision of how palpable and proximal performances may recreate communities.

* * * * *

The floorboards creak, and I reach for a stone wall to steady myself. The warm smell of baking bread mingles in the damp air of this church basement. I have found myself in an environment that avant-garde artists might call an "installa-tion" and that church-members might call a "community project." The stone wall is the foundational support system for the church's belltower; immediately surrounding it, pillows cover the floor. A child runs past me and throws himself excitedly on the pillows, looking up to notice what I had not. "Stars!" he cries with glee, settling himself into the softness and looking up at an installed ceiling of flickering lights. As adult visitors and two more children gather in this sequestered space, recorded voices fill the environment, extending a cautious invitation that will never settle into perfect intimacy. One voice describes life in the fishing village that he left, recalling early morning sunrises. Another tells of how her Polish grandmother came with her brother to work on a farm in the United States because her parents could not afford to keep either of them. As the voices proceed, I become aware of a shadow figure moving quietly behind a scrim that covers the stairwell. The figure steps carefully and halts, extending arms in an embrace that is not returned.

This small space is one of many inside a larger maze created in the basement of the First Baptist Church in Boston's Central Square. As I move through each site, the "installation cum community project" will ask me to think about Boston activism and neighborhood memory, about domestic violence and domestic comfort, about nuclear dumping and environmental protection. At the same time, it will ask me to hang an ornament on a paper maché tree and to help a senior citizen hang hers. It will ask me to linger near a pool of water and let me watch as a child delights in getting her fingers wet. This first space, however, is about immigration, and it is called "Homeland," a reminder that, before 2001, the term could have compelling resonances in the United States beyond the anxieties of national security. I watch as this child stares at stars and turns his head to hear. I watch his parents as they listen, and wonder what it means for them to enter this space and to hear these stories. I watch the other visitors watch this child as he listens.

The title of my essay takes its terms from the name of a Boston community arts group called *Touchable Stories* and from my preoccupation with the way performance and memory interact with the apparatus of art-making. The idea that *memory* can be *infrastructural* goes against some of the conventional ways of understanding both terms, paradigms that would relegate memory to the evanescent and individuated realms of the psychic rather than to the material, political, and economic domains of the infrastructural. However, if, after Lacan, the formation of psychic subjectivity is understood to be necessarily relational, then the notion of infrastructural memory is my attempt to broaden our sense of that relational field. In this chapter, I am interested in understanding how performance-based uses of oral history might position speakers and listeners in environments that induce a kind of infrastructural awareness of a shared material relation. This means extending the central questions of oral history to consider not only its role as a documentation of individual experience but also its capacities for forming a partial collectivity. While oral history is often used to create a group awareness of different experiences, I am interested in considering how performance might also induce a more radically contextual consciousness of the shared operations that produce that difference. My simplest metaphor for this kind of infrastructural awareness is the construction signs on highways that say, "Your tax dollars at work," a type of representational practice that reminds its addressee of the tacit and material support system made possible by an often abstract or alienated public operation. I am interested in how artistic oral history projects such as *TS* might similarly induce a reminder of our interdependency with the operations of the public, the economic, and the social. In some ways then, my preoccupations revolve around old questions about the relation between culture—or what used to be called the "superstructural"—and the domain of political economy—what used to be called the "base." The notion of an infrastructural imagination is my way of characterizing how an aesthetic structure and a material structure might engage rather than oppose each other. To imagine infrastructurally in this domain involves not only listening to stories of class difference at the level of content, but also unsettling the apparatus of art-making at the level of form, indeed, using performance to expose the material and environmental enmeshment of artists and audiences, of rememberers and listeners, of citizens and civic space. As this essay continues, I hope to illustrate the radical contextuality of *Touchable Stories'* infrastructural imagination and to consider its effects. At the same time, I also argue that the interdisciplinary field of performance studies provides a fruitful site with which to conduct this exploration and, moreover, that such explorations can extend or revise some of the operating assumptions of performance studies scholarship. Along the way, I consider how the status of oral history has been routed through a host of critical paradigms in performance art, in memory theory, and in post-structuralist criticism. That interrogation in turn reflects upon the conceptual possibility of a tangible story and a material remembering.

But first, let me introduce *Touchable Stories*. The articulated mission of this Boston-based arts group is to create installation and performance environments that "highlight the often unheeded voices and concerns of low income and working class communities."[1] Each production selects a particular city or neighborhood in the Boston area—Upham's Corner in Dorchester, the city of Allston, the unevenly gentrifying Central Square in Cambridge, the Fort Point artists' neighborhood in Boston—and focuses on creating dialogue around the issues that press most heavily on the minds and bodies of its inhabitants. The yearlong process behind each performance begins by collecting oral histories from neighborhood residents; in multiethnic neighborhoods, interviewers are found who speak a variety of languages— Spanish, Mandarin, Portuguese, Russian. Meanwhile, the group's director and founder, Shannon Flattery, works to develop relationships with local leaders and civic organizations. She contacts historical societies, activist organizations, immigrant community centers, and churches as well as mayors, popular historians, homeless activists, and store owners, groups and individuals whose civic memory is particularly acute and often politicized. Through these relationships, *Touchable Stories* secures a site in which to develop the project—the Brighton Street Baptist Church in Allston, the First Baptist Church in Central Square, the Maxwell Community Business Park in Dorchester. Flattery then schedules an array of community dinners in which the artists and volunteers share a meal with different community representatives—many of whom have not met together in the same room before. From oral history interviews and these discussions, the *Touchable Stories* team derives focused themes—housing, language, racial prejudice, urban renewal, domestic abuse as well as conceptual themes such as "home," "spirituality," or "longing"—with which to construct an installation and performance environment. Using the aesthetic of a "living maze," *Touchable Stories* transforms church basements and community halls into environments of urban memory and civic education, creating individual "rooms" in which particular issues are addressed. For Flattery, the gathering and presentation of oral narrative propels the construction of the maze. "Basically, we start with the oral history and then create a setting for you to hear it in."[2] The techniques for creating that setting are varied. In some projects, sections of the taped oral histories are piped throughout the space; in others, visitors try on different headphones attached to taped voices in different languages. Such auditory techniques are then matched to imagistic, tactile, and/or embodied modes of representation such as the display of black and white photos, the presentation of slowly moving shadow figures, the opening and closing of secret drawers, the sipping of tea, the winding up of a toy. Other techniques are linguistic, including traditional didactics as well as textualized walls and community "guest books" in which visitors record responses or write down more stories. A run of performances ends with more community dinners to reflect on the event, to discuss the themes dramatized, and to make suggestions for future projects.

Before founding *Touchable Stories*, Shannon Flattery had been working with a number of Boston-based art groups—*Ruby Slipper Productions, Gardening at Night, Mobius,* and *Invisible Cities*—ensembles that sought expressly to reform the concept of "audience participation" and to develop Conceptualist practices that refined the nature of the interaction in so-called interactive art. Much of this approach was toward multisensory activation, emphasizing the Proustian possibilities of smell and taste, creating environments that elicited the spectator's touch, and generating auditory installations that enabled careful and sustained practices of listening. Inspired by such Conceptualist techniques, Flattery still felt ill at ease with the limited demographics of the audiences with whom such projects "interacted" and wanted to adapt their methods for people who were not well-versed in the artistic legacies of the avant-garde. A turning point occurred during the preparation of a site-specific installation on a city lot, one that was separated from a row of houses by a bike path. The night before the opening, the group of artists realized that their power generator made too much noise, drowning out the music and other auditory components of their installation. They decided to leave flyers in the neighbors' mailboxes informing them of their predicament and searching for an alternate power source. When they returned the next morning at 7 A.M., they looked down the bike path to see dozens of orange extension cords coming through the fence, an offering that would obscure materially any sense of where this neighborhood ended and the art installation began. To me, the obscurity of that boundary propels the formation of an infrastructural imaginary. The orange cords not only "showed the seams" behind the production of art (à la Brecht) but productively confused inherited oppositions between inside and outside, figure and ground, frontstage and backstage by which we conventionally delimit the art object. In their absolutely essential mundanity, the cords performed the precarious connection between art and its material substrate. As material that could have been withheld, as a substrate that has been placed on view, the infrastructural vulnerability of art-making is exposed and, with it, the radical interdependence of art and its community.

A desire to maintain this fusion of aesthetic practice and neighborhood space now drives the dramaturgy of *Touchable Stories*. Indeed, at a time when "community art" endures no small degree of condescension, *TS'* mode of culture work promises to radicalize our formal sense of the relation between such terms. Oral history functions uniquely in this mission. It both provides the themes of the production and inspires the techniques of its presentation. On the one hand, the voices of oral history have the appeal of the experiential. "I came from Leningrad when I was exactly 6 years old," says one voice. "I am from mainland China . . . Shanghai," says another.[3] On the other hand, the repetition and placement of oral history within the living maze highlights their representational status. (See figure 3.1, floorplan.) As each Allston immigrant story is repeated, for instance, they progressively expose the tropes and conventions of immigrant narrative as well. As the source of civic information and the medium of artistic innovation, *TS'* oral histories exemplify the mutual saturation of politics and aesthetics. Memories provide the content and the form, the message and the material, of civic arts. Furthermore, by incorporating narratives with images and spaces of urban life, *TS'* performances show the enmeshment of representation and experience, illustrating how everyday practices produce and are produced by the narrative constructs in which we perform them. As I hope to show, this coincidence of aesthetics and politics, of memory and materiality, and of representation and experience makes *Touchable Stories* an exemplary site with which to think through the larger connections of oral history and performance. In what follows, I explore these issues as a form of avant-garde art practice, as an alternate way of thinking about memory and museumship, and as a comeback to deconstruction's critique of presence and orality.

For scholars of performance art and theater, the use of oral narrative has a varied history. More recently, it has been broadly situated as a force extending the Conceptualist Art movement and as a technique propelling theater for social change. The first genealogy is derived from the artistic experiments of the 1960s when painters and sculptors began to work across the medium of performance, incorporating space, embodiment, and voice into their innovative practices. The results of such experiments were wide-ranging and, as many have noted, are inappropriately homogenized under any single artistic movement. They include the efforts of "Happening," "Fluxus," "Event," and "Activity" performers to create environments of immediate encounter or pure action. They include the use of voice and embodiment by groups such as the Living Theater to create a scene of authentic interaction. They include the confessionals of a variety of solo performers—the matter-of-fact disclosures of the Wooster Group's Spalding Gray, the taboo monologues of video artist Vito Acconci, and the boundary-crossing verbalizations of performance artist Karen Finley. To other art communities and critics, the appearance of bodies, voices, and

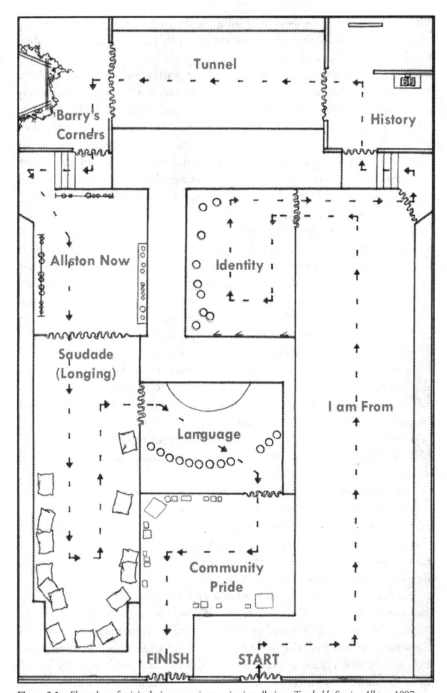

Figure 3.1 Floorplan of original nine room interactive installation. *Touchable Stories: Allston*, 1997.

words in museum galleries and site-specific installations marked a larger shift in the goal of artistic representation more generally. This transformation was lauded by some and derided by others as an orientation away from the art object and toward the experience of the art spectator. Its most famous derider, art critic Michael Fried, condemned the "theatricality" of artists influenced by the Conceptualist and Minimalist goals of creating a discomforting scene of spectatorial encounter: "Art must somehow confront the beholder—they must, one might almost say, be placed not just in his space but *in his way*."[4] While Fried found such a theatrical goal to be cumbersome, sculptor Robert Morris relished it. "It is in some way more reflexive because one's awareness of oneself existing in the same space as the work is stronger than in previous work."[5] For some, it was precisely this cumbersome realization of "oneself existing in the same space" that characterized, in Alex Potts's terms, "the sculptural imagination" of the late 1960s and early 1970s.[6] Whatever the value judgment, it was also through the shared goal of creating such encounters that artists working in a variety of media could be seen in relation to each other. When a sculptor offered a display of Minimalist blocks, when a dancer performed everyday rather than stylized movement, and when an installation artist narrated a story about himself, all three attempted to move viewers into a hyperawareness of their own presence. They thus raised the stakes of spectatorship, incorporating the act of reception into the art object itself. In such a genealogy, oral performance emerges as intriguingly sculptural in its effects, borrowing and reworking the capacity of experimental sculpture to create a material consciousness of one's existence in a shared space.

This genealogy of avant-garde art practice provides one way of contextualizing the experimental use of oral narrative. As artists openly sought to address their audiences, as artists challenged the autonomy of the art object by incorporating themselves into their work, the performance of oral narrative became a useful technique. For many, orality took form as an unconventional and often self-consciously inappropriate form of autobiography. In his reading of *Sex and Death to the Age 14* when Spalding Gray describes playing strip poker with his cousin, critic Henry Sayre focused on the moment when "we overhear something in this monologue we wish we had not." This shaky moment makes use of a kind of narrative presence, one that "involves its audience by creating a cognitive dilemma—usually social in character—with which the audience must come to grips and which it must at least seek to understand."[7] That kind of explicit address was used in different museum contexts by artists like Vito Acconci. In the notorious *Seedbed*, an unseen Acconci shared sexual fantasies through a microphone and speaker as visitors entered the gallery. Akin to the experimental sculptor, these and other works tried to induce in receivers a corporeal consciousness of their own role in the structuring of the art event. Meanwhile, feminist performance artist Karen Finley extended the technique and, in some cases, called its bluff. If anxiously masculine figures such as Gray and Acconci discomforted audiences with tales of private sexuality, then Finley pushed the bounds of appropriateness with politicized narrations of abusive sexuality. While these and other productions received very mixed reviews, they shared a commitment to using oral performance to invite audiences to reckon with their own status as receiving subjects.

The artistic use of oral performance is also part of a slightly different genealogy, one that explicitly deploys theater in the service of community formation and community interrogation. Ever since the 1930s when the W.P.A. sponsored newspaper theaters, socially committed theater practitioners have made use of documentary texts to create a theater of public dialogue. Oral histories have since become another type of resonant document in service of these goals, often incorporating issues of class, race, gender, and national difference as a central theme. The work of Anna Deavere Smith is perhaps the most widely recognized recent example of this kind of project. To prepare productions like *Fires in the Mirror* and *Twilight: Los Angeles, 1992*, Smith responded to moments of social crisis by interviewing hundreds of individuals representing various demographic groups and types of involvement. After the 1992 Los Angeles uprisings following the Rodney King verdict, for instance, Smith re-performed oral narratives of police chiefs, store owners, college students, gang leaders, city activists, senators, academics, fathers, mothers, and aunts from different ethnic and classed constituencies. Combining "verbatim" oral narratives with vocal and gestural representations of each of her subjects, she used her theaters to present multiple viewpoints and to offer an alternate public sphere for social deliberation. Within performance studies, Smith's use of oral performance is interpreted alongside the work of other socially committed artists such as Emily Mann's performances of Vietnam war narratives in *Still Life* and—even more recently—Moisés Kaufman's oral excavations of Matthew Shepard's fatal beating in *The Laramie Project*. These oral performances differ from the performance art described above in that the disclosure is not—or not only—focused on the autobiography of the artist or performer. Furthermore, they more overtly address the community politics from which they derive and to which they address themselves. Their theatrical techniques also bear more of a resemblance to the traditional structures of the dramatic stage. However much they experiment with the theatrical form, Mann, Smith, Kaufman, and other theatrical artists use theater spaces more often than gallery environments, presenting verbal material to spectators who sit in rows and watch as performers play selected characters.

The oral performances of *Touchable Stories* share aspects of both of these genealogies, providing an opportunity to consider the relationship among visual arts and theatrical genealogies of performance studies. Both contribute to the particular kind of infrastructural consciousness induced in *TS'* living mazes, using the radically contextual techniques of experimental sculpture to allow the highly local performance of oral history to materialize an unsettling relationality. As a trained sculptor whose work gradually began to extend its spatial and temporal reach, Shannon Flattery herself fits more easily into the visual arts trajectory. Her steady incorporations of performance into installation environments were a late-twentieth-century extension of the goals of Conceptualist art, focusing particularly on its interaction with the receiver in a shared structure. Like other performance art experiments, there is also in *Touchable Stories* the occasional overhearing of "something we wish we had not." Rather than tales of explicit sexuality, however, the narratives of racial prejudice or an unequal urban economy might require receivers to come to terms with ("and at least to understand") their own racial and class position in Boston's urban space. By forming *Touchable Stories* and allowing the interviewing and recording of oral narrative to drive her work, Flattery now shares many of the goals and techniques of documentary theater as well. Equipped with headphones, a social mission, and a desire to hear the voices of everyday experience, *TS* artists are akin to the community investigators associated with theaters for social change even if their methods of representation differ from those of documentary theater. *Touchable Stories* is thus best understood as a place where (at least) two artistic trajectories meet, where the reform goals of interview-based theater are refracted in "living mazes" that reuse the interactive techniques and site specificity of a Conceptualist environment. By gathering "voices" and then "creating a setting" in which to hear them, *Touchable Stories* places political theater's democratic focus on verbal expression inside the time/space experimentation of a Fluxus "Event."

The infrastructural dimensions of material remembering are not wholly accounted for by an excavation of the environmental practices of the avant-garde. Theorists and historians of memory also provide a significant intellectual trajectory in which to account for performed uses of oral history. In many ways, the idea of a memorial infrastructure extends and, in the case of *Touchable Stories*, possibly reverses aspects of Frances Yates's theorizing in *The Art of Memory*. Yates studied the ways that classical orators developed *mnemotechnia* by associating different topics with different parts of the building in which the oration took place—its columns, its atrium, its furniture.[8] In some ways, a kind of mnemonics of space propels the living mazes of *Touchable Stories* where the audiences and not just the orators are invited to remember. Visitors walk down a staircase to think about immigration, linger in a corner to recall a legacy of political activism, or look up at the ceiling to contemplate urban renewal. Whereas the practice of mnemotechnia conventionally preassigned the variables of infrastructural space, *TS* places its receivers in a more unsettling relation to memory. To encounter these staircases, corners, and ceilings is often to be positioned as unwitting rememberers, recalling an urban memory that receivers did not always know was theirs. Familiar environments become loaded with alternate histories; mundane spaces become the repositories of extraordinary narratives. The jolt of an infrastructural consciousness both exposes the obscured material history of civic and neighborhood space and turns it into the site of an alternate imagining.

Historian and theorist Pierre Nora extends Yates's discussion with his investigation of what he calls *lieux de memoires* and their relation to the ironies of modernity, providing another paradigm with which to understand the material extensions of *Touchable Stories*. Opposing such modern "places of memory" to earlier *milieux de memoires* (or environments of memory), Nora discusses the rise of a self-conscious historicism that broke from the unself-consciousness of earlier memorial transmissions where "[t]he remnants of experience still lived in the warmth of tradition, in the silence of custom, in the repetition of the ancestral have been displaced under the pressure of a fundamentally historical sensibility."[9] Whereas earlier *milieux de memoires* restored "true memory" and "real memory" repeatedly through "skills passed down by unspoken traditions, in the body's inherent self-knowledge, in unstudied reflexes and ingrained memories," now self-conscious *lieux de memoires* live in the push and pull between memory and history—"moments of history torn away from the movement of history, then returned; no longer quite life, not yet death, like shells on the shore when the sea of living memory has receded."[10] For Nora, the spatial shift from "peasant culture—that quintessential repository of collective memory" to the alienation of urban culture most paradigmatically embodies this epistemological shift. A new, detached sensibility drives the creation of formalized, bounded memorials. Now, monuments, archives, cemeteries, and museums do the work of remembering that society itself no longer does "naturally."

Nora and other theorists of memory have influenced historiographical experimentation in history and performance studies, providing ways of theorizing the performance of history at the level of both explicit spectacle and implicit embodiment. The concept of a *lieu de memoire* responds to the interests of cultural and performance historians in the means by which museums and other historical sites "display" history. Its bicameral division and self-conscious spectatorial strategies offer a structure in which to theorize the overt and explicit performances of history that occur in museums, monuments, parades and other sites of official history. Meanwhile, if the *lieu de memoire* responds to a performance studies interest in spectacle, then the *milieu de memoire* responds to a performance studies interest in bodily habit. The notion of a *milieu de memoire*'s embodied "self-knowledge" and "unstudied reflexes" coincides with the covert and implicit acts of gestural behavior that repetitively perform and reconstitute the structure of everyday life. This tacit realm of what Paul Connerton calls "incorporated" memory, figures centrally in Joseph Roach's theorizing of a "kinesthetic imagination" in his landmark *Cities of the Dead*.[11] What is perhaps less uniformly accepted by these and other theorists, however, is Nora's notion that the tacit realms of the *milieu de memoire* are "natural" in some pure or absolute sense. If bodies do the work of remembering in performance studies scholarship, those bodies are also subject to the pull of politics and the play of representation. The incorporated memory of a *milieu de memoire* is thus the site of social difference and the means of its reproduction, a memorial infrastructure whose habits and gestures may come to feel "natural" but are no less social than the alienated displays of a *lieu de memoire*. Indeed, for many scholars, the desire to maintain the notion of a pure, authentic space of embodied memory is the result of a misguided and ultimately unhelpful nostalgia.

I find it interesting to use Nora's concept of memory next to the sites of *Touchable Stories*, both to understand the techniques of the latter and to question the nostalgia of the former. It is important, for instance, to note that the supposed "unself-consciousness" of peasant culture also existed within a power structure, a feudal system whose unequal economic rituals between lord and subject neutralizes the impulse to celebrate this *milieu* unproblematically. *TS* seems acutely aware of the connection between memory and economic infrastructure, creating an aesthetic in which to represent both the comfort of the former and the ironies of the latter. The Allston and Central Square projects engaged an environmental consciousness on several levels, invoking a concept of hospitality with its rituals of entrance, welcome, and offering as well as its feelings of enclosure, protection, and intimacy (see figure 3.1). Visitors hung decorative ornaments on a large puppet tree in one space and sat across a row of empty chairs in another (see figures 3.2 and 3.3). The rooms created miniature spaces that were simultaneously sequestered and interrelated as visitors encountered one exhibit while having a haptically environmental awareness that something else was going on next door. It thus invoked the environments of home and neighborhood at once, performing the oft-disavowed interdependence of the private and the civic. At the same time, the performance of comfort coincided with a performance of politics. In *Central Square*, the tree-shaped puppet welcomed visitors who also listened to stories of a contested nuclear plant and illegal chemical dumping in their neighborhood.[12] Each room offered mnemonic devices for activating shared recollection and, in most cases, for creating the realization that the recollection was shared in the first place. To listen was to be a witness not only to the oral narration but also to one's own enmeshment in a collective, power-ridden, and often disavowed interactive structure. In a sense, *Touchable Stories* infrastructural imagination offered the embodied and environmental setting of a *milieu de memoire* while making the self-conscious politics of a *lieu de memoire* available for reflection and debate.

The corporeal gestures of environmental memory consistently align and collide with the overt display of historical politics. *Allston's* Urban Renewal room provides another example. The space was filled with bottles of water hanging from the ceiling while taped oral histories recalled the spaces, rituals, and routines of a different civic life (see figure 3.4). "There were no supermarkets or department stores then. The Allston business district was where we used to do our shopping."[13] Inside each bottle was a black and white photo of a different site from Allston's past—"the five and dime," "the produce market," "the meat market," "the shoe store"—all described by the taped voices heard. The bottles parodied the display mechanisms of a museum. Hung at eye level, they elicited the conventional behavior of museum performance as spectators moved carefully and quietly from picture bottle to picture bottle down the line. The room thus juxtaposed such detached spectatorial movement before a miniature five-and-dime with the rituals of coming and going recalled in the memory of a five and dime that was, at one time, "life sized." Later, an anonymous and disembodied hand appeared from the wall to shake up each bottled image with a tab of alka seltzer. Echoing the rhetoric of urban renewal, the plop/plop of the antacid promised comfort and calm. Its fizz was figured here differently as an agent that destroys urban space in the name of urban relief. A similar recreation of museum performance

Figure 3.2 Tree Hands, detail, "Spirituality." Interactive installation/performance by artist St. Suzan Baltozer. Performer is hidden in tree structure with wires attached to arms that lower hooks on which audience members may place brass dragonflies handed out upon entering the installation. Audio discussion revolves around the places from which we draw strength. *Touchable Stories: Central Square*, 1998. Photo by Bob Raymond.

Figure 3.3 Chair Room, "Community Pride." Interactive installation by artist/founding director Shannon Flattery that paced the spotlighting of individual, audience participant chairs (illuminating one at a time) with the projection of different voices. Audience participants were served with warm cider. *Touchable Stories: Central Square*, 1998. Photo by Bob Raymond.

occurred in the *TS*' use of headphones. It is a convention of many museum visitors now to don headphones. Walking from exhibit to exhibit, visitors press handheld tape players to hear erudite contextualizations of everything that they see. In *Allston*, the *TS*' use of headphones cited but revised museum practice. Rather than giving each visitor the same tape, visitors chose from an array of oral history recordings of different voices representing different immigrant experiences and national languages. Rather than directing listeners about when to turn the tapes on and off, listeners made their own decisions. Rather than anticipating how recorded words would inter-act with successive exhibits, visitors structured the mix of space and sound in their own unplanned and spontaneous movements, lingering and listening, tuning-in and tuning-out, turning and tuning-in again.

In other places, the comfort of what might be retroactively posited as an element of a lost *milieu* was placed in intimate coimbrication with a less than harmonious memory. In the *Upham's Corner* maze, visitors were invited to sit at a table of Latin American food, to adjust their plates, to pick up forks and knives. As they recreated these everyday gestures, their motions activated tapes of oral histories from the neigh-borhood's Caribbean community.[14] In *Allston's Saudade*, a room named after the Portuguese word for longing, visitors were invited to sip tea while listening to stories of aging and illness. In the *Central Square* project, the issue of domestic violence was addressed through the oral histories of social workers at a nearby shelter, their taped

Figure 3.4 Fire Museum then and now, detail, "History." Installation by artist/founding director Shannon Flattery. Two of approximately sixty paired jars contrasting images of the Fort Point Boston neighborhood from the early 1900s and the present day. Jars are filled with water; immersed xeroxed acetates give the images a 3-D effect. Also used prominently in *Allston*. Photo by Lolita Parker Jr., London Parker-McWhorter, and Anthony Feradino; historical photos courtesy of The Boston Wharf Co. *Touchable Stories: Fort Point*, 2001–2003.

voices piped from inside individual mittens that each visitor was asked to place on her hand and hold to her ear (see figure 3.5). Such techniques refuse to accept a neat opposition between the embodied behaviors of past *milieu de memoire* and the detached spectatorial structures of modern *lieu de memoire*. Without lapsing into rose-colored nostalgia, *TS* instead finds in urban culture a "repository of collective memory," albeit a remembering that links unstudied memorial reflexes—such as tea-sipping, memorial senses—such as baked bread, and memorial objects—such as mittens—to issues of struggle, violence, and inequality. By mixing the form of the *milieu* and the politics of the *lieu, Touchable Stories* finds a way to create an experience that is both empathetic and critical, intimate and alienated. These living mazes use oral history to

Figure 3.5 Laura Open, "Domestic Violence." Interactive installation by artist Laura Mack. Canopy is lowered over seated participants; 1950s family reunion/dance party is projected onto the canopy; stories about domestic violence are heard through speakers embedded in red felt mittens. *Touchable Stories: Central Square*, 1998. Photo by Bob Raymond.

show the weight of oral history. Deploying memory and materiality, representation and experiential gesture, they dramatize the deep connection between the psychic and the social, between bodies and the world that they (in)habit everyday.

To bring the phenomenon of orality into the disciplinary domain of performance studies is both to appropriate and to test a series of critical paradigms and art practices. In addition to the legacies of the avant-garde, in addition to theoretical discussions of the nature of memory, there is an even more broadly influential philosophical movement that impinges on current theorizing of oral performance. At the center of much recent critical discussion lies a deconstructionist critique of metaphysics, one that questions the irreducibility of experience—or "presence"—by recognizing the role of representation in structuring daily life. At the center of the deconstructionist critique, furthermore, lies a critique of "orality," one that questions the presumption that the non-written oral is a pure incarnation of experience. In *Of Grammatology*, Jacques Derrida offered the most exemplary and widely cited version of the deconstructionist critique. Asserting that Western intellectual thought is governed by a series of binaries that present themselves as given rather than constructed, Derrida was particularly concerned with the binary between "speech and writing" in which the former is assumed to have ontological primacy.[15] Citing Rousseau's *Confessions* as a case study, Derrida used the concept of orality to characterize a metaphysical search for a realm of pre-discursive being and immediate, unmediated encounter. Barbara Johnson offers a helpful précis:

> Derrida's critique of Western metaphysics focuses on the privileging of the spoken word over the written word. The spoken word is given a higher value because the speaker and listener are both present to the utterance simultaneously. There is no temporal or spatial distance between the speaker, speech, and listener, since the speaker hears himself speak at the same moment the listener does. The immediacy seems to guarantee the notion that in the spoken word we know what we mean.[16]

Writing, by virtue of its distance between speaker and receiver, is assumed to produce a less authentic kind of encounter. Derrida argues against this kind of premise. He asserts that the assumption of authenticity in a non-written exchange is produced by the phenomenon of writing itself. Written representation produces the assumption of its opposite and, with it, a longing for a mode of being outside of writing, one where the representational gaps between signifier and signified would be closed. As such, "presence" always bears the trace of the differential representation it would seek to transcend.

It is hard to overstate how fundamentally the deconstructionist critique has influenced and, in some cases, short-circuited, the basic assumptions behind oral performance. To the extent that some proponents of oral history still invoke the authenticity of the oral encounter—to the extent that they laud its immediacy and assume its self-evident access to experience—they would seem to reify a regressive metaphysics.[17] Indeed, such assumptions have contributed to the somewhat conflicted status of oral narrative in the disciplines of critical theory and even in history, where experiential authority is methodologically suspect. As I have argued elsewhere, the conflicts also appear in the field of performance studies, where the appeals of artists and scholars to the immediacy and presence of performance sound naive to deconstructionist ears.[18] That kind of reception is certainly possible when it comes to *Touchable Stories*. Like other arts, activist, and oral history groups, *TS* uses a fairly literal vocabulary to characterize themselves—words and phrases like "actual," "immediate," "real," "truthful," "empathy," "authentic relationships," "presence," "true connection" populate their self-descriptions. To watch and listen to *TS* practice, however, is to be aware of the skill and sophistication required to create immediacy and of the critique of authenticity that is embedded in the material components of the living maze. Orality is deployed in these exhibits with a varied rhetoricity. It is sometimes ironic, sometimes descriptive, and sometimes partial but always overtly mediated by the environments, tape-players, gestures, and images that represent it. As theorists of orality and performance, therefore, it is necessary both to understand why the language of presence might be important to practitioners and to consider the complicated representational practices to which it might be referring all along. For me, this is where the notion of an "infrastructural imagination" becomes more resonant. Analyzing the time and space requirements of a *TS* event makes it clear that continuous co-presence—the moment when "speaker and listener are both present to the utterance simultaneously"—is a mediated moment. This mediation requires too much skill to be shunted to the realm of an outdated metaphysics either by the supporters of deconstructionist critique or by its antitheoretical detractors. Indeed, such techniques of time–space coincidence—inherited from both sculptural and theatrical practices—have been a central means by which artists attempted to expose the disavowed relationality of speaker and listener.

Together, the auditory, imagistic, tactile, embodied, and textual techniques of representation that I described above provide a way to frame the material means of art-making in *Touchable Stories* as well as the representational issues such art-making addresses. The creation of a "setting" in which to hear oral history is a self-consciously mediated endeavor and one that explicitly foregrounds its production of history. To hear a tale of a produce market or a five-and-dime while viewing hanging bottled photographs is to be invited into that production. With oral histories variously synchronized, tales of urban life differentially interact with each photograph. As visitors match word to picture, they craft multiple historical narratives rather than singular historical truths. Received in specimen bottles that are touched and turned by each visitor, the desires of historical preservation are both honored and ironized. Showing that our access to the past is necessarily incomplete, each visitor is invited to construct a relationship to remembered stories and, along the way, to discover how those stories have constructed them. In room after room of each part of the living maze, *TS* oral history is placed inside environments that are figurative rather than literal, partial rather than falsely comprehensive in their chronicle of historical truth. The anonymous hands, disembodied voices, shadowed bodies, miniatures, dolls, scrims, tapes, and videos resist literality and testify to the multiple technologies available to enable a moment of human connection. If this is "presence," it is one that is explicitly aware of its own production and unafraid to present a sense of discontinuity in the act of remembering. Together, *TS*' oral performances illustrate the indirect, roundabout work of tangible storytelling.

As it happens, that work also expands beyond the setting of the living maze. Indeed, to focus only on a reading of the exhibits would be to create boundaries around my object of inquiry, to shore up the measure of its time and space to a synchronic reading of a circumscribed event, albeit one whose multi-sensuality seems to resist singular inscription. Other technologies of time and space are equally necessary to understand *Touchables Stories*' production of presence. The lengthy time commitment of the group's process and its members' continuous presence in local neighborhood space is a case in point. In descriptions of *TS* method, the concept of time emerges again and again as a representational medium. "*Touchable Stories* takes the time to become a part of civic life," says one grant proposal, "time that is essential to making commitments and following through, to grounding empathy in real and enduring relationships."[19] Through a long process of participatory fieldwork, the team learns of unanticipated concerns and refines their perspectives on topics that they thought that they had understood. While they began with the issue of gentrification in Central Square, *TS* artists eventually learned that service-industry workers who now complained of being displaced had themselves earlier displaced a previous generation of residents, especially those who worked in the candy factories and refineries that were eventually shut down. While *TS* members began with concerns about child abuse in several projects, they soon learned that it was equally important to track the unintended effects of the 51A Child Abuse Law—a rule allowing children to report their parents—that children themselves had begun to abuse.

If this kind of participation stretches the concept of time in avant-garde practice, the neighborhood location of the final performances pushes beyond the conventions of space in site-specific art. Shannon Flattery spoke of the importance of "hanging out" continually in the Baptist Church in the months before the Allston performance, how neighbors came to expect her presence there, knowing that they could stop by to discuss its issues, to disagree, or to tell another story. Such episodes are less interestingly understood as an extra-aesthetic process than as themselves aesthetically produced instances of democratic sociability. They are also central to the infrastructural production of "presence," a commitment to geographic continuity that can disrupt as much as concretize founding intentions. Indeed, Flattery can be seen continuing the longer history of the settlement movement, an early-twentieth-century effort in social change where reformers and artists moved into immigrant and working-class neighborhoods.[20] By the time of her third project in Dorchester, Shannon Flattery decided to formalize this aspect of her artwork by moving in to the Upham

Corner neighborhood where she lives now. The temporal reach of each project also extends long after the maze has been dismantled, for *TS* sets up an infrastructure that ensures transformation over time. Making use of abandoned church basements, seeing in the wood planks of old coal-carrying tracks the pathways of future installation visits, *TS* leaves such spaces ready for continued use after departure. The once unlit, untraveled basement of Central Square's Baptist Church became a permanent recreational center after the *TS* performance. At a time when a number of cynical associations are attached to the term, *TS* members have revitalized the concept of urban revitalization by incorporating an infrastructural ethics into each element of their art practice. This is where the mediating work of artistic representation participates in a material future, not only reproducing a site's specificity but also transforming a site's potentiality. Indeed, creating the context for future imaginings is an integral part of *TS'* infrastructural ethic.

Of course, appeals to transformation can occasionally rationalize contemporary social control in palatable form. *TS'* improvised artistic processes inventively address that concern, for most of the spatial methods of this ultra site-specific work are based less in attentive planning and more in spontaneous disruption. On numerous occasions, group members have had to accommodate unexpected behavioral responses. Chairs that were supposed to remain hauntingly empty in *Central Square* were sat upon. In the same production, visitors were supposed to hang ornaments on the puppet tree but began hanging them in every corner of the maze, an unanticipated practice that Flattery decided to adopt for each new performance. At *Upham's Corner*, *TS* artists realized that their exhibits were vulnerable to "vandalism" and decided to welcome rather than to resist it. Flattery periodically let the neighborhood teenagers come into the installation "to trash the place."[21] Working with the reflexes and bodily practices of their neighborhood's *milieu de memoire* means that *Touchable Stories* cannot feel too precious about the carefully composed trappings of their *lieu de memoire*.

In their most recent production, the infrastructural incorporation of civic life and art practice took on new dimensions and, in many ways, reversed the historical gaze. As *TS* artists and their colleagues embarked upon various projects, they found themselves increasingly vulnerable to changes in Boston's rent control laws as well as to the surrounding pressures of urban development. A large number of Boston artists were living in the Fort Point neighborhood in former industrial buildings. As the city began to turn over various parts of the neighborhood to the construction of new highways, stadiums, and corporate buildings, as higher income Boston professionals sought out the boheme aesthetic of "loft-like" living quarters, Fort Point artists were evicted or priced out of their living and working spaces. Living under the threat of displacement, artists mobilized themselves and became newly attuned to the urban politics of their city. For Shannon Flattery and other *TS* members, this meant adapting an acquired infrastructural consciousness to their own neighborhood. If *TS* had previously used art practice to expose the political economy of Boston communities, they now became aware of the political economy of art practice itself. Sustaining the infrastructural imagination of other neighborhoods meant attending to the infrastructural politics of their own. It was thus logical that *Allston, Central Square*, and *Upham's Corner* would be followed with an installation maze called *Fort Point*, an excavation of the history, labor, and dreams of this artist community. In addition to tales of immigration, shopping, or holiday celebrations, the oral narratives in this exhibit contained stories of the "first time I saw a Jackson Pollock . . . it just knocked me over."[22] Whereas previous installations recreated the everyday gestures of eating, decorating, or self-adornment, the incorporated gestures of Fort Point's *milieu de memoire* included painting and sculpting. In mirrored reflections and video displays of artists at work, the exhibit dramatized how the production of neighborhood depended upon artistic practice, arguing that Fort Point itself came into being with each push of a brush and each press of clay. The *Fort Point* installation thus further radicalized the concept of infrastructure and the artistic phenomenon of presence. Here the artists' own presence as workers and storytellers was represented as fragile and contingent (see figure 3.6). Those who had been responsible for producing *TS'* aesthetic frame were now inside the frame themselves.

To consider the relationship between oral history and performance is, in some ways, to ask how it is that a story can touch. How can the telling of a story move us? How do the tropes and plots of narratives come to feel fundamental to our ways of working in the world? What makes us realize that a story is ours? What makes me realize that my story is yours? In very different domains of performance studies, scholars and artists have been asking themselves similar questions. Whether it is by assessing the innovations of the recent avant-garde, by excavating the constitutive role of memory, or by testing the complex paradigms of critical theory, the exploration of performance has meant the exploration of the tangible story. The work of *Touchable Stories* provides a site with which to explore these legacies as well as a vehicle for thinking through them differently. That thinking means questioning a number of inherited paradigms, paradigms that still find useful the oppositions between content and form, art and apparatus, foreground and background, product and process, art and politics, representation and experience, human and world, my backyard and yours. It is by asking us to ask ourselves just how far we are willing to challenge these inherited philosophical, political, and aesthetic formalisms that *Touchable Stories* builds its infrastructural practice. The "indiscrete" nature of such work often derives from a political or social mission. It also derives from the fundamentally broad and varied nature of oral history, especially oral history performed. By experimenting with different ways to hear a story, *TS* offers an oral history performance that values the mediated nature of the "presence" that orality produces. Along the way, *Touchable Stories* shows that remembering has an infrastructural politics. In narratives collected, in mazes constructed, in gestures, words, images, and motions, the memories of the psyche interact with the materiality of space in encounters that are mutually constitutive, unpredictable, and ongoing.

Figure 3.6 Lolita, "Mirror/Mentor." Interactive installation by artist/founding director Shannon Flattery. A room of mirrors incorporated 12 two-way mirrors wired to sensors that triggered illumination of hidden dioramas and video sequences on the theme of artistic mentors. Red jeweled pull-cords accompanied each of the mirrors; pulling switched on 1–3 minute soundtracks. *Touchable Stories: Fort Point,* 2001–2003. Photo by Shannon Flattery.

Notes

1. Shannon Flattery, unpublished grant proposal in author's possession.
2. *Touchable Stories, Fort Point*, video documentation of *Touchable Stories, Fort Point* installation/performance (2001–2003).
3. *Touchable Stories, Allston*, video documentation of *Touchable Stories, Allston* installation/performance (1997).
4. Michael Fried, "Art and Objecthood," *Art and Objecthood: Essays and Reviews* (Chicago: University of Chicago Press), p. 153.
5. Robert Morris, "Notes on Sculpture, Part 1," *Artforum* 4.6 (February 1966): 42.
6. Alex Potts, *The Sculptural Imagination: Figurative, Modernist, Minimalist* (New Haven: Yale University Press, 2001).
7. Henry M. Sayre, *The Object of Performance: The American Avant-Garde since 1970* (Chicago: University of Chicago Press, 1989), pp. 27, 28.
8. Frances Yates, *The Art of Memory* (Chicago: University of Chicago Press, 1966).
9. Pierre Nora, "Between Memory and History: *Les Lieux de Mémoire*," *Representations* 26 (Spring 1989): 7.
10. Ibid., 13, 12.
11. Paul Connerton, *How Societies Remember* (New York: Cambridge University Press, 1989), p. 72; Joseph Roach, *Cities of the Dead* (New York: Columbia University Press), p. 26.
12. *Touchable Stories, Central Square*, video documentation of *Touchable Stories, Central Square* installation/performance (1998).
13. *Touchable Stories, Allston*, video documentation of *Touchable Stories, Allston* installation/performance (1997).
14. *Touchable Stories, Upham's Corner*, video documentation of *Touchable Stories, Upham's Corner* installation/performance (2000).
15. Jacques Derrida, *Of Grammatology*. Trans. Gayatri Chakravorty Spivak (Baltimore and London: Johns Hopkins University Press, 1974), pp. 97–164. Originally published in France in 1967 by Les Editions de Minuit.
16. Barbara Johnson, "Translator's Introduction," in Jacques Derrida, *Disseminations* (University of Chicago Press, 1981), p. viii.
17. The work of Alessandro Portelli, "What Makes Oral History Different," *The Oral History Reader*, ed. Perks and Thomson (New York: Routledge, 1998, 2002) and Michael Frisch, *A Shared Authority* (Albany: SUNY, 1991), among others, have clearly located oral history within relational contexts, establishing that it is a definitively creative and partial practice. Nonetheless, some historians continue to use oral history as a primarily evidentiary source, and some oral historians and scholars of personal narrative continue to insist that oral narratives provide unmediated access to the experiential.
18. Shannon Jackson, "Practice and Performance," *Professing Performance: Theatre in the Academy from Philology to Performativity* (Cambridge and New York: Cambridge University Press, 2003).
19. Shannon Flattery, unpublished grant proposal in author's possession.
20. See, e.g., Shannon Jackson, *Lines of Activity: Performance, Historiography, and Hull-House Domesticity* (Ann Arbor: University of Michigan University Press, 2000).
21. Shannon Flattery, interview with the author, January 2000.
22. *Touchable Stories, Fort Point*, video documentation of *Touchable Stories, Fort Point* installation/performance (2001–2003).

FOUR

Bringing Old and Young People Together: An Interview Project

Laurie Lathem

As she recounts here, Laurie Lathem faces a group of kids who need to know something more than appropriate techniques for acting or playwriting. They need to connect with the world that makes sense of those techniques as means of re-imagining the world in which they live. With the courage of convictions learned through many prior writing workshops, Lathem introduces a new element into the summer playwriting course at the Berkeley Repertory Theater school—an interview project that, in turn, introduces her, her students, and us to the powerful alchemy of young and old voices, histories, and memories engaged in a creative process of mutual witness.

In 1995, I began working with Fred Rochlin, a man who became a performance artist at the age of seventy-four by telling stories about his World War II experiences. I was teaching a solo performance workshop at Highways Performance Space in Santa Monica, California, a place that attracts mainly queer and bisexual artists, transsexuals, transgender, and people exploring all manner of sexual and gender issues. My class was filled with young actors in their twenties, most of whom sought stardom via the highly successful one person show.

There was no formula for this workshop. From the beginning, I found myself inventing the process on the spot, based on the needs of the student before me. Roughly, the workshop would begin with written work, getting ideas onto paper and beginning to shape them dramatically. Then it would shift into performance work, with discussion and feedback. I wanted to include all performance styles, and, indeed, the clarification of style was one of the cornerstones of my work with these students. During the four years in which I taught this class, I had students doing everything from conventional, confessional monologue and stand-up comedy to nonverbal, conceptual performance art. I even had a student who was working on a solo opera. Because of the variations of style and genre that the students brought to the class, my approach was, by necessity, flexible and spontaneous. For this very reason, the process never ceased to be anything but a deeply challenging and thrilling experience for me.

On the second night of class, Fred Rochlin walked in, a nondescript-looking old man and I thought he must have entered the wrong room. I could sense everyone getting a little uncomfortable. Who was this old man and what was he doing here? And what kind of kinky story did he have to tell?

One of the first stories Fred read in class was called "Milk Run to Genoa" about a kid named Shorty who was one of Fred's buddies in the Army Air Corps during the war. Shorty was a sweet boy who went to church and collected china cups for his mother while the other guys were off chasing women and getting drunk. One night after a day off the base, Fred came back at midnight.

> Shorty was there, still awake, and waiting for me and he was just gushing, alive with excitement and he said, "Oh, you'll never guess what I found today."
>
> I said, "What?"
>
> And he said, "Look here," and he opened the lid to his foot locker and there was his clothes and three little cups and saucers.
>
> So I said, "Look at what?"
>
> He blurted, "At these, at these," and he took out those little cups and saucers and said, "Aren't they just precious? Can you believe this one is a genuine Wooster, late eighteenth century? Can you believe how lucky I am? Aren't you jealous? And this is a Miesner, and this is turn-of-the-century Wedgwood, not really rare but still very nice."
>
> I tried to be enthusiastic; I didn't want to be a wet blanket.
>
> I said, "Swell. Where'd you find them?"

The story went on to tell how on their very first mission, a supposed "milk run," Fred and Shorty were attacked in midair by the Germans. Shorty's head is literally blown off inches from where Fred is sitting in the plane. As the navigator, Fred then has to pull the plane and the remaining crew out of danger by plotting a course back home. Fred prays for the first time in his life.

> "Momma, I don't know what I'm gonna do. This is a milk run. Mama, this was the first one . . . Mama, I don't think I can do this fifty times . . . And look, there's poor Shorty. What about his Ma? What about those cups?"

When he finished reading, everyone in the room was in tears. We didn't quite know what had hit us. I was struck deeply by the detail in the story, in particular the image of the precious little china cups in the army foot locker. In the midst of catastrophe, there were these delicate things. I pulled Fred aside after class and told him

I thought he had something really special and that I would like to work with him on it. He didn't believe me. He was an architect, not a performer. He didn't think he could memorize lines, he didn't think anyone would be interested in his stories.

Every week for the next few months, Fred came to class with another one of his stories. One was about how he was shot down over Yugoslavia and had to walk to Italy with a female Partisan named Marushka, and how, along the way, he and Marushka had a love affair and how Fred had to shoot and kill three young Nazi boys. In another story, Fred helps deliver a baby by Caesarean section in a dirt hut in Italy and the following day obliterates a Hungarian farming village that he knows has no military value. They kept coming week after week, each more simple and heart-wrenching than the last. They came to be called the "Rockets" stories after Fred's nickname in the army.

It took several years for me to coax Fred into performing a full evening by himself. Over three years at Highways, I concocted seven evenings of group per-formances of work in progress from the workshop. They were a tremendous success. Over three years, I directed six or seven of these evenings. Each time, Fred had the honored last spot in the lineup, and each time, he blew the audience away. One day I told him, "OK, Fred, you've done about three hours of performance. You can mem-orize your lines, and people are interested in your stories. So how about now we work on a show of your own?" He finally agreed. We took two of the eight or so stories in the Rockets canon, and put them together in a show called *Old Man in a Baseball Cap*, scheduled a night at Highways and rehearsed for a few weeks. Then he took the stage by himself, and kept a standing-room-only audience rapt for seventy-five minutes. At the curtain call, people were standing and weeping and shouting.

His show, *Old Man in a Baseball Cap*, was told in the voice of his nineteen-year-old self, but filtered through the perspective of Fred as an old man. It was this unique combination of the young and old voice that caught people's hearts and minds. The show went on to the Actors Theatre of Louisville and to the La Jolla Playhouse, among others.[1] *Old Man* mainly attracted elderly audiences. That was the way the theaters marketed it and it worked. Here was a show old people could relate to. World War II veterans and their families nodded their heads in recognition and then stood on their feet at the end, sometimes with tears running down their faces in gratitude for the courage to tell stories that had been long buried in the hearts of many members of the audience.

What was most exciting for me, however, were the occasional nights when young people were watching. This was rare because the show was almost always advertised "for mature audiences only," as though Fred's frank accounts of sex and birth and death were any more graphic than the lyrics a teenager might hear on a favorite CD. On the nights when some brave parent thought better of the warning, I would watch the young person watching Fred, and see the glimmer of recognition mixed with sur-prise at being so interested in what this old man had to say. The teenage boy seeing himself in the old man was terrifically moving, and fueled my passion for bringing old and young people together in a joint creative project.

In the summer of 2001, as Creative Director of the Berkeley Repertory School of Theatre, I saw an opportunity to make this hope a reality. The Berkeley Repertory Theatre is a midsized regional theater in Berkeley, California with two full-size houses, a school and perhaps the most educated subscription audience in the country. Berkeley Rep has a nationwide reputation for artistic excellence (it won the Tony Award for Outstanding Regional Theater in 1997) and is one of the top-ranking professional resident theater companies in the United States. In 1999, Berkeley Rep was given a donation to expand its education programs by opening a school in the unused building next to the theater. I was hired to create the school from the ground up, to design both the summer and the year-round programs, to develop outreach programs, to hire the staff, and to teach courses in playwriting. Here was a chance to go beyond the usual acting, voice and movement classes and to get young people to write and perform their own material. I was tired of theaters being located in neighborhoods that saw only the comings and goings of the nice cars of the audience members. Too often we as artists are blind to people who coinhabit our communities, walking past them or stepping over them to get to rehearsal on time. I wanted the boundary between neighborhood and artistic endeavor to break down. It was through young people that I saw the chance to attempt this.

Stretching the conventional parameters of "drama school" to include oral history, playwriting, and some aspect of community service was very exciting for me. It would help the young actor go beyond the usual limits of self-consciousness and to develop a love of language. While there is nothing wrong with a desire for the spotlight, I wanted my students at Berkeley Rep to learn to take responsibility for their own vision rather than to be in constant service to someone else's. My previous work with incarcerated, on-probation, and gang-affiliated youth had confirmed my conviction that at the heart of the hardship of many young people is the absence of a belief in the self and in the cultivation of a personal vision.[2] Sadly, the notion that they may actually have an idea of their own is a foreign one for many of today's young people, and our society does little to foster any such notion. Several years ago, I worked with a sixteen-year-old boy named Johnny who had been arrested for gun and drug possession and was flunking out of school. We were working on his play together, with me taking dictation because his literacy skills were so poor, when I said offhandedly, "Good idea," and wrote down the line of dialogue he had come up with. He looked at me, stunned, and said, "No one ever told me I had a good idea before." Johnny went on to graduate from high school and to attend college. He cited our work together as the thing that turned him around.

At Berkeley Rep, it was important to me that the summer students get out in the community and do something, anything, to be of help to someone else. I asked myself what seemed to be self-evident: is it an essential part of what makes an artist to be mindful of the struggle of others? Again, so much of the teenage actors' focus is on herself: "How do I look?" "Am I good in this play?" I wanted them to engage in an activity that would not obviously lead them toward the goal of becoming a better actor, but that would make them better artists, better writers, better thinkers. Isn't this the goal of the artist after all, to inhabit the skin of another, and in so doing, to perhaps tell something of him or herself?

Identifying what constitutes community service was a tricky business. Even trickier was getting the parents to swallow the notion that their kids, for whom they were paying one thousand dollars tuition for one month of theater classes, might spend even ten minutes per week cleaning up a space for community use or any such menial labor. They wanted their dollars to count, for every minute to be accounted for and for us to be accountable for every dollar spent. In initial meetings with parents and board members at The Berkeley Repertory Theatre, I met strong resistance to the idea that sweeping the sidewalks outside the theater, for instance, might benefit the growing sensibility of the young artist. It was in these meetings that I finally came to terms with the fact that this was a program that had to be marketed and that these parents were the customers upon whom the survival of the program depended. This did not mean, however, dropping my commitment to community service. It would have to be wrapped into a creative project, something that stretched the limits of what might be required learning for a budding actress, but that would also not insult her parents' pride.

As part of my job description, I was expected to teach courses in playwriting. Under that rubric, I developed what came to be called the Interview Project: part playwriting, part oral history, and part community service. Two groups of sixteen teenagers would go to a senior citizen center to conduct interviews that would be the basis for short plays that they would write. The plays were then performed by members of the students' writing class at the senior citizen center for an audience made up almost entirely of the interview subjects. (The summer program was broken into two sections, one month each. The second month of the Interview Project was different in that professional actors from the Rep company, rather than the students themselves, performed the students' plays at the senior center. This proved to be much less interesting for reasons that I will go into later.)

Perhaps paradoxically, self-expression would be achieved by way of interviewing people whose lives differed markedly from the young students' own. In order to tell their own stories, the teens would first have to listen to someone else's and to create something for their communities. The project would get them into dialogue with old people, it would get them writing, it would get them out into the neighborhood. In the process of finding something to talk about with the old people, maybe even finding some common ground where there appeared to be none, they might also find a story that would reveal as much about themselves as about their interview subject. Whether or not this qualified as community service remained to be seen. The project also raised some serious questions. Whose stories were ultimately told at the senior center? Why engage the life stories of elderly people at all only to depart from those stories and create one's own? What, if any, was the benefit to the community? Because of the Interview Project and the kinds of questions it raised, the playwriting course would depart from traditional playwriting. At the same time, because of the playwriting course, the Interview Project would depart significantly from traditional oral history. The way in which both were different proved to be the fertile ground from which an entirely new entity was created, something that was not readily classifiable as either playwriting or oral history, but which combined elements of both to great effect. It is this aspect that I would like to explore here.

Preparing

Prior to the first class meeting, I enlisted the help of Gretchen Case, a doctoral student in performance at the University of California at Berkeley and a professional oral historian, to help me prepare the students for the interviews. In keeping with the idea that the Interview Project should have some value to the community, I suggested that the interviews themselves deal with the subject of neighborhood. Gretchen and I went over a list of sample questions, as well as interview protocol and what to do in case of trouble. Because of the ways in which this project would veer sharply from traditional oral history methods of collection, it was helpful to have someone with Gretchen's expertise to define exactly where those diversions might—for better or worse—occur.

Getting the young people to think about the neighborhood was the first step in the process, so in the first class meeting I led a discussion about what defines neighborhood. This turned out to be a revealing glimpse into the socioeconomic reality of these children. One student said: "I don't really have a neighborhood. I live on a ranch and can't see any other houses from our land." It was no surprise that the kids who lived in the wealthier areas (and most of the kids in the pricey summer program were from such backgrounds) had less invested in their neighborhoods than those who lived in less affluent communities. While location mattered, "neighborhood" had little or no meaning to them. I pressed them to discuss characters in their neighborhood, and places of community interest, but the conversation kept stalling.

My one full scholarship student, an African American fourteen-year-old girl named Tania was from a world completely different from that of the other students. Because her mother had lost custody of her, Tania lived in public housing in a poorer section of San Francisco with her aunt and cousins. I had worked with Tania in an arts program called Young Artists at Work at the Yerba Buena Arts Center in San Francisco earlier that year. This program required that the participants' families earn no more than twenty thousand dollars a year for a family of four. Tania was extremely focused and extraordinarily talented. I was thrilled to give her this opportunity to study acting, and to validate her hard work and talent. However, putting her in this program with mostly white, upper-middle-class kids from the East Bay gave me pause. I wanted it to be a good experience for her and worried about what not being accepted in this strange new world where artistic ambition is unquestioned might do to her sense of self. During the course of the month-long program, I watched with terror and helplessness as Tania was mostly shunned by the other kids. She exasperated her classmates by her lack of academic skill. She had never tried to memorize lines, for example, whereas her classmates had been in countless school plays. My heart sank a dozen times as Tania fearlessly blurted out oddball questions or comments that made the other kids roll their eyes. But it wasn't long before her raw and unquestionable talent gained her a kind of exalted, if reluctant, status among them. During acting class improvisations, Tania shined. "I got to show my stuff," she told me recently. "I wanted to send out a message. I think that everyone was paying full attention." The kids may not have wanted to have lunch with her, but Tania made it impossible for them to dismiss her.

Tania had more to say about her neighborhood than almost any of the other kids. The socioeconomic stereotype in her case was, in many ways, true: unlike the idyllic, safer neighborhoods of the other students, Tania's was full of crime and danger. Still, Tania felt like she came from somewhere that mattered. She had family there, people to whom to answer should they spy her walking around after dark. There was a park across the street where she liked to watch the children play. Neighbors would watch out for each other's children and loan each other money. The concept of neighborhood already lived within Tania, and unlike most of the other kids, she didn't have to go searching for its meaning.

On that first day, we also discussed the idea of symbols. What is a symbol? The students mostly knew that it was something that represented something else, but it took some prodding to get them to go deeper. First I had them look around the room (a bare, unadorned classroom) and pick out things that were symbols. Items of jewelry, a Nike sneaker, a book were some of the things that sparked discussion. Then I had them think about things that existed in their neighborhoods that might be symbols. They mentioned statues of war heroes, a haunted house, a public pool, a mural. Tania talked about the park and also about a community center that she described as "clean," which meant that people cared about it and were proud of it. The discussion became excited and heated, and finally the notion of neighborhood seemed to gain some ground.

Finally I prepared the students for the interviews that would take place the next day. We would meet one hour in advance of setting out for the senior center so that they could prepare a list of questions. I explained that they wouldn't have tape-recorders and that they wouldn't take notes during the interview, and that they needed to be prepared with many more questions than they would likely need. Conducting the interviews this way would require them to listen more carefully, with their whole selves, I explained, instead of relying on notes or recordings. These interviews would become the basis for their own plays. But before anything else happened in the creative process, before the names could be changed or the drama recreated, the students had to do something important. They had to *listen*.

The next day, we met on the stage of the Berkeley Rep Thrust Theater, and the students began creating lists of questions for the interviews. Some had to do with neighborhood, and others focused on the interviewees' upbringing and childhood. Still other questions had to do with the scope of a life already lived. I encouraged the students to think of questions that they truly wanted to ask. What did they want to learn from these elderly people?

"What was your favorite neighborhood?"

"If you could go back and change one thing about your life, what would it be?"

"What was your happiest day?"

"When was a time that you learned something?"

I cautioned them not to treat the interviewees as people whose lives were entirely in the past tense. They are still alive, I reminded them, and might take offense at the assumption that they had already packed it in.

We went over the protocol for conducting the interviews. It was not necessary for them to make it through all the questions on their list. In fact, ideally they would only need one or two questions to get the conversation rolling onto unforeseen topics. Under no circumstances were they to argue with their subjects, or to go to their rooms with them. If they were unlucky enough to have a subject who was unwilling to talk, or who gave monosyllabic answers, they could call me over and I would see what I could do to help the situation. I assured them that they would most likely encounter the opposite reaction. These people had agreed to the interviews because they wanted to talk about themselves. I had personally spoken to each one of them on the phone, and they were enthusiastic about the project. Plenty of other prospects had declined to be interviewed. The ones who agreed did so because they were excited about the idea of helping teenagers write plays. Among the elders were Holocaust survivors, retired teachers, artists, civil rights activists, engineers. As one former teacher and writer said, "I think it's a wonderful thing to get young people to write plays."

Above all, I advised the students to treat the interview subjects with the utmost respect, both during the interviews and when they were recreating them in play form. Sharing life stories with no control over the outcome was an incredibly generous act. The students could change people, places, events, as the stories took shape in their minds, but under no circumstances would they be allowed to ridicule or mock. I asked them to keep in mind that their plays would be performed in front of the interview subjects at the end of the month, and that whether the people they spoke with would be able to recognize themselves in the plays or not, it was imperative that they feel good about having participated in the project.[3]

Listening

We arrived at the senior citizen center, took our place in a multipurpose room, and waited for the interview subjects to join us. The students were nervous, glancing over their lists of questions, slouching in corners. One by one the interview subjects came in, looking skeptical, sheepish, and a bit lost. They weren't quite sure what was expected of them, and I tried to be as welcoming as possible as I set each one up with a pair of students.

The students began tentatively and slowly. "What?! I can't hear you!" shouted one impossibly deaf old woman to Ben, a shy interviewer who looked stricken. Several students buried their faces in their lists of questions, refusing eye contact and alienating their subjects. I paced the room, offering what I hoped was a silent reminder to the teenagers of our purpose here. One interview had already ended with the subject and the interviewers staring silently at the floor. "What happened?" I asked the student, John, a somewhat arrogant, acne-scarred boy. "I asked him all my questions. It didn't go anywhere," he answered somewhat defensively.

Meanwhile, the rest of the room was starting to buzz. Many of the teenagers in the room were leaning forward in their seats, listening with their whole bodies now as the interviews heated up. Most of the girls were laughing and nodding their heads. Tania's interview with a man in a wheelchair was going well. The old people were smiling, delighted by the contact, talking, telling stories, remembering out loud to the delight of the students. It didn't seem like interviewing anymore; this was storytelling. And most important of all, the young people were *listening*, not as to a lecture, but with a kind of spirited wholeness you could see in their bodies and feel in the room. It was electric. More seniors came in, wondering what all the ruckus was, and then they asked to be interviewed as well. I took students whose interviews were not going well, like John's, and set them up with the new subjects. And now the room was packed and alive with teenagers and elderly people engaged in real dialogue. The strain was gone. The participants seemed to be enjoying each other. This was everything I had hoped for. The entire meaning of the Interview Project was evolving in the room in this moment. Whatever writing came of it would be gravy.

When forty-five minutes had passed, I reluctantly went around the room and told the students to begin to wrap up their interviews. More than one cried out, "Oh, no! We're just getting started!" An old woman named Myra jumped up and hugged her interviewer, a fifteen-year-old named Jean. "This young lady is a real gem," Myra announced with her arm around Jean. Jean, a heavyset, confident young woman who took her acting training very seriously looked at me and said, "This was the most AMAZING thing! Myra is the most AMAZING person! Is it OK if I give her my phone number?" I had to think fast about this one. There were, it seemed, a mountain of liability issues attached to every aspect of having minors under one's direct supervision, and I wasn't sure if facilitating a private relationship between Jean and Myra was entirely without consequence for me and for Berkeley Rep. When I said, "Sure," Jean just about jumped out of her skin. "Thank you SO much!"

Driving back to Berkeley Rep, I had three of the kids in my car. On the way there, they had been cool and polite, asking if it was OK to eat in my car, showing me and each other how adult they could be. Now they were all squealing and babbling at once as though they had all just met Sting backstage at one of his concerts.

"My guy escaped from the Nazis when he was a kid!"

"He always fought racism his whole life and even marched with Martin Luther King."

"My person is Einstein's cousin!" (Later, when Tania would hear this, she would ask, "He the guy with the hair?")

I sat back in my seat and soaked it up. That the sophistication of these teenagers had given way to childlike excitement meant to me that the Interview Project was already a success.

Repeating

When we got back to the theater, the students spent the rest of the remaining hour writing down everything they remembered from the interview. It didn't have to be important, or dramatic or relevant in any way to what they eventually might come to write about their interview subject. Body language, facial expressions, phrases, and whatever ideas that sprung into their own minds were all to be recorded. The students spread out in the 400-seat theater, and fell into delicious concentration. The sixteen students remembered and recorded in silence, all but for the scratching of their pens on paper. In doing so, they were taking the first step toward interpreting the interview material and creating from it their own characters and ideas for short plays. I had encouraged them not to treat the interview material as particularly sacred. Instead they were to use it as a springboard for their own ideas, and for dramatic possibility. Where was the drama in the stories they heard? Before they took off for their next class, I asked them to give the character of their interview subject a different name in order to make room for their own characters to take shape.

The next time we met, I had the students get up one by one on the big stage at the Rep and tell the story of their interviewee's life in the first person. What they didn't know, they could fill in however they wanted, extemporaneously. They could attempt to tell the whole life story or they could focus on one time period or episode. What I wanted was for them to get up on stage and talk. They were, after all, students of acting, and I wanted to exploit the desire to act as much as possible. In order to demystify the writing process, I would use this "up/down" method all throughout our month together. The student-actor would get up on her feet to let the creative subconscious do its work, and then the student-writer would sit down to record and rework the material. As it turned out, this was not only good for their writing but for their acting: as a result, some of the best "acting" in the program ended up being done in the writing classes.

Some of the students had a hard time with the idea of changing the story of their interview subject. "It's her story," a lovely, sensitive student named Emma said. "Who am I to change it?" I told her she could be as faithful to the original interview material as she wanted, but that choice should be made on the basis of what would make for a good play. Emma said, "OK," but she was uncomfortable. Here is where the values of playwriting and oral history began to compete with one another. Some of the students found themselves caught between the goal making of a "good" play with dramatic conflict, clear characterizations, and an emotional arc, and the their sense of faithfulness to the personal histories of the interview subjects. But much of this tension began to dissolve with their first performances of the stories they had heard.

The improvised monologues went something like this:

"When I was three years old, my mother died. I still miss her sometimes even though I can't remember her very much. My father and I planted an apple tree in her memory. Two years later, my father got sent to a concentration camp and I had to go live with my aunt in Hungary . . ."

"There was a water tower in my neighborhood. One day I woke up and someone had painted a huge Swastika on it. I didn't know what to do. I wanted to go out and paint over it, but my friend told me not to. She said it was too dangerous. My friend was never really my friend after that, not that way she used to be . . ."

And this from Tania:

"Nobody was supposed to be at the school at night. So I got some of my friends together one night and we went in and played around. I got them in that position, and we could have gotten in big trouble. But we didn't. No one caught us."

Somewhere between the interviews and the monologues we were now watching, the line between listening and creating had been crossed. Could anyone say where that line was any more? One by one the students got up and embodied their newly imagined characters, characters that one week ago would have been entirely outside their vocabulary. The listening part of the exercise had clearly been a success. The next step, that of repeating and refining, had been much more than that, as evidenced by the drama and conflict in the monologues we were now seeing. An orphan recreates the image of her dead mother; two friends split over issues of racism and civil rights; a boy ropes his friends into a risky adventure. Through the act of repeating others' stories, the students were already creating their own stories, stories that were being told through the eyes of the "other." As Tania later noted, "I had to put my own words from his [the interview subject's] perspective, but also from mine." Before any writing had officially begun, the question had already been raised: whose stories were these?

Creating

At the next class meeting, I had the students identify their main character. This distinction between "interview subject" and "main character" was important in continuing the sometimes difficult work of freeing themselves creatively from the interview material. The plays were no longer focused only on the interview subject, but also on the character that the young playwright had envisioned as a result of the preliminary work of listening and repeating.

Then I asked them to write a paragraph describing an event from a particular time in the life of this main character. It was little surprise to me that most of them chose events from their characters' adolescence, whether these were wholly invented, or taken directly from the interviews, or something in between.

A fourteen-year-old named Sarah wrote a story about a teenage girl in prewar Germany who wants to go out of the house wearing a necklace with the Jewish Star of David, but, fearing for her safety, her father forbids it. Here was an event that encapsulated all of what it means to be a teenager: the struggle of a young adult to assert her own identity against the overbearing protectiveness of her parents. The necklace was the non/fictional girl's way of defying her father and of asserting her identity through her own history. It was a symbol of adulthood and identification with her cultural and religious past. Sarah's story could have been set in suburban America in the year 2001, and the bones would have remained much the same. What, then, was gained by having the student arrive at her story by way of what was, for her, an extremely foreign, historical setting? Why the detour? It required her to put herself in the shoes of someone in an apparently faraway time and place, and therefore to begin to think of history as *close*: like the interviewee him or herself, alive and breathing, and close enough to *touch*. The same way that the teenage boy watching Fred Rochlin playing his nineteen-year-old self sees himself in the old man, these young drama students put themselves in place of the old people they interviewed and made their struggles their own. This was not a matter of vandalizing the interviewees' personal stories as some of the students had worried it might be. This was the empathic response of the emerging artist seeing global concerns in personal, intimate stories. Perhaps herein lay the community service aspect of the project, as it got these young privileged students to think about the life struggles of a marginalized group within their own communities, a group of people who had been until then largely invisible to them.

Now that we had zeroed in on the main character and the central event of the play, we spent the next several class meetings shaping scenes, and the students began to write their plays in earnest. We went over basic play format and play structure; the main character had to want something; there had to be an obstacle; through the ensuing conflict, something had to change. I had them write down what their main character wants, what he/she fears and what stands in his/her way.

For most of the students, these were familiar concepts, ones they had studied in previous acting classes. The challenge for them was to apply these same principles to the less familiar craft of writing. I assured them that they knew these ideas, that writing a play would draw upon much of the same knowledge they had gained as actors. For others, like Tania, these concepts were entirely new. Yet Tania knew these things instinctively. She knew them in her body. This was what made her such an exceptional actor. But in order to apply them to her writing, she would have to understand them intellectually. I told Tania not to worry too much about these ideas, that they would become clearer to her once she got down to writing her play. If the characters were there, and there was a relationship and a dramatic conflict, the rest would follow. She trusted me, and plowed ahead with the curiosity and laser-like focus that made her such a joy to have in class.

The next few class meetings were spent in silent concentration as the students wrote their plays. One by one, they would come to me whispering questions and asking for help. Was it okay if there was a third character? (It was, but two characters gave enough to work with for first time writers, and I discouraged them from adding other characters arbitrarily.) Was it okay to use flashbacks? (Absolutely, as long as they were not used as an easy way "out" of potential dramatic conflict.) But most of the questions revealed a lack of clarity about the essential dramatic conflict. "I'm not sure where to go from here," was a common dilemma that led me to ask the writer to define the central driving desire of the main character in specific terms. The answers were often vague and general such as "she wants to be happy," or "he never wants to have any pain anymore." Trying to create drama from a non-specific foundation, I told them, was like trying to build a house on Jello. You would only get so far and then everything would come tumbling to the ground.

I believed that, based on their previous acting training, they knew how to create specific intentions for their characters, but that, like Tania, they were unsure of how to translate these principles to the page. The scenes were too talky, and rambling. It was time to stop writing and work on some improvisational scenes. Inventing the exercise on the spot, I had each writer cast his or her two-character play with fellow students and then, in front of the whole class, give basic direction to his/her actors. This consisted mainly of defining the time and place of the scene and, most important, identifying the separate desires of the two characters and the specific obstacles that stood in the way of each character realizing those desires. It was extremely helpful for the class to listen as the writers struggled to define the conflict for their actors. The familiar context of improvisation made creating dramatic conflict less intimidating for the writers: trying to help out their fellow writer-actors "on their feet," as it were, under the pressure of very little available time, each student seemed better able to articulate the dramatic conflict in their plays. In turn, the actors' improvisation fed back into the writers' basic ideas, helping them to crystallize the central action. This exercise involved risks but I trusted that the students would, by this point, treat each other's work with respect and care, and hoped that they would generously reveal to each other the strengths and weaknesses in their overall concepts.

The improvisations proved to be more helpful than I could have imagined. They were an invaluable lesson in collaboration. The actors took seriously the responsibility and opportunity of creating conflict where it was lacking in the student-playwrights' draft scripts. The writers were thrilled to have their work improved upon, and the actors respectfully and artfully made bold, intelligent choices based on the writers' basic concepts. Charged with keeping the scene alive through conflict, the actors added an urgency that was often missing from the scenes as written. Relationships took on emotional depth and color and entire histories were created by way of such off-the-cuff lines as: "You never want me to be happy," or "I always knew you were jealous of her." The writers took furious notes as they watched their scenes unfold before them in ways they could not have foretold. The scenes were so much fun to watch that there was little room for any sense of private ownership. It was particularly gratifying to me that many of the scenes incorporated the theme of neighborhood and made use of symbols to distill the dramatic conflict to its essence. The water tower, the necklace, the apple tree, the forbidden school. It took two class periods to complete the round of improvisations. Then the writers began rewriting their plays.

Telling

Nervousness set in among the young writers as the day of the performance at the senior center grew closer. "What if my person doesn't like what I wrote? What if she gets mad at me for changing her story around? My play has nothing to do with the interview . . ." These were some of the concerns voiced during the final class hours. I took it as a good sign that the teens were nervous; it showed an investment in their work, and also in their relationships with the interview subjects. They read and reread their work, changed lines of dialogue here and there, tweaked and refined their scenes, all with a view to the final telling.

We arrived at the senior center and repaired to the same all-purpose room where the interviews had been conducted. While we waited for the seniors to come in, the writer/directors gave last minute directions to their actors (mostly the same casts as in the improvisations). I gave final instructions; the actors should enunciate and be heard; the writers should bow after their plays were read; all should enjoy the experience.

When the audience of seniors had finally trickled in and were seated, I made a short announcement reiterating that these short plays were works in progress inspired by the interviews that took place a month earlier. Then the two-player casts began reading the plays one by one on a small, makeshift stage at one end of the room. The actors were nervous, as were the writers. It didn't help their anxiety that the elderly audience had a hard time hearing, and the readings were punctuated by shouts of "Louder!" so that after a while, the students on stage were practically yelling out their lines. It was this interaction between student/performer and interviewee/audience member that distinguished the student readings from those featuring professional actors, and that made me value them so much more. What remains important about hiring professionals, it seems to me, is that the young writer has the best possible voice for his work, as well as the pure "playwright's" experience of sitting back and listening without being in the spotlight. In our case, the young writers had the same opportunity to listen to others performing their plays, but with the additional benefit of having worked with students like themselves to create the plays and performances. Indeed the student actors had been instrumental in the writing process, and therefore had more invested in these creative relationships. It also brought the audience closer to the real experience of the teenaged writers. The fact that the actors were being shouted at to speak up also brought the audience closer to the real-life experience of the teenaged writers, creating a strange intimacy between the old people who were yearning to hear and the young actors for whom there was now no longer a "fourth wall" or invisible barrier between themselves and their listeners. Moreover all the people in the space—the senior interview subjects, the actors, the writers—were in it together; they had all joined in the creation of these plays. When the professionals took part in the Interview Project the following month, something crucial was lost in the distance created between the audience and the writer/actor.

I tried to pick out the interview subject whose story was being told from the faces in the audience, and often it was not difficult. There was usually one person listening to the story, watching the young actors on stage, whose face showed a particularly vivid mixture of pride and vulnerability. He or she would giggle shyly and strain forward in his/her seat. He/She would say "Hmm," in dramatic punctuation as though watching a familiar story whose twists and turns were unknown. As they were. All the material, by the time I heard it, was already in transition from "fact" to "fiction." Indeed, the process of transformation had begun with the listening during the interviews themselves, interviews which I myself did not hear. I was, however, witness to the process by which this material became what it was on the day of performance. The student who heard the story about the teenager wanting to wear the Star of David transformed the single narrator's tale into a two-person drama. Two actors played father and daughter, each reading from scripts that shook slightly in their anxious hands. The scene rose to something like this:

FATHER: If you go out of the house wearing that, you put your own life at risk. I cannot allow you to do that.
DAUGHTER: It's my life. If you're so weak to hide yourself and who you are from the world, the least you can do is allow me to be who I am, to be who you made me.

During the reading of this play, an elderly audience member broke down in tears. Did the interviewees see themselves in the plays? How did they see their personal life experiences reenvisioned by the young writers? Did they feel disappointed that they were not more directly represented? And finally, were these still their stories?

Della Pollock says "a story is not a story until it is told; it is not told until it is heard; once it is heard, it changes . . . a story is not a story until it changes."[4] It can be said, then, that these stories had not existed until now. However often told or long buried, they were living a new life through the voices of these teenagers. Here was another turn on the Fred Rochlin experience. While watching Fred, the young audience member saw a reverse image of himself in an old man playing his young self. Here was an older person watching her young self as told by the young playwright. The teenagers had to see themselves in the old peoples' lives in order to identify creatively with them, and they had to put themselves in the skin of another. To the very extent that listening is a form of bearing witness, it also spurred these students to engage their own stories in performance. And yet then, as it turned out, there was another, deeper form of bearing witness, that of telling stories that were not entirely their own. To bear witness, not from outside the story, but to inhabit it from within had been the point, the goal of the Interview Project. During the readings, the listener and teller had switched places. Now the audience member who had been the original narrator witnessed his or her history as well as, through the body of this young person carrying it on, his or her future, all at once.

Something entirely new was being created on the stage of this bland room. The stories were taking on a new shape, a new life. They were becoming the property of teller and listener alike, of subject and writer, of young and old. None could claim sole ownership. The extraordinary act of generosity on the part of the seniors in telling their stories, knowing that they would be recreated without any further input from them, was having its payoff. Why did they agree to this? Watching the faces of the audience members it became clear to me: they did it not only because they wanted to tell their own stories but because they wanted to hear someone else's.

After the readings, the students and seniors milled about socially for a few minutes before we had to leave in time for the end of the school day. There was a palpable sense of relief on the part of the students and their interview subjects. So much risk had been taken, and yet no one was hurt, no one offended, no expectations dashed. Several of the seniors beamed at their interviewers with parental pride. Some of the teens brought along thank-you cards for their interview subjects. Most of the audience members commented on how interesting the plays had been, and how intelligent and thoughtful. All were glad to have had the opportunity to hear what was on the minds of these young people, and to have helped in the process.

What had occurred here? What had changed? And what, if any, was the effect on the community? Certainly some of the early class discussions had gotten the students to think about the idea of neighborhood. But a true sense of community was cultivated more in the act of entering the senior citizen center than in all the class discussions put together. A group of teenagers listened to a bit of history, put it through the transformational rigors of a creative process, and came back to tell what they had made of it. Speaking someone else's story in their own voices, they became aware of something outside themselves. Some of the students were struck by how much easier their lives were now in contrast to people of past generations. Others were impressed by how similar were the struggles of past and present life. Tania would later tell me: "What I learned is that things never change. My guy, he moved around a lot.

His brother died. The same things happen now that are hard." She could see the outline of history set against contemporary life and it made that history come alive.

Los Angeles playwright and community activist Luis Alfaro conducts a program in which teenagers and senior citizens living in the same community are paired to collaborate on a neighborhood monument. They must decide together what the monument commemorates, where in the neighborhood it should live, and what it should look like. The object (and genius) of this exercise is obviously not the monument (which after all never gets built), but the hard won agreement between young person and old. The imagined monument becomes their joint project, their joint property, something for which they have come together in the spirit of community. The monument of The Interview Project was the story. Telling stories has always been a way to join people together, a way of humanizing that which is in danger of becoming dehumanized, of bearing witness and keeping history alive. For the participants of the Interview Project, the story was the initial meeting point and the final product. It was the thing that lives between the generations, the place at which they meet. And through its metamorphosis, it changed those who were witness to it. A story is not a story until it changes; it is also not a story until it somehow changes us, listener and teller alike.

Notes

1. Fred Rochlin's *Old Man in a Baseball Cap* was eventually published as a memoir by Harper Collins (1999).
2. Previous work with incarcerated youth included a recent Playmaking Project at the Alameda County Camp Sweeney division of Juvenile Hall; work with *EachOne ReachOne* of Matteo County, CA at the San Francisco Juvenile Hall; Playmaking with the Virginia Avenue Project of Los Angeles; and playwriting workshops at A *Place Called Home* in South Central Los Angeles.
3. As a happy coincidence, the production running at the Berkeley Rep at this time was *The Laramie Project*. Here was a chance to illustrate the theatrical objective of The Interview Project to the participating students and to demystify it. Not only were the students in the summer program all invited to see the production, I arranged to have them speak with the actors after the performance in a "talk-back." I had mixed feelings about *The Laramie Project* as a piece of theater. While powerful in its style and message, I found it lacking in the complexity its subject matter demands. It felt, to me, more of an homage to the town of Laramie than a probing examination of the bigotry that led to the murder of Matthew Shepard. However, when I saw the production again with my students, I appreciated it much more. Much of my criticism fell away in the face of the students' enthusiasm and emotional response to the play. Not only was it a show that might make young people want to come to the theater again, it was a living embodiment of oral history. While I still maintained my reservations about *The Laramie Project*, the students' response in some ways challenged my critique. Jack, an exuberant, sixteen-year-old bear of a boy, said to me after the play, "I am not the same person after seeing *The Laramie Project*."

The discussion with the actors was exciting. The actors were generous and intelligent in the discussion, happy to be of help with the students' own interviewing process. It was fortunate that the production was largely composed of the original cast who conducted the actual interviews and who played themselves on stage (unlike many subsequent productions, in which actors played the actor/interviewers). The playwriting students had the chance to ask questions about the interviews in Laramie, how the actors felt about them, and how the interviews ultimately came together to make the play that had so moved them.

"Did you ever get angry at the person you were interviewing?"

"Were the words of the play taken verbatim from the interviews?"

"How did you feel about being in Laramie after what happened there?"

One of the actors revealed that as a gay man, he had to confront his own fears in order to do the work at hand. Another talked about growing emotional during one of the interviews. These actors, stars in the young actors' eyes for being on the big stage at Berkeley Rep, were now colleagues, and the world of living history seemed full of purpose and creative possibility. The Interview Project was to differ in many ways from *The Laramie Project*, most notably in the absence of any reference in the final plays to the writers and interviewers themselves. Interestingly, none of the students had any inclination to write themselves into the story, and, as this aspect of *Laramie* was one about which I had serious questions, I was pleased that this never came up. Nevertheless, the exposure to *The Laramie Project* and the fine actors involved with the production was an invaluable asset to the students' deeper understanding of oral history.

4. Pollock, paper presented at the national meeting of the Oral History Association, San Diego, 2002. See also Pollock, "Memory, Remembering, and Histories of Change: A Performance Praxis," *The Performance Studies Handbook*, ed. Judith Hamera and D. Soyini Madison (Thousand Oaks, CA: Sage, 2005).

FIVE

Memory and Performance in Staging *The Line* in Milwaukee: A Play About the Bitter Patrick Cudahy Strike of 1987–1989

Michael Gordon

Michael Gordon, a senior labor historian, shows what can happen in the risky and passionate collaboration among historians, interviewees, and theater practitioners. In the production of The Line, *which Gordon rehearses here, we see the possibilities not only for amplifying under-heard voices but, in so doing, gaining more precise understanding of the ideological pressures that constrain them and the strike negotiations they initiated. Accordingly, good history may not only make good theater but good theater may make better history.*

In plays based extensively on oral history, interviewees help to shape how the plays depict their lives and the events they remember. Interviewees' memories provide details and perceptions that can determine the interpretive authority of the play and provide engagement and immediacy. Yet in developing scripts about historical events that use oral interviews, playwrights should not rely on individual and collective memories alone, not just because memory can be unreliable, but also because evidence from written and other sources may be needed to create scripts that reflect history's complexity and depth. For these reasons, playwrights will find it helpful to work closely with historians, and with interviewees and the cast. This kind of collaboration can result in plays about history that are both good theater—and good history.

My own work on a play about a strike in the Milwaukee area between 1987 and 1989 suggests how difficult and rewarding such collaborations can be. It also suggests that plays about labor history, specifically, can also stimulate public discussion about such important issues as attacks on unions, plant closures, job loss, and declining living standards long after the events that are depicted in such plays have passed. The project I was involved with, *The Line*, dramatized the twenty-eight-month long strike by members of United Food and Commercial Workers Local P-40 at the Patrick Cudahy meat-packing plant in Cudahy, Wisconsin, a city of about 19,000 people just south of Milwaukee. Although reviving memories of the strike was painful for many, oral history interviews that I conducted for the play gave former P-40 members an opportunity to help shape the historical content and orientation of the play. In addition, other research I conducted, along with post-performance discussions with the audience, gave union members and others in the community new insights about their lives and the strike and helped reaffirm the values that led P-40 members to strike in the first place.

The project began in 1993 when I first approached John Schneider, the artistic director of Milwaukee's Theatre X, asking if the theater company would be interested in producing a labor play based on oral history that would spark discussion about the plight of American workers and unions over the last twenty-five years. Formed in 1971, Theatre X is an experimental collective known for its determination to present theater in a spirit that is embodied in its motto, "Vision, Industry, Nerve." Schneider and his colleagues eagerly agreed, and we quickly decided to focus on the Patrick Cudahy strike because it typified the plight of workers and unions. It also included many features that we thought would make for provocative drama and discussion.

Key events in the company's history and the strike seemed especially typical and relevant. Formed in 1893, Patrick Cudahy remained under family control until 1971 when it was sold to a succession of out-of-state companies, including its current owner, Smithfield Foods of Virginia, which purchased it in 1984.[1] Smithfield installed new local managers at Cudahy who believed they had to make drastic changes in order to be more competitive and to reverse the financial losses suffered under the previous owners. They especially worried about their aging hog slaughtering operations, lower wage scales at competing firms, transportation costs from distant hog-raising centers, and the increasing number of costly grievances filed by employees since Mark Rosenbaum had become the P-40 president in 1981. For over a year, company officials explored options and plotted strategy. In the spring of 1986, they received important new advice from a Milwaukee law firm that had just finished helping a Hormel meatpacking plant in Austin, Minnesota, to defeat a UFCW Local P-9 strike there. The firm now helped Cudahy officials to formulate a set of demands for steep concessions that they hoped to impose after the contract with P-40 expired on January 1, 1987. When bargaining sessions began on November 10, 1986, Cudahy officials, under new legal advice, launched a carefully orchestrated campaign for sweeping changes. The company's most staggering blows were released in its economic demands in mid-December: wage cuts of up to $3 an hour, "the right to subcontract work," the elimination of plantwide seniority and insurance benefits for retirees, an increase in the number of part-time workers to twenty percent of the workforce, and massive changes in contract language.[2] P-40 members were incensed. They had agreed to wage reductions totaling $2.50 in 1982 and 1984 under the previous owner. They now argued that Patrick Cudahy could remain profitable without the new cuts and other changes, and that union members could not withstand additional decline in their standards of living. The new wage cuts were indeed steep. Workers who were making $9.00 to $9.80 an hour would be paid $6 to $8.65 an hour. With these cuts, many workers in 1987 faced the prospect of making the same wages they had received at Cudahy in 1967. P-40 members alleged that the company tried to force the strike, hoping that it could break the union, an allegation the union eventually formalized in an unfair labor practice complaint to the National Labor Relations Board. On January 4, 1987, nearly all 850 P-40 members voted to strike. P-40 resigned itself to defeat and ended the strike on April 30, 1989, after workers failed in their last-minute bid to buy Patrick Cudahy during company bankruptcy proceedings.[3]

There was much about this strike to recommend it as an oral history study and a play. The project unfolded quickly. In the summer and fall of 1994, I conducted research in printed sources and interviewed twenty-three former members of P-40 and two company officials. By January 1995, I had given Schneider of Theatre X my narrative history of the strike and a set of transcribed interview excerpts. During the spring and summer of that year, as he transformed the information into a script, Schneider and I had many long conversations about recent labor history and the strike. Joining us were former P-40 members, and, once rehearsals began, members of the cast and crew. This collaborative effort culminated in twenty performances of *The Line* during January and February, 1996. The following September, the play was revived for a performance at the University of Wisconsin-Milwaukee in connection with a program on "Theatre and Social Justice in America," and for two perform-ances at the University of Wisconsin-Madison.

The Line is divided into two acts of about one hour each. Approximately seventy-five percent of all dialogue in the play is taken directly from the oral history interviews, logs of bargaining sessions, and quotations from newspapers. The rest was created by the playwright to flesh out scenes and provide background. Act I begins in 1984, shortly before Smithfield Foods purchased Patrick Cudahy. Plant workers are just realizing that a failed attempted buyout by a former company president may have been part of a plan to soften them up for more wage concessions. Subsequent scenes depict how Smithfield's new managers devised their strategy over late-night dinners at a local hotel. Interspersed are scenes in which workers, dressed in shop-floor clothes, vividly describe how hogs were slaughtered, disassembled, and made into pork products. The action then shifts to the heated bargaining sessions that occurred from December 3, 1986, until the contract expired without a settlement on December 31. Occasionally the scene temporarily shifts to workers testifying about the implications of company demands for tighter worker supervision and limitations on breaks. For example, "Sharon" explains her difficulty breaking into traditional male jobs in the 1970s, and her subsequent harassment by supervisors. "Marie" explains that she has just seven minutes to race two departments over and one flight down for a bathroom break. "I quite often eat my lunch on the toilet stool," she says, "because I don't have time" (see figure 5.1). Act I ends early on the morning of January 1, 1987, when a supervisor informs "Sharon" that she has to go home because the contract has expired and "You don't work here any more."[4]

Act II opens with picket line confrontations and the company hiring unskilled strikebreakers. Workers struggle to make ends meet on $40 a week strike pay and donated food. The action explores their belief that executives and consultants tried to force the strike. The play concludes with a confrontation among workers, company officials, and company attorneys over the firm's motives, and how and why the strike ended as it did after the failed union buyout.

Three key points emerged from my research and our discussions that formed the main interpretive points of the play: the difficulty of meatpacking work, the sources of workers' anger, and the union's claim that the company violated the National Labor Relations Act by not bargaining in good faith. All these themes were largely absent from public discussion during the strike, but the collaborative, retrospective nature of this project—the "shared interpretive authority," as the historian Michael Frisch would call it[5]—*forced* these themes into the forefront and provided new insights about the strike.

What emerged from my interviews and from discussions with former P-40 members at their annual reunion is that many workers believed their jobs were simply too arduous and demeaning to do for just over $6 an hour. Former meat packers pointed out that media coverage focused largely on wage issues but never conveyed a sense of the work conditions. At the time of the strike, workers in the "kill and cut" processed eight thousand hogs a day. Elsewhere in the plant, workers produced and packaged hundreds of thousands of pounds of pork products—sausage, bacon, hot dogs, ham, lard, and much else. In creating the play, the workers, Schneider, and I agreed that we needed to convey a sense of the intensity and pace of this work so that audiences would understand that company demands for drastic wage cuts meant more to Cudahy employees than just a loss of purchasing power. Workers believed that company officials no longer valued the enormous effort required to process and produce products of quality. "It was just amazing how fast these guys would work," former P-40 member Don Korinek remembered of workers on the kill floor. "How hard they would work. I mean [company president Roger Kapella] had a labor force there that was killin' themselves for him, you know. He never gave that an idea, I think."[6] Schneider, collaborating with set and lighting designers Richard H. Graham and Melanie Graham, devised an ingenious approach to convey the nature of shop-floor work and its context. The set resembled a section of the abandoned kill floor, which Rick Graham, Schneider and I toured in the summer of 1995. The set powerfully evoked the grim context of death and sweat, but nothing we could have done would have adequately conveyed the stench of dead hogs that still seeped from damp walls seven years after the "kill and cut" had been closed. Workers' accounts helped stimulate the audience's sensual imagination. Some work descriptions were graphic. The character "Steve" (who is a composite of several interviewees) describes how he wore earplugs as he drove hogs up several flights of narrow stairs to the kill floor because as they near their death "hogs scream at exactly the same decibel level as a Lear jet taking off." "It's something you can't imagine," he says later. "I remember a hog that must have been pregnant, and she was aborting. And the hog in back of her was eating it. And I thought, 'I can't believe I'm watching this.' Another time a guy took one of those little piglets and threw it up in the air, and hit it across the room with a stick, like a damn baseball bat, and I thought, I can't believe I'm watching this, either."[7]

Other workers tell how they lost fingernails and skin from pulling hot resin off hogs in the de-hairing process in temperatures of well over one hundred degrees. They note each step in the cutting process, from cutting eyelids, ears, and cheeks, to the organs and the intestines, which were still pulsating and steaming as they reached workers on the line. The small intestines were sent to the chitterlings department. The large went to casings, where "Marie" worked. "And we all know what's in casings," she says during Act I:

> That's the only job I never talked in, 'cause the casings would burst and you didn't want to have your mouth open. Oh, sure. (*She laughs*) You put the casings on this tube—almost like a stuffing horn—that blows water through, which blows out all the crap. And maybe there's a little tear or a thinner membrane somewhere, and they break. And you get splattered with shit. Literally. And, boy, were you a mess! It reeked in there, and no air-conditioning in that department. At night I'd go to eat supper, and I'd put my hand up to my mouth with a fork or spoon, and I could smell that. I'd go: Oh! (*She shudders.*) The dogs in the neighborhood loved me. I was always getting chased by dogs.[8]

The actors describe accidents that workers had endured. Fingers were cut off. One worker died after being shifted from the extreme heat of the kill floor to the cooler. Another, "Andy" in pork sausage, perished when an ammonia pipe exploded above his head and froze him black.[9] Workers who pulled fat shaped like a leaf from the chest cavities of the hogs faced hellish conditions. "It's used in baking," Steve explains:

> The leaf puller grabs the bottom of the leaf with one hand, and with the other, fists the fat free from the back and the ribs, and then pulls the whole leaf out in one piece: A thousand per hour, times two. It's so exhausting, each man works for twenty minutes and then rests for forty. They'd be soaking wet, even their jeans. Rainstorm. Imagine working in a rainstorm.[10]

The demanding nature of meatpacking work was inseparable from the second major theme that emerged from discussions and interviews: workers' anger toward the company and the extent to which it was deeply embedded in generational memory. Generational memory is formed by shared experiences that shape life-course values and behavior—and by the joint recollection of such experiences.[11] The workers whom I interviewed explained that company wage demands were not just an affront to the comforts, necessities, and occasional luxuries of middle-income lifestyles. They believed the wage cuts and other demands betrayed the powerful value system that they internalized from the larger culture since childhood. These values helped shape their expectations and governed their behavior. Their anger therefore was rooted in the intertwining of personal and class history with national history.

Kathryn Dudley has helped us understand much about the sources of workers' anger and their sense of betrayal in similar situations elsewhere. In her study analyzing how 5,500 Kenosha, Wisconsin, Chrysler workers responded to jobs that were lost after Lee Iacoocca closed the plant in 1988, she learned that former Chrysler workers lived by cultural and moral precepts that were embodied in an unwritten social compact. In exchange for a lifetime of hard work, they believed they would receive job security and freedom from economic insecurity. They viewed their commitment to Chrysler as a commitment to their community and their children too: they worked hard to keep the company profitable as an investment for their children, whom they believed would also get good paying jobs at Chrysler. Dudley also found that many workers linked their hard work to a larger national purpose, believing that their contributions created a solid industrial base that would help keep America strong. In the light of these cultural beliefs, Chrysler workers attributed their loss of jobs to corporate leaders who had no commitment to the national purpose.[12]

This strong moral code was shaped by a series of events and forces that emerged after World War II and continued into the 1960s. The events included the massive strikes of 1946; the conservative anti-union reaction that resulted in the Taft-Hartley Act of 1947; the purge of radicals from the CIO in the late 1940s; the beginnings of the Cold War; McCarthyism; and the enormous postwar economic boom. Some of the more important forces that shaped workers' attitudes and expectations derived from the massive ideological campaign conducted by business leaders to "sell free enterprise" to America after the war. In *Selling Free Enterprise: The Business Assault on Labor and Liberalism, 1945–1960*, Elizabeth Fones-Wolf shows how business used schools, churches, community institutions, and the media to reorient workers to American capitalism, and to discredit the postwar liberal agenda.[13]

The former Patrick Cudahy workers with whom I talked helped me to understand the effects of this campaign. They said they had grown up internalizing what their teachers, clergy, politicians, parents, and business leaders said they had to do in order to become good citizens and achieve a middle-class lifestyle: work hard; remain loyal to their employer and their country; stay out of trouble; provide for their families; and live frugally. Workers who abided by these powerful precepts were rewarded accordingly. But in the 1980s, these same workers became angry when they discovered that employers like Cudahy still wanted them to follow such rules but were no longer willing to reward them for doing so.[14]

The play's creators decided that it was important to incorporate expressions of this anger into the script to make the play historically accurate, as well as to clarify the sources of the anger. In the interviews, workers often explained their feelings about this betrayal in long monologues. Schneider interspersed salient excerpts from the interviews at various points in Act II as the strike careens to its end, sometimes incorporating the words of several interviewees into the voice of a single character. In one scene, for example, as company president Roger Kapella explains his position to a reporter in his office, "Barbara" presents *her* views to a reporter on the picket line down below (see figure 5.2). She says:

> You can see what they're doing. I think it's the times, isn't it? They're trying to bust unions everywhere, they're trying to knock people's wages down, they're trying to make this instead of a middle-class job, a . . . I don't know the term to use. A low-class job? A peon job? We're not uneducated. We're not stupid. We're hard workers. We're family people. We're good people. We're not just people who come from the bottom of the barrel, people that only want to work a few weeks just to get by, people that don't care or that don't know any better. We're not those kind of people. And I think they're trying to make it that way—that there won't *be* any middle class! That you can't graduate from high school and make a living. You know what I'm trying to get at? I think that's what's so humiliating for me.

In yet another soliloquy, "Barbara" again speaks for other workers as she focuses her sense of their common betrayal by corporate America:

> I loved the people. I was eighteen tears old when I left my parents' house. I'd never talked to a black person in my life. I go there . . . and I felt such a family bonding there.
>
> People were genuinely concerned. I don't know if people were more compassionate in that era, or . . . Things were good. We made good money, people felt good about themselves. We had goals. People would strive to get their kids through school, or . . .
>
> At the time I started, there were a bunch of kids my age. Our goals were—we were all getting married. We all planned our weddings together. We threw little showers at work.
>
> And my goal was—I was gonna work there forever. (*She laughs*) My goal was a house, a family. Children were a big priority. And vacations. We all kind of planned vacations.
>
> A comfortable life. And you cannot do that to a person! You cannot take a person who is making ten dollars an hour and make him work for six! You understand what I'm saying? Six dollars an hour—You're not gonna do anything but put food on your table and a roof over your head. You can't have any more than that. You can't have goals like that of sending your kids to college, or being able to plan a Florida vacation, or buy a bigger, better house, or a new car. I thought that's what America was![15]

The historical anger in *The Line* explodes even more forcefully in a scene near the end of the play in a discussion about the union's effort to purchase the company during bankruptcy proceedings through the union's Cudahy Equity Co-op. The contract package P-40 submitted to the bankruptcy judge called for increased benefits but a base wage of just $7 an hour, far less than many workers made under the old contract, and just one dollar more than the amount proposed by the company. Company vice president Dan Habighorst tells the audience—as he told me in his interview—that the package was ironic, because after the company abandoned slaughtering and focused solely on processing it actually *increased* base wages to $8.08 an hour. "Marie" quickly retorts (these are the actual words of a confidential interviewee, not the real Marie): "I would have worked for the co-op for six dollars an hour, but I'd rather go on welfare than work for you, because you are a liar. If you offered me twenty dollars an hour, I'd tell you to stick it up your ass."[16] The word "liar" is significant. Marie believes that company officials not only lied about the need for concessions, but more fundamentally that they lied to workers about what they had to do to make it in America.

A third theme in *The Line*—that company officials bargained in bad faith—was widely believed by P-40 members both during the strike and afterward, even though none had direct evidence to support the charge. At the time of the strike and during the interviews I later conducted, company officials flatly denied they had tried to force the strike in order to break the union.[17] Although no evidence available to the public conclusively supports the union's claim, two sets of documents that I uncovered in files of the National Labor Relations Board's (NLRB) Region 30 in Milwaukee suggest how company attorneys helped Cudahy officials devise a bargaining strategy and carry it to the bargaining table.

My examination of documents filed with the NLRB revealed a complicated legal dispute. The NLRB in Washington ultimately ruled that 220 company documents subpoenaed by the union to support its charge of bad faith bargaining could not be introduced because the items were subject to attorney–client privilege. The case went back to the Milwaukee level for another hearing, but the hearing was never reconvened and the issue never decided.[18] When P-40's buyout attempt failed, Patrick Cudahy agreed to pay the union $515,000 if it would agree to drop the NLRB charges and end the strike. By then, P-40 had no money to continue the legal proceedings. Union officials were desperate to gain at least some compensation for their beleaguered members and accepted the deal.

Because the subpoenaed documents were never introduced into evidence, they are not public records and not open to researchers. Available NLRB records do contain a detailed description of the documents prepared by Cudahy attorneys for the hearing. One item of interest was a "Strategic Planning Guide Book" that outlined legal constraints, legal tools, cost information, and other items that gave an insight into the company's objectives during negotiations.[19] Other documents in this set include "The strike manual," which "describes in detail the probable legal consequences of a range of employer responses to a strike"; advice about negotiating strategy and how to determine whether an impasse had been reached in negotiations that would permit the company to implement its final offer unilaterally; and opinions, notes, and summaries regarding layoffs, unemployment compensation, proposals, replacement workers, picketing, and much else.[20] Also in the NLRB files was a log of all bargaining sessions that summarizes each person's remarks and includes many verbatim excerpts that helped us understand how company strategy actually unfolded at the bargaining table. Schneider and I believed that the logs lend much weight to the claim that Patrick Cudahy was preoccupied with pressing the limits of legally permitted negotiating options while really seeking to create an "impasse," which would permit the company to unilaterally implement its final offer and force a strike.[21]

Schneider imaginatively brought this important hidden history into Act I by staging excerpts from the logs covering many bargaining sessions. We see negotiators arguing over lie detector and drug tests, the length of bathroom breaks, the meaning of contract language regarding "maximum productivity" standards and employees' sexual preference, wages, and other issues. Schneider helps the audience follow the negotiations by staging them on a raised platform that rolls two feet onto the kill floor set with each new bargaining session (see figure 5.3). A slide projects the date on the wall. The company's strategy to force the strike creeps into the discussions—as it did in the actual bargaining logs—until it holds a prominent place by the end of December.

In the play, as in real life, on December 15, the union president, Mark Rosenbaum, and the company attorney, Thomas Krukowski, haggle over the company's desire to subcontract work. "I think you know we won't agree to something that will eliminate half the jobs in the unit," Rosenbaum says. "This is our last best proposal," Krukowski snaps back. "This theme will carry throughout the rest of the negotiations. We'll listen to anything you have to say. Try and persuade us. But this is our last best proposal. What you see may be all you'll be able to see." On December 16—two weeks before the contract was to expire—the company finally presented its economic demands, including a base wage of $6.15 an hour. "It's an initial proposal," the lawyer assures. "The language proposal is our last best proposal. . . . The current contract expires December 31. That's coming right up." "We've never had a problem extending the contract before," Rosenbaum says. "We do now," Krukowski replies. "We do have a problem with extending it now. When the train leaves the station, we hope you're on it." On December 22, the union suggests the need for a mediator. The company quickly jumps at the chance to press a position that will enable the company to impose its new contract unilaterally. "If you feel you need a mediator because we're at impasse . . .," the lawyer says. "A mediator is generally used when at impasse. Is that why you're requesting it?" A union attorney, Robert Bartell, flatly retorts that "It has nothing to do with impasse," but Krukowski keeps pressing his agenda.

On December 24, Krukowski reads a letter to union officials that he has drafted for the company vice president, as the vice president looks on over the lawyer's shoulder. Schneider took the wording verbatim from the actual letter, which accompanied Patrick Cudahy's final contract offer. "After carefully reviewing all of the union's proposals, responses, and positions, we believe that we are deadlocked and that we are in a position, after having bargained in good faith with you, to be able to furnish you with our final proposal. Because the parties are at impasse on the central issues, and because the contract is set to expire six days from the receipt of this letter, the company intends to implement its wages, hours and other conditions of employment as set forth in this final proposal, at 12:00 AM on January 1, 1987."

On December 29, Krukowski presses the impasse issue one last time. "So there's nothing to consider," he says. "Struck work, diametrically opposed. Part time employees, diametrically opposed. Chain bumping, diametrically opposed. And wages, diametrically opposed." When a union official requests an extension of the contract, this exchange between the Cudahy attorney, Krukowski, and the P-40 attorney, Bartell, ensues:

KRUKOWSKI: The company is ready to meet with you around the clock until midnight, December 31. We will not agree to an extension of the contract. We're prepared to drop forty items. You have our list. On key issues, we're diametrically opposed. That's impasse.

BARTELL: We don't feel we're at impasse.

KRUKOWSKI: We've been at impasse since December 23.[22]

Did Patrick Cudahy bargain in bad faith? Because we lacked concrete evidence, this major question remains unresolved in *The Line*—as it did in the strike. It was important, however, to bring the issue out of the hearing room shadows and to restore its place in the strike's history. The bargaining struggle and the company's tactics remains a theme throughout the play. It returns in Act II, as the characters at first rejoice at an administrative law judge's initial finding of company misdeeds, only later to lament the NLRB's decision to send the case back for rehearing. It reemerges at the end of the play when all the characters confront each other and plead their cases to the audience, reviving the themes of work, anger, and the company's strategy. Audience members, among them interviewees and other former P-40 members, Cudahy managers, local residents affected by the strike, people learning about the strike for the first time, indeed had much to consider—and to discuss. Some stayed for up to an hour after performances to talk about the strike and the play with me, Schneider, the cast members, and others. Could the strike have been averted? Did the company bargain in bad faith? When it was clear Patrick Cudahy would close the kill and cut jobs permanently, should P-40 members have granted the concessions to save their jobs? Were the union's positions unreasonable in light of the company's previous losses and its need to be more competitive? Did Patrick Cudahy officials play fast and loose with the bankruptcy laws by resorting to protection after they first gambled on keeping the plant open with strikebreakers? Does the National Labor Relations Act adequately protect workers in such situations? What role should government play in bitter labor–management struggles that have such serious effects on workers and communities? Overall, the discussions suggest that Schneider's determination to take his subject seriously helped audiences understand the complexity of these and related questions.

Discussions among actors and former P-40 members during rehearsals and over beers at a favorite bar near Patrick Cudahy's headquarters provided even more insight about workers' beliefs and values for cast members and the audience. This collaboration especially helped to shape the play's interpretive authority, and especially Schneider's decision to let the workers summarize their view of the strike's meaning at the end of the play. Participants in these discussions believed that the results of the strike were mixed. By the mid-1990s, when these discussions occurred, Patrick Cudahy employed over one thousand people in its successful processing operations. The company was unionized, although P-40 dissolved after the strike, and very few of its 850 former members then worked for their old employer. Despite its own serious problems during the strike, it seemed that Patrick Cudahy had clearly prevailed. Yet in other ways, we all agreed that perhaps it had not. That is why Schneider decided to give workers the opportunity to voice a final judgment about their experiences in the last scene of the play. In this scene, the company's attorney triumphantly congratulates the company and begins to leave them when Barbara pulls him up short. "We didn't win anything . . . And people suffered. I saw what it did to people. It brings tears to my eyes when I think about it. But if I had to do it all over again, I would do the same. Because you have to take a stand. You shouldn't be afraid to stand up and say—*This is wrong! You do not treat people like this! You do not treat human beings like this! You cannot do that and come out on top! You cannot!—AND I DON'T THINK THEY CAME OUT ON TOP!*"[23]

Figure 5.1 In a scene from *The Line*, "Marie" explains how difficult it is to take a bathroom break: "I have to take my metal mesh glove off, my arm band, my belly guard, my rubber glove under the mesh glove, my cotton liner under that. My rubber apron. And then the bathroom is two departments over and another floor down, and I have to be back in place and dressed again in seven minutes! I quite often eat my lunch on the toilet stool, because I don't have time." Flora Coker as "Marie." Photograph by Fred Fischer.

Figure 5.2 "Steve" and "Barbara," who is visibly pregnant, discuss the strike. By creating actual picket signs such as "Who Can Stay Alive on 6.25," creators of *The Line* sought to make the play both accurate history and provocative theatre. They modeled "Barbara" on a striker who walked the picket line while in the last term of her pregnancy. Rodd Walker as "Steve" and Marcie Hoffman as "Barbara." Photograph by Fred Fischer.

Figure 5.3 *The Line* depicts a bargaining session between P-40 president Mark Rosenbaum and Patrick Cudahy vice president, Dan Habighorst. David Rommel as Rosenbaum and John Kishline as Habighorst. Photograph by Fred Fischer.

Notes

An earlier version of this essay appeared as "Staging the Line: The Creation of a Play About the Patrick Cudahy Meat Packing Strike of 1987–1980," *Labor's Heritage* 9 (1997): 58–77. Used by permission of *Labor's Heritage*.

1. *Patrick Cudahy Ink*, April 1977, March 1980, Summer 1985; Mary Becker and Del Hauenstein, *Patrick Cudahy: A Journey through the Past, Present, and Future* (Milwaukee: Patrick Cudahy, Inc., 1990), pp. 2–4, 13, 15–16.

2. Author's oral history interview with Roger Kapella and Dan Habighorst, October 5, 1994, Cudahy, Wisconsin, for the *Patrick Cudahy Strike and Plant Closing of 1987–1989 Oral History Project*, University of Wisconsin-Milwaukee Urban Archives, Tape 1, Sides 1 and 2; Tape 2, Side 1 (all interviews cited hereafter are in the *Cudahy Oral History Project*); Hardy Green, *On Strike at Hormel: The Struggle for a Democratic Labor Movement* (Philadelphia: Temple University Press, 1990), pp. 32, 292; *Milwaukee Journal*, June 17, 1986; "Patrick Cudahy/Local P-40 Negotiations" (bargaining log), November 10 and 18, December 3–5, 9, 11, 15–16, 1986, Patrick Cudahy Case Files, National Labor Relations Board, Region 30, Milwaukee, Wisconsin (hereinafter referred to as Cudahy Case Files, NLRB Region 30); "Final Offer for an Agreement between Patrick Cudahy, Incorporated, and United Food and Commercial Workers, International Union Local P-40," December 31, 1986, 3, 6, 34–43, Exhibits "A" and "B," and passim.

3. *Milwaukee Journal*, January 4, 11, 25, February 25, April 26, September 11–12 1987; *Milwaukee Sentinel*, January 13, 21, November 26, December 12, 1987, April 19, May 1, 1989; *Cudahy Reminder Enterprise*, January 8, 15, 1987, May 4, 1989.

4. John Schneider, *The Line* (Milwaukee: Theater X, 1996 [unpublished]) 39–40, 42, 43, 46–47, 56 (Sharon and supervisor), 35 (Marie). Excerpts are from oral history interviews with Sharon Swaner, August 2, 1994, New Berlin, Wisconsin, Tape 1, Sides 1 and 2, Tape 2, Side 1; and Marie Machniewicz, July 20, 1994, Oak Creek, Wisconsin, Tape 1, Side 1. For the most part, characters are named after the actual interviewees whose words they speak. In one case, several perspectives seemed to blend easily into a single voice. We named this person after one of the people in the composite.

5. Michael Frisch, *A Shared Authority: Essays on the Craft and Meaning of Oral and Public History* (Albany: SUNY Press, 1990), xxii–xxiii.

6. Oral history interview with Donald Korinek, July 28, 1994, Milwaukee, Wisconsin, Tape 2, Side 1.

7. Schneider, *The Line*, 15, 17; oral history interview with Steve and Julie Pauley, July 30, 1994, Greenfield, Wisconsin, Tape 1, Side 1; Machniewicz interview, Tape 1, Side 2.

8. Schneider, *The Line*, 30; Machniewicz interview, Tape 1, Side 1.

9. Schneider, *The Line*, 67, 85; Machniewicz interview, Tape 2, Side 2; oral history interview with John Becker, August 18, 1994, Cudahy, Wisconsin, Tape 1, Side 2.

10. Schneider, *The Line*, 48; Korinek interview, Tape 2, Side 2.

11. Historians and others have long been interested in how generational memory shapes working-class identity and consciousness. Studies of people who lived through the upheavals of the 1930s to the 1970s especially have noted how events in those years shaped values and political views in subsequent years. John Bodnar has challenged this "deterministic paradigm" by arguing that generational memory is formed by individual and collective experiences over time, and not solely by cataclysmic events like the Depression or the antiwar and civil rights movements of the 1960s. He views generational memory "as the result of long-term encounters with economic forces and powerful

authorities." "Regardless of the past," he adds, "generational views are also under constant review and discussion in the present." Bodnar, "Generational Memory in an American Town," *Journal of Interdisciplinary History* 26 (1996): 636. On generational memory, see Tamara K. Hareven, "The Search for Generational Memory: Tribal Rites in Industrial Society," *Daedalus* 107 (1978): 137–149; Alan B. Spitzer, "The Historical Problem of Generations," *American Historical Review* 78 (1973): 1353–1385; Glen H. Elder, *Children of the Great Depression: Social Change in Life Experience* (Chicago: University of Chicago Press, 1974); John A. Clausen, *American Lives: Looking Back at the Children of the Great Depression* (New York: Free Press, 1993); Todd Gitlin, *The Sixties: Years of Hope, Days of Rage* (New York: Bantam, 1987); Wade Clark Roof, *A Generation of Seekers: The Spiritual Journeys of the Baby Boom Generation* (San Francisco: HarperSanFrancisco, 1993); and Howard Schuman and Jacqueline Scott, "Generations and Collective Memories," *American Sociological Review* 54 (1989): 359–381.

12. Katherine Marie Dudley, *The End of the Line: Lost Jobs, New Lives in Postindustrial America* (Chicago: University of Chicago Press, 1994), chap. 9.

13. Elizabeth A. Fones-Wolf, *Selling Free Enterprise: The Business Assault on Labor and Liberalism, 1945–1960* (Urbana: University of Illinois Press, 1994).

14. There are many useful studies that shed light on workers and unions in the postwar years and after, though not all of those cited here interpret workers' experiences as I do. See Walter Galenson, *The American Labor Movement, 1955–1995* (Westport, CT: Greenwood, 1996); Kim Moody, *An Injury to All: The Decline of American Unionism* (New York: Verso, 1988), chap. 2; Robert H. Zieger, *American Workers, American Unions, 1920–1985* (Baltimore: Johns Hopkins University Press, 1986), chaps. 4–6; David Brody, *Workers in Industrial America: Essays on the 20th Century Struggle*, 2nd ed. (New York: Oxford University Press, 1993), chaps. 5–7; George Lipsitz, *Class and Culture in Cold War America: "A Rainbow at Midnight"* (New York: Praeger, 1981); Stanley Aronowitz, *False Promises: The Shaping of American Working Class Consciousness* (New York: McGraw-Hill, 1973); Eli Chinoy, *Automobile Workers and the American Dream* (Urbana: University of Illinois Press, 1992); Richard Feldman and Michael Betzhold, eds., *End of the Line: Autoworkers and the American Dream, An Oral History* (Urbana: University of Illinois Press, 1988); David Bensman and Roberta Lynch, *Rusted Dreams: Hard Times in a Steel Community* (Berkeley: University of California Press, 1987); Gregory Pappas, *The Magic City: Unemployment in a Working-Class Community* (Ithaca: Cornell University Press, 1989); Paul Blumberg, *Inequality in an Age of Decline* (New York: Oxford University Press, 1980), which also contains useful discussions of previous views of working-class life by sociologists and others; and Katherine S. Newman, *Falling from Grace: The Experience of Downward Mobility in the American Middle Class* (New York: Free Press, 1988). See also Rick Fantasia, *Cultures of Solidarity: Consciousness, Action, and Contemporary American Workers* (Berkeley: University of California Press, 1988).

15. Schneider, *The Line*, 60, 80, 90; oral history interview with Barbara Linder, July 27, 1994, Milwaukee, Wisconsin, Tape 1, Sides 1 and 2.

16. Schneider, *The Line*, 97; oral history interview with confidential informant identified as "PC 100," August 3, 1994, Tape 2, Side 1.

17. *Cudahy Reminder-Enterprise*, January 8, 1987; Kapella and Habighorst interview, Tape 2, Sides 1 and 2.

18. Local P-40, United Food and Commercial Workers International Union, "Charge Against Employer," Case 30-CA-9462, February 2, 1987; details of the charge in Kenneth R. Loebel (P-40 attorney) to Joseph A. Szabo (Director, Region 30, NLRB), January 30,

1987; Joseph A. Szabo, "Order Consolidating Cases, Consolidated Complaint and Notice of Hearing," Cases 30-CA-9462 and 30-CA-9535, March 27, 1987; untitled response by Patrick Cudahy, April 7, 1987; Subpoena Duces Tecum for above cases served on Patrick Cudahy officials Roger Kapella and Dan Habighorst, and on Smithfield Foods, Inc., May 14, 1987; "Petition of Patrick Cudahy Incorporated to Partially Revoke Subpoenas Duces Tecum," May 20, 1987; and NLRB Region 30 General Counsel's "Opposition to Petition of Patrick Cudahy, Incorporated to partially revoke Subpoenas Duces Tecum," May 26, 1987; all in Cudahy case files, NLRB Region 30.

19. A complaint filed by P-40 with the NLRB on February 2, 1987, alleged that Patrick Cudahy had violated the National Labor Relations Act because the company had "bargained in bad faith without any desire to reach an agreement and then unilaterally imposed new wages, hours, and other terms and conditions of employment prior to any bona fide impasse having been reached." P-40 alleged that by so doing, "the employer forced the employees to engage in a strike in order to protest such employer conduct" which the employees believed "was designed to destroy their right to bargain collectively" and the union itself. On March 27, NLRB Region 30 agreed with P-40 and ordered the company to comply with the law. When the company continued to deny the charges, the board subsequently subpoenaed scores of documents prepared by Patrick Cudahy and its attorneys which it believed would support its charge of bargaining in bad faith at a hearing in June before NLRB Administrative Law Judge Donald R. Holley. The company objected that the subpoenas for over 220 of the documents were protected by the attorney–client privilege rule, and asked Holley to conduct a preliminary hearing so that their witnesses could support their claim of attorney–client privilege. Judge Holley privately examined the documents at the evidentiary hearing that began on June 3 and ruled against the company, finding that the company's law firm, Krukowski and Costello, gave the company "business" or "financial" advice, but no "legal" advice as the company claimed. On the final day of the hearing, Holley referred to a document called "Planning—Contract Expiration" which he considered especially revealing. Company attorneys said "the document outlines specific responses Patrick Cudahy would make to a strike, . . . estimates the value of compensation concessions the firm was seeking in negotiations, and details certain changes Patrick Cudahy wanted in the successor agreement." Holley, however, said that pages 8 and 11 of the document indicated "that Cudahy intended to participate in bargaining with an intention to take action which would bring about what they would claim to be an impasse as of December 31, 1986. And reading those pages causes me to conclude that Cudahy did not intend to enter negotiations with the earnest desire to reach agreement with the Union." In fact, Holley said, "Patrick Cudahy intended to engage in bargaining in bad faith . . ." Holley then ordered the company to produce the subpoenaed documents for trial. The company refused and appealed to the NLRB in Washington. Holley recessed the hearing without making a final ruling on the complaint pending the appeal and other legal actions. On May 12, 1988, the NLRB in Washington ruled that the documents indeed were subject to attorney–client privilege, removed Holley from the case, and sent the case back for another hearing.

In Judge Holley's words, the "Strategic Planning Guidebook" was "A description of Company and union strategic objectives in negotiations; an analysis of legal constraints on communications with employees by agents of Patrick Cudahy; a description of effective communication with employees from a psychological/persuasive point of view; a detailed analysis of legal constraints on negotiating behavior; an analysis of Patrick

Cudahy labor cost under the 1983–86 contract; a detailed analysis of legal constraints on Patrick Cudahy's responses to a strike; as well as, an analysis of legal tools available to Patrick Cudahy to use affirmatively as a means of minimizing the cost of a strike."

Hearing transcript, Patrick Cudahy Cases 30-CA-9462, 30-CA-9535, 30-CA-9565, June 10, 1987, pp. 558, 560; "Index of Documents Claimed As Attorney/Client Privileged by Patrick Cudahy Incorporated," p. 2. See also statement of facts and other case history details in "Trial Brief of Patrick Cudahy on Privilege Issues" for the above cases, June 9, 1987; Patrick Cudahy's "Motion for Special Permission to Appeal," June 11, 1987; the entire transcripts of the hearings for the above cases for June 3–4, 10, 1987; the company's "Motion for Special Permission to Appeal," June 11, 1987; the "General Counsel's Opposition to Respondent's Motion for Special Permission to Appeal," June 15, 1987; "General Counsel's Opposition to Respondent's Motion for Disqualification of Administrative Law Judge," June 27, 1987; Judge Donald R. Holley's Order, July 2, 1987, denying the company's motion that he disqualify himself because of bias; NLRB, "Order Granting Appeals," May 12, 1988; and "NLRB Settlement Agreement," May 1, 1989—all in Cudahy case files, NLRB Region 30.

20. "Index of Documents Claimed As Attorney/Client Privilege by Patrick Cudahy Incorporated," Cudahy case files, NLRB Region 30.
21. The NLRB in Washington did not see these records because the logs were not among the contested documents which the company claimed should not be made public. The logs are called "Patrick Cudahy/Local P-40 Negotiations," covering fourteen sessions from November 10 through December 30, 1986, Cudahy case files, NLRB Region 30.
22. Schneider, *The Line*, 47–48, 49–50, 52, 53, 54; "Patrick Cudahy/Local P-40 Negotiations," Session #2, November 18; Session #3, December 3; Session #4, December 4; Session #7, December 11; Session #8, December 15; Session #9, December 16; Session #11, December 22; Session #13, December 29, 1986; and Dan Habighorst to Robert Waters and Mark Rosenbaum, December 31, 19986—all in Cudahy files, NLRB Region 30.
23. Schneider, *The Line*, 100.

Remembering Toward Loss: Performing *And so there are pieces . . .*

Rivka Syd Eisner

Rivka Eisner gives us an inside-out view of oral history performance. Having worked extensively and intimately with her interview subject, "Chị Tôi," a Vietnamese national pursuing a legal education in the United States, Eisner describes how she developed a performance that began in movement—in small gestures, in play with symbolic objects, in expressive, bodily response to Chị Tôi's stories—and gradually moved toward incorporating Chị Tôi's words into the performance event, And so there are pieces. . . . *This essay is about the process of translating an intimate stranger's memory, history, and life through the life and language of one's own (social) body and then again into and through those other bodies and selves that make up the "audience." It is about, in one of the many senses in which Rivka uses the word, "doubling" non-identical others in ourselves—even as we reckon with both the beauty and difficulty of irresolvable differences.*

In the spring of 2002, I developed a performance based on the life-narratives of "Chị Tôi," a Vietnamese woman I first met at a dinner with friends held while she was attending law school in the United States. As our friendship deepened, I gradually heard more about her and her family's experiences of living in Vietnam during the "American War." The array of perspectives she offered though her family narratives and commentary were new to me. Prior to speaking with her what I knew of the "Vietnam War" was limited to news accounts and personal perspectives from an American standpoint, usually pertaining to the 1960s era protests or the combat hardships of U.S. soldiers. I did not know about the struggles of Vietnamese individuals and families, or about the complex divisions between Northern and Southern Vietnam. Wishing to hear more, I asked Chị Tôi if we could continue our conversations as part of an independent project for an ethnography class. She agreed, and the discussions that started over dinner gradually grew into a class project, a Masters' thesis, a series of public performances, and now, a dissertation based in part on extensive fieldwork in Vietnam.[1]

We crafted Chị Tôi's life narratives together in an intensely collaborative year and a half of interviews, informal visits, interaction at social events, phone and email correspondence, and gift and letter exchanges. As part of my M.A. and continuing doctoral work, I created *And so there are pieces . . .*, a movement-centered perform-ance intended to honor Chị Tôi and her family, to reflect our deep-rooted coopera-tion, and to offer carefully selected pieces of her history to a greater community.

The sole performance of *And so there are pieces . . .* took place on the campus of the University of North Carolina at Chapel Hill, on March 22, 2002 in a small black box theater space seating sixty to seventy people. The audience comprised invited guests and their guests. While most of the words spoken in the performance were Chị Tôi's, many were her quotations of family members and some were my own reflec-tions and attempts at contextualization. Still, the words were at best in concert with the stylized movement and gesture with which I tried to communicate their mean-ings. The performance lasted approximately fifty minutes and culminated in a sam-pling of traditional Vietnamese cuisine (what proved to be a small feast).[2]

In the following pages, I hope to offer glimpses into the experience of working with Chị Tôi to develop what I would call a living archive of her life story.[3] The term "Chị Tôi" means "my older sister" in Vietnamese. Although a Vietnamese citizen, Chị Tôi has lived in the United States for the past several years to attend law school. At the time of this writing, she is working in the United States as a legal researcher on issues pertaining to Vietnam, in particular, trade relationships and the effects of chemical dioxins used during the war. She grew up in Ho Chị Minh City, then Saigon, during the Vietnamese–American war. A transnational citizen at this point, Chị Tôi's early years were inextricably bound up with political upheavals in Vietnam during the mid-twentieth century.

Chị Tôi was born in 1954, in a time of transition between French and American involvement in Vietnam that scholar Stanley Karnow calls "an interlude between two wars—or rather, a lull in the same war" in her country's battle-scarred twentieth cen-tury history (Karnow, 199). It was the year the French army, after nearly a century of colonial rule and almost ten years of outright warfare, was defeated by Viet Minh forces at Dien Bien Phu. Following this momentous battle, and amid the ensuing turmoil, government representatives from major world powers met in Geneva to work out a ceasefire agreement. In Geneva, it was decided that Vietnam would be temporarily divided into North and South at the seventeenth parallel, and that nationwide elections to reunify the country would be held in two years. The French agreed to leave the North and the Viet Minh were, in turn, to withdraw from the South. Having financed much of the French war effort, Americans now began increasing their participation in Southern Vietnam both economically and by their physical presence. In the wake of World War II and in the midst of the Cold War, American involvement in Vietnam was primarily motivated by fear of what the United States perceived as a great and mounting threat: the growing number of communist revolutions, governments, and sympathizers in the world, especially in Asia. As a consequence of Vietnam's division, and the uncertainty of political power struggles in both regions, 1954 also became a year of massive migration. Almost a million people, primarily Catholics from the North, moved to what they hoped would be greater safety in the South, while many people—like Chị Tôi's parents—who supported the communist Democratic Republic of Vietnam, transitioned to the North (Karnow, 207).

A nationalist seeking an end to colonial rule, Chị Tôi's father sadly "bid farewell" to Chị Tôi's mother in November of 1954 in order to fight for the North, for what he thought would be just "a couple of years." It is told, and written in his diary, that he boarded a ship and sailed northward, fleeing the South, at the precise moment of Chị Tôi's birth. His departure, coupled with Chị Tôi's birth, marked a simultaneous making and breaking of their family. A month after giving birth, Chị Tôi's mother, fearing that her own affiliation with and activism on behalf of the communist North put her life at risk, went underground. After several years of living in dangerous shadows, Chị Tôi's mother also fled the South for the North where her sister and husband had preceded her. During this tumultuous time, Chị Tôi stayed in the safety of her grandparents' home. There she was raised by her grandmother and grandfather, as well as aunts and uncles who identified as "traditionalists" and worked for the South.

From the moment her father left, Chị Tôi's immediate family was separated and divided. In and out of imprisonment, forced hiding, and combat, Chị Tôi's mother visited her sporadically, suddenly stepping unannounced into Chị Tôi's life for only short spurts of time. Having chosen to ally herself actively with the North, Chị Tôi's mother became exiled from her Southern home. The times Chị Tôi spent with her mother during the war were desperate and few, and grew increasingly rare as the war escalated. This is why Chị Tôi says she really only met her mother at the war's end, when she was 21 years old. Chị Tôi never met her father. He died fighting in the streets of Saigon during the 1968 Tet Offensive. Burnt into the memory of many Vietnamese and Americans, the Tet Offensive was a massive series of surprise attacks in Southern towns and cities that began on Tet, the Vietnamese New Year. The wave of attacks were planned and carried out by the Democratic Republic of Vietnam army from the North and their communist supporters in the South (called "Viet Cong" by the South Vietnamese government and the Americans). Chị Tôi notes that because so much information was "shrouded in secrecy," she learned she "had a father" and "by the way, he is dead" on the "same day, same morning." During the war, "nobody told me anything," Chị Tôi says, "because nobody really knew what was going on, and because it was really dangerous, and risky also, to talk about it. So they prefer to just pull a veil." After the war, "I discovered I had a past. I discovered I had a mother. I discovered I had a father." Chị Tôi's father was an acclaimed Vietnamese writer. Pieces from his war diary were later published. It is primarily through these written remains, and a few stories preserved orally, that Chị Tôi has come to piece together a father figure and reconstruct a sense of family. As I began to write and rehearse the performance, I found myself moving in ways that echoed Chị Tôi's frayed family ties and broken memories. Emotionally fractured and torn, at the same time I was stretching and reaching to pull this story together for and with Chị Tôi. In the process I realized, of course, that I was literally moved by the force of a history that was not my own in any conventional sense; that I was becoming part of this history through the performative exchange of memory. Memory seeks mobility within, across, and through time and living bodies. Without movement, it may become static and forgotten. Memory must move or die. In a sense, it is mortal. It needs mortal bodies to take it up and carry it in and through time. In movement and gestural-based performance I became something like a fleeting guardian of the vitality of Chị Tôi's memories—a sister-by-memory.

Over the course of approximately six months, Chị Tôi and I met over twenty-five times and recorded approximately fifteen hours of interviews. Our exchanges were more like "intimate conversations," however, than pre-scripted interviews (Conquergood, 10). As the weeks and months passed, I attended more and more closely to the art and craft of Chị Tôi's story-making and to the narrative dynamics that were claiming both of us. The storytelling event proved just as vital and insepa-rably linked to the meaning of her stories as their content. I heard clips of incomplete stories that stopped too soon, leaving me curious and wondering. I listened as she repeated the same narratives in different contexts, noting how the purpose and focus of each changed—sometimes discretely, at other times drastically. Stories are both original and a copy. They are new and familiar. Their beauty exists in the extent to which each storytelling event yields not a perfect replication of a previous telling but layers of sedimented interpretations, re-creations of experience, and associative remembering. A living story is one fraught with change. Over time I came to under-stand this project not as an attempt to perfectly mirror Chị Tôi's stories through performance, but as an endeavor to uncover, witness and represent *pieces* of her life experiences for audiences unfamiliar with her particular, generally untold and unknown history.

I decided to retell her stories, as well as the narrative of our time together, using Chị Tôi's own words interspersed and framed with my interpretive and affective responses. Her pasts, performed into the present and future through story, are now within my memory. I know them intimately, yet they are not mine. "In this chain and continuum, I am but one link," for the story is "neither me nor mine [and] does not really belong to me [yet] I feel greatly responsible for it" (Trinh, 122). Her stories, experiences, and memories are now doubled differently within me. They are the same and completely different. Though seemingly far removed in time and place from Chị Tôi's life, my history is now shaped by hers. As storyteller, Chị Tôi "takes what [s]he tells from experience—[her] own and that reported by others . . . and [s]he in turn makes it the experience of those who are listening to [her] tale" (Benjamin, 87). I do not lay claim to her experiences, yet my perceptions are changed—painfully and lovingly, inescapably altered—by knowing Chị Tôi.

In transmitting Chị Tôi's stories, I bear the knowledge that while helping to sustain their life, I inevitably reshape them. Consequently, I sought respectful fidelity, although not mimetic accuracy, in re-presentations of her stories. I worked hard to discern and to pass on the pressing vitality and heart of her stories even if some of the details would inevitably fall askew. After grounding her narratives in the historical context of the Vietnamese–American war, I was most concerned with tapping into and communicating her narratives' *affective force*. The truths within her stories derived not simply from facts, but from her narratives' detailed, sensitive recognition of the vulnerability, beauty and resilience of individual lives and from the consolidation of our perspectives in appreciation of and respect for those lives-in-story. Chị Tôi and her narratives acknowledge and savor a world of specific lives often painfully and thankfully bound together in basic pursuits of freedom, friendship and survival, for despite differences, as she says, "our hearts beat and bleed the same way."

The performance I developed from our interactions in some ways followed a linear chronology, both with regard to the phases of Chị Tôi's life, and the order in which they were told to me. But in the end it was impossible to affix a neat timeline. Chị Tôi's earliest stories were told to her later in life, through the retrospective eyes of many different people. With Chị Tôi, moreover, the performative moment of speaking opened a space in which meanings and memory were being constantly made and remade. As I listened, Chị Tôi pieced together disparate and previously buried story fragments. Through self-narration, she restored/re-storied the events of her life in narratives that remained distinctly incomplete. Some of these rested, frankly, on historical gaps. For others, she relied on me to supply missing parts and explanation.

As I anticipated the performance, I could only hope to tell what little (and how much) I had learned from her and to "translat[e] between the lines." Working as much with gaps and contradictions as with explicit narrative content, I pursued the creation of a similar, yet distinct, collage of her life stories (Benjamin, 82). Taking Chị Tôi's own fragmentary creation as my model, I came to view the process of story-making and storytelling as one of translation and adaptation. In performed and written adaptation of her life stories, I claimed both "fidelity and freedom" (79). I wanted my re-performance (on the understanding that Chị Tôi had already variously performed and re-performed her stories) to be like an "echo of the original," in which my words and embodied gestures were guided and "powerfully affected" by Chị Tôi's

(76, 81). Cutting and refashioning her life narrative, I struggled with myriad story pieces that often seemed crudely cut from anything like a whole text or life fabric. At the same time, I felt gratefully pierced through by the power and magnitude of her otherwise small and modestly told stories. In this context of adaptation and translation, I came to think of re-performing Chị Tôi's life narratives as a way to "cut" and circulate her often unknown and unspoken knowledge and experience into others' lives.

Chị Tôi is my dear friend and cultural guide. With trust and respect, I followed her through the spectred landscapes of her memory. Finding myself suddenly in the midst of the yellowing images, gestural shards, and pieces of stories that often seemed ripped on the sly from a (nonexistent) family scrapbook that made up her tattered past, I became caught between two inseparable findings. First: that memory may embed itself within bodies like pieces of glass pressed into the palms and hearts of the tellers and listeners, and secondly then: that these lovingly painful "cuts" are both wounding and life-giving. With the general aim of exploring the generative and damaging potentials of being "cut by" and "cutting into" memory, I begin here by remembering the performance itself, and then proceed to reflect on some of the implications of witnessing this complex life and history.

And so there are pieces . . .

It is the night of the performance. I wait nervously behind the curtain. The people who have responded to my open invitation to attend talk in a polite hush and turn their programs in their hands. The lights dim, fading and softening the sparse stage. *I want the stage to be humble, exemplifying Chị Tôi's desire for her life and stories to be understood as* "one among many." The space is all black, nearly empty except for a small prop table in the back and a few streamers of red and gold triangular paper cuttings hanging from ceiling to floor. *The cuttings are emblematic of Chị Tôi's narrative* "pieces." *They slowly twirl, sharp and glittering, on invisible threads.* In the center of the nearly bare stage lies an open umbrella, waiting for me to enter, to hide behind it, and to begin the performance—not with talk, but with quiet movement, accompanied by the rising chords of one of Chị Tôi's favorite pieces of music, a Chopin piano concerto.

I walk across the dark stage and crouch behind the umbrella. *My heart is pounding.* In this opening sequence I want to show, through movement and gesture, a trajectory of Chị Tôi's experience from childhood to present adulthood. I begin with a prolonged, partially obscured gaze at the audience, peeking out over the umbrella's rim as the child Chị Tôi once was might have tentatively observed her explosive surroundings. *I remain quiet, looking out from behind the umbrella. Chị Tôi survived the early years of her life through silent observation. She watched and wondered wordlessly as the war erupted, and splintered her family, her life and life-narrative, into pieces.*

The performance begins with me *imagining into* the possible experiences and thoughts of Chị Tôi as a young child, watching violence explode all around. This opening scene developed primarily out of a worn photograph in which there was no umbrella but there were the piercing, lost eyes of *Chị Tôi* at four years old. As the music and movement progress, years pass and we grow older. She/I—we are angry at having lost so much in the waste and wake of this war. I twirl the umbrella and "punch it" confrontationally toward the audience. They do nothing. During the unfolding movement sequence I come to realize that what Chị Tôi seeks, what would be most meaningful, is some kind of effort at reconciliation with her embittered past. I attempt to show her gradual, unfolding trust by looking directly at the audience, holding my hand out beyond the umbrella's edge to see if the "rain" and "war" have stopped their incessant pounding. Setting the umbrella down, I tentatively move toward the audience. I am ready to speak with Chị Tôi, to retell her stories through the voice and movement of my body, to make contact with "real Americans." A story of Chị Tôi's life begins . . .

Part I: Skin

(Music from the opening movement sequence with the umbrella fades. Lights rise slightly. The stage is set with a visible prop table, simply draped in red cloth, upstage left. On the table sits: a tube of red paint, paintbrush, glass of water, roll of gold paper, silver scissors, crisp white shirt, red Asian bowl, and chopsticks. The shirt, bowl and chopsticks are gifts from Chị Tôi. The black umbrella sits open on the floor at the back of the stage, where I leave it at the end of the introductory movement sequence.)

In my own words and voice, I tell the audience the bare essentials of what I feel they must know about Chị Tôi. I pause a second before telling those gathered:

I have a friend I call Chị Tôi. Chị Tôi means "my older sister" in Vietnamese. She grew up in Saigon during the Vietnamese-American war. She lived with her grandparents and younger aunts and uncles who worked for the South. Her mother, father, and eldest aunts fought for the North. Chị Tôi tells me she really only met her mother when she was 21. She never met her father. Her father was a praised Vietnamese fiction writer, and he kept a journal throughout the war. Some of the diary was later published. (*Take picture out from under my shirt.*) This is a picture from the diary. She tells me it is a family photograph.

Standing close to the audience, I pause and shift into the voice and taut bodily posture that seems to claim me when I wish to speak as, or really with, Chị Tôi. I embody her words, voice, and bodily affect. We speak together. *The voice that spills forth is plural.* I pull slowly at the top of my shirt with one finger. *I am about to reveal intimacies of others' lives. In doing so, I too feel somewhat splayed open. Who knew it would feel so vulnerable to tell someone else's stories? Speaking this way puts both of us at risk. At risk of being misunderstood. At risk of being presumed rather than perceived. At risk of being heard and then forgotten.*

Slowly, I reach for the photograph that has been hiding beneath my shirt. *I grasp its edges. It peels away like a layer of skin. This gesture never felt quite so revealing in rehearsal. This small, stark movement surprises me with its impact.* I speak cautiously while looking into the picture's past. Chị Tôi told me the secret buried within this family photograph. *I am about to tell it to you.* I seek to step into the lilting flow, the rhythms and intonations, of Chị Tôi's familiar speech. Embodying Chị Tôi's vocal rhythm and posture, I tell the audience as Chị Tôi told me:

> "This is the only picture of the three of us, the three of us together."[4] You see it is a picture of my parents when they are very young. But what you do not know is that my mother is holding a cloth over her arm to hide her pregnancy. To hide me. So, I am also in this picture. It was taken in a place called Tha La, a beautiful place in the countryside. "I think it was the last time they saw each other. This is the only picture of the three of us [. . .] together. This is the only time the three of us were ever together."

Jumping and gliding back and forth between transcribed, remembered, and interpretive text fragments, I patch together a retelling of both the photograph's story, and the story of how I learned its secrets. Next, I tell the audience what I imagine as I look into the family photograph:

The picture shows Chị Tôi's parents standing close together, holding hands. Their faces are expectant. They are looking away, gazing out beyond the edge of the picture's frame. I ask Chị Tôi:

RIV: Where do you think they are looking?
CHỊ: Oh, they looking, towards like, you know, the horizon [pause]
   new life [pause]
   future [pause]
   that's what they want.

> *(Place the picture downstage center near audience. Start transition movement back to the table for red paint, gold paper, brush, and water to be used in next part of the performance.)*[5]

Chị Tôi's family picture is the first of several symbolic props I arrange and leave near the audience, starting a kind of memorial made from tokens of Chị Tôi's life-stories. As more objects gather throughout the performance, this rough altar becomes a site of memory, mourning, and honor for Chị Tôi's father, family, narratives and lived experiences. *It is a kind of plural grave. A place where the remains of stories, the incomplete pieces of lives, memories and narratives, accumulate.*

Part 2: Bone

The next narrative cut is one version of Chị Tôi's birth story. I say the word "bone" to mark the beginning a new section. While speaking, I unroll a scroll of gold paper on the floor. Lying parallel to the audience and next to Chị Tôi's family photograph, the paper stretches from one end of the stage to the other. The paper is the next addition to the developing altar. Crouching over the thin gilt paper, I unscrew the lid of a tube of bright red paint. Plunging back and forth over the paper, I paint the impossible timeline, or lifeline, of Chị Tôi's family as I speak. This is a dividing line as much as anything else. A huge, rough red scar on gold. *My body bends and curls, sweeping the brush over the gold paper. I point and arc the paintbrush as I speak, illustrating and emphasizing words, images, and the multiple voices—Chị Tôi, her father, her mother, "the people of Vietnam"—that make up this narrative.*

CHỊ: And they say, okay, in '56 there would be a big election [pause]
   then the people would choose whether to go entirely North.
   Or to go entirely South.

   . . .

   [pause] So [pause] my, my dad left.
   My dad left thinking,
   "okay,
   in two years there will be an election
   and we were sure that, you know,
   the people of Vietnam would choose Ho Chi Minh as their leader
   and we would have a unified country.
   So for the time being, let those Americans and those French do
   what they want,
   but in two years,
   I'm going to come back [pause] to see my family."
   So he left, with that hope in his heart.

As Chị Tôi did to me in our interview, I look toward the audience, pausing a moment to make sure they are following the story before I say more.

   H'he was a soldier, right?
   And my mother was in town because she was going to give birth.

   . . .

   So, so they had parted before that [pause]
   before he left South Vietnam.
   [deep sigh] And, uh, . . .
   afterwards, afterwards when, after years and years,
   when you know, my mother recovered his diary [pause]

RIV: How did she find that?
CHỊ: That is another story [slight laugh/sigh].
  She finally [pause] corroborated the dates, and she found that
  [pause] his ship was heading North and he was standing on
      the deck of the ship, looking Southward, to where my
      mother would be [pause]
  on the same night I was born.

The water streaks red, like blood, as I dip the paintbrush in the glass. With the word "born," I strike the paintbrush against my open palm. *Droplets of paint-blood spatter across the stretch of timeline, marking Chị Tôi's birth. This is a story of family being made and broken. All at once.*

  Yeah, he wrote the hour and the night.

  . . .

  Yeah, and he, uh, he said that he was on the deck, and thinking of her and of *me* [happy].
  Didn't know that I was *being* born [laughs].
  But he remembered that his last thought was that [pause]
  "okay, you know,
  goodbye my loved,"
  right,
  "my loved wife and, and child.
  [pause] I'll, I'll see you in two years."

  . . .

  But, in fact, he never came back.
  [quietly] And we never saw him.

As I embody Chị Tôi speaking her father's "last thought," I stand straight and still as if I were on the bow of the ship, staring out over the water as he is said to have done. I speak as Chị Tôi, imagining into her father's life. On the words "And we never saw him," I look back to the audience, indicating a change in narrative voice, time and place. Now we all know: he never attained this wish.

After pausing, I bend down and deliberately rip the painted timeline into pieces, leaving Chị Tôi's family photograph central amidst the ruin. *Red paint, like familial blood, rouges over my hands and fingertips as I rip the paper out of sadness, frustration, anger, love and irretrievable loss.* I spread my fingers open wide in the glaring stage lights. Chị Tôi tells the stark truth of it: "he never came back" and "we never saw him."

  (Leave glass, paint, paintbrush and ripped timeline as part of the growing altar downstage at audience's feet. Transition to table to get silver scissors for upcoming haircut movement sequence.)

Part 3: Flesh

Each part of the performance is named by a single word referring to a vital part of the body: skin, flesh, sinew, bone, heart, and blood. Each points to the visceral nature of life and death within the stories, suggesting both the fragility and strength of the actual bodies that lived-out and made these narratives. Collectively, the titles also perform the bodily life of these stories themselves, as they linger within individuals and pass through generations. "Flesh," composed of two key sections, marks the muscle and fiber of the storied lives in these sections, which are equally taut and tender.

a. Scissors

(Move to prop table and hold up the scissors, with blades open, while speaking "Flesh." Return downstage with scissors. Carefully begin "cutting" Chị Tôi's hair.)

This part of the performance developed out of giving Chị Tôi a haircut. It moves from a very concrete memory of tediously cutting her hair to a more symbolic mode of thinking about the entire project as a process of adaptation and translation characterized by the reciprocal sensations of "cutting into" her narratives and feeling viscerally "cut back" by her stories.

In this movement sequence, I begin with my feet planted. Holding the large scissors, I clip into the air, imagining Chị Tôi sitting in front of me in the kitchen chair, swathed in her bathrobe. *Clip. Clip. I was afraid of cutting off something irretrievable. Slowly. Clip. Snip. The silver scissors flash clean and sharp in the light.* This is trust, I remember thinking. I had better be careful. *Holding the scissors in one hand, I extend the other as if holding the small hand mirror Chị Tôi used to observe my progress. Snip. Slice. I tell the watching eyes:*

> One day, I was at Chị Tôi's house and she asked me if I would cut her hair before a fancy dinner party. I looked at the dull scissors and said . . . "okay." She watched me cut her hair through a small hand mirror.

(Movement sequence shifts from cutting Chị Tôi's hair to symbolically "cutting" into my own body.)

With arms outspread, I turn the scissors toward myself. It is only right for me to feel the visceral weight and demand of these stories. *These are real people, actual lives. They depend on me to tell it right. I slide the shimmering scissors down the stretch of my inner leg from hip to heel while speaking. Concentrated beams of light dance on the blades. Trembling and on tiptoe, I aim the shears slowly toward my stomach. Ready to puncture. Chị Tôi is here, in my guts as a lovingly-sharp and aching shadow:*

> I have been performing Chị Tôi, or performing with Chị Tôi in mind, for over a year. Every performance, planned or unplanned, practiced or unpracticed, contains

pieces of her. I could not extract her if I wanted to try. Her sliver narratives are embedded into my skin. Sometimes I find her in my breath. In fleeting dreams as I rub my eyes awake. She inhabits my thoughts as I move through the day. I wear her clothes. I eat from her spoons and bowls. Ghosted, doubled-selves, she is here whether I ask her to be or not.

(Bending down with the scissors, cut segments of timeline into even smaller pieces. When finished, place scissors at the altar. Next, transition back to the table to pick up the white shirt. Movement sequence of putting on, stretching, and taking off white shirt lasts through scene.)

b. Shirt

The next piece of story is spliced together, borrowing and combining moments from two separate interviews in which Chị Tôi speaks about her present life. She describes feeling as if she exists and lives in at least "two worlds." Her life's work and interests move her from country to country. She rarely lingers in one place for more than a couple of years. Chị Tôi knows how to adapt and survive in many environments. It is a useful skill to possess. But living this way, as someone who moves within and travels between different worlds of thought and landscape, often leaves Chị Tôi feeling misunderstood, as she says: like a "monster" or "an enigma."

In this second section of "Flesh," I use a white button-down shirt, a gift from Chị Tôi, as a symbolic prop. The shirt becomes a second skin. *My arm slips through the narrow sleeve, and my shoulders roll and shift, adjusting to the feel of the softly encompassing cloth.* The shirt becomes like the social roles Chị Tôi plays in different locales. It is the monstrous and enigmatic sheath that sometimes fits perfectly and at other times stifles her.

The white shirt performs double meanings within the scene. Moving with the shirt and putting it on, I am trying to convey something about Chị Tôi's life in constant diaspora by "trying on" Chị Tôi's voice, words, bodily gestures, experiences, and stories in this physical form. It is an imperfect fit. For both of us. *I pull, and shift, and itch* (see figure 6.1). Chị Tôi feels she doesn't fit any better in her home country than she does in this one. She struggles to be understood and accepted within different contexts; I struggle to make sense of her life-narratives for her, for myself, and for our audiences. We twist and stretch the shirt, buttoning the sleeves, straightening and straining at the collar separately and together. Chị Tôi explains her predicament:

CHỊ: Men in my country see me as—[pause]
    some of them think I am half man.
    And I wouldn't be surprised if some of them
    think I prefer women over men.
    Because I wouldn't kow-tow,

Figure 6.1   From "Flesh: in the middle." Photo by James Cahill, Jerry Eisner, and Nathan Epley.

I wouldn't run after them.

.   .   .

I am an enigma to them.

.   .   .

I am always in the middle.

> *(Standing planted with arms outstretched, I tug the shirt's arms right then left. The fabric is almost splitting apart. "I am in the middle." The shirt seems always on the verge of tearing.)*

I mean,
I am in the middle
and I feel so bad
because my own kind rejects me
and here also,
they, they
don't accept me.
So where [pause]
where am I?
Where am I, really?

.   .   .

Too foreign.
Too unknown.
Right?

. . .

And *I* like a fool
thought that that was good
like, you know, I have [pause]
compiled,
or reconciled
the best of both worlds.
But to some,
no
they don't accept that

. . .

Too unpredictable.
But, you know,
Rivka

. . .

I want things that are so alien to my culture [pause]
and on the other hand
I want things that are alien to this culture.

. . .

So, am I a monster?
In, in, that want of mine?
In that need of mine?

I almost have the shirt on properly now. Attempting to button the cuffs, I pull at the shirtsleeves. In the end, I give up, leaving the cuffs undone. They swing down and fall over my hands as I continue the narrative. *This shirt is swallowing me, stifling me, surrounding and enveloping me. I arch my shoulders and arms back to lessen its tension-hold. It feels tight as a tourniquet.* My discomfort with the shirt peaks, and on the word "monster," I flip my arms over my head, bringing the blouse with them (see figure 6.2). The cloth covers my face and I crouch down, my body becoming contorted with the effort. Then, slightly lifting the fabric from my face so I can see the audience, I ask Chị Tôi in my own voice the question I asked her in our conversation:

RIV: Who would let you be you [pause] would let you be who you really are?
CHI: Almost nobody.
   I don't think a man of my generation [pause]
   would be able to do that
   because men of my generation would be so
   anchored in their traditions.

. . .

Figure 6.2 From "Flesh: monster." Photo by James Cahill, Jerry Eisner, and Nathan Epley.

Unless it is a really free spirit.

. . .

That is that cross I have to bear
I, I don't fit anywhere [pause].
That is my misery actually.
I don't fit with the older ones [pause]
I don't fit with the younger ones [pause]
I am floating in this life.

Part 4: Sinew

(Still wearing the shirt and standing in the middle of the stage, take a pause to mark the end of the past narrative and begin the next. Speak the word "sinew," stretching and extending arms and legs, attempting to embody something of Chị Tôi's tenacity.)

CHỊ: There is a tenacity in me.

I proceed carefully, preparing the audience, and also myself, for the telling of Chị Tôi's most sensitive story. It seemed critical to explain how this narrative, the story of her father's death, finally emerged in our conversations. She told me the story unexpectedly, as we looked through a handful of recent photographs sent by her mother. To help the audience understand the context out of which the story was told and on which it was dependent, I begin with a rough description of our conversation on that day. I then offer spoken and gestural depictions of several of the photographic scenes that kept haunting me long after our exchange:

> On one visit, we look at family pictures. We look at recent family photographs sent by Chị Tôi's mother. I ask endless questions. We come to a series of photos taken at her father's empty tomb in the cemetery. It is the New Year so Chị Tôi and her mother have made a little altar of offerings in front of her father's memorial. Red apples, oranges, flowers, and incense sit in contrast to the wash of gray-granite stones. I ask Chị Tôi what it says on her father's headstone.

As I talk about the photographs, I embody what I take to be an essential "gest" of each photograph. Gest, or gesture, in the Brechtian sense, "is not supposed to mean gesticulation; it is not a matter of explanatory or emphatic movements of the hands, but overall attitudes" (Brecht, 104). This form of gesture distills social structures and power relations in a simple pose or condensed scene rather than in a naturalistic imitation of a past occurrence or the impression of history coming alive before-your-very-eyes. With a few stark gestures and movements, I hoped to invoke something of the personal and political complexities bound up in the photographs.

The "crucial technical device" of gest, says Brecht, is "historicization," the process by which the performer knowingly "play[s] the incidents as historical ones" (140). Gestures then, here and throughout the performance, were not meant to imitate aspects of the photos, but rather to act as the embodied condensations of complex social attitudes. *I kneel like Chị Tôi's mother kneels at the gravesite. I lean in as Chị Tôi did when she told me the ever-painful story of her father's death.* With each of these gestures, I suggest the personal and political gravity of their loss:

CHị: We do not know the day of his death.

. . .

Nobody knows where he died.

. . .

Nobody knows where he fell [pause]
we only know the area.
So it says that he fell in that offensive in 1968 [pause]
the Tet Offensive.
They had to leave him behind.
Did I tell you about it?

RIV: [I make a sound that indicates no]
CHỊ: Because he was mortally wounded.
   And [pause] he told them to go.
   He said, "No, I will delay you,
   so leave me behind with my pistol and a couple of bullets."

.   .   .

   Nobody knows.

Throughout Chị Tôi's life, during our interview, and now in performance, this story continues to bleed out its age-long sadness into the present. "He died with the diary in him." *In him*:

   He knew that it was a very hard offensive [pause] and he could die.
   I think he [pause] he went ahead [pause]
   knowing [pause]
   he could have avoided altogether [pause].
   it wasn't his business to go and fight because he was a writer.
   And he had the *right* not to go into combat [pause].

.   .   .

   He *did* it, he did it of his own will.

.   .   .

   He wanted to go into the city to find me.

.   .   .

   So [pause] he *was* in the outskirts of Saigon.
   He said, "Okay she is in there somewhere."
   Me.

(The tape of the recorded interview beings to play. Chị Tôi's voice is heard telling the story.)

Here I yield to Chị Tôi's voice on the interview tape. She tells me, and now the audience, what she knows of her father's death. This is her story to tell. It is the epicenter from which all of her other stories flow and into which they are drawn back.

   "She is in there somewhere.
   If I make that extra effort [pause] I can go to the house."
   My grandparents' house.
   "And I could get her."
   It is like a Hollywood movie.
   In a Hollywood movie, he *would* have attained the house.
   He would have reached the house.
   But, he didn't reach the house.
   He was on the outskirts.
   And [pause] yeah, they were fighting really hard.
   And they couldn't retreat [pause] all them [pause] all the retreat were cut.

And so [pause]
and he was wounded.
And so his friends started to carry him [pause]
and he said, "No, leave me."

Like a defensive shield, the shirt I put on in the last section now becomes something that I hold against the hailstorm of bullets. I double over and begin thinking of my entire body as lungs reaching for breath. *I spread my arms out like bellows, attempting to inhale all the air left in the room. There is not enough.* Still bending, nearly crouching, I draw the shirt completely over my head and squeeze it into a tight ball. Quietly repeating Chị Tôi's own repetition of her father's charge, "No, leave me," I place the shirt at the altar.

Over a dreamlike cello concerto, Chị Tôi tells of her father's last breaths. He asks for a pistol. He asks for his comrades to "leave me." Here, in the act of speaking, Chị Tôi is performing the past into the present. She recalls the images, sounds, and words her father's soldier friends expressed when they first told this story to her more than twenty years ago. Piercing a veiled past with precise recollection, Chị Tôi pauses, searching for the right word for "his . . . bottle . . . how do you call it?" *Startled, I realize Chị Tôi is asking me a question.* Unexpectedly called into the narrative, I answer awkwardly, offering the word she searches for with some difficulty:

The next day they came back [pause]
and the Americans had bombed everything.
[so softly] Everything burnt.
[pause] That battlefield was burnt down to the ground.
[deep sigh] They found his [pause]
[pause] bottle [pause] how do you call it?
RIV: Canteen?
CHỊ: Yeah.
And he had a *very* special canteen.

Chị Tôi and I continue this most difficult cut of narrative together, my voice and body underscoring hers, periodically repeating words and phrases that need to be spoken—uttered, heard and felt—at least twice:

CHỊ: [pause] And the canteen was burned black.
[deep pause] That is how they presumed that he was dead.
[deep pause] They kept hope in their heart for long time [pause]
thinking that maybe somebody saved him [pause].
[. . .]
I didn't know anything.
The day they came to tell me, "Hey you've got a dad.
Your father name was blah, blah, blah"

. . .

"Your father name is so-and-so-and-so [pause]."
And I said, "Oh, really?
[softly] Where is he?"
"By the way, he is dead [pause]."
So, I had three news, same day, same morning.
That "You have a father, you are not an orphan.
Your father's name was [pause]"
and third [pause]
"by the way, he is no more."

. . .

On my birth certificate, my dad was three dots. [taps the table three times]
So, I thought that I was, ah, uh, bastard.
An illegitimate [pause].
Orphan [pause] [deep sigh out].
I had all kinds of questions in my head.
And nobody told me anything because nobody *really* knew what
    was going on, and because it was really dangerous
    and risky also, to talk about it.
So they prefer to just pull a veil.

   (*Second music cut fades in over Chị Tôi's voice. Music and movement last approximately*
   four minutes. Chị Tôi's voice returns as music diminishes.)

I have pictures that you would be curious to see
where I am the only girl, and I was wearing [pause]
and I was very demure, ladylike [pause]
and I was sitting among a group, of
hardened, hardened fighters
all in fatigue, combat fatigue.
And they would be men in their fifties.
Right.
And
I would be sitting there, and all of them would be around me, staring at me.
Crying.
I wouldn't cry, but they cry.
Because I would remind them so much of my dad.
He was *loved* by many.

. . .

And his friends, yeah, all of them [pause]
and, what they did for me very beautiful
after the war, I came to see them
and each of them reminisced something that they *knew* about him
    [pause].

Yeah [pause] and so I wrote it down.

. . .

How could I get to know my own father?
They described what a man he was.
They described the way he walked.
They described what dishes he liked.
They described how his laugh *sounded* [pause].
[so softly] I did *not* know him [pause]
And I was supposed to be the *closest* to my father,
and at the same time, I was the *farthest* [pause] oh [pause]
that is the irony of everything [pause].
So I wrote it down in my diary
And then I burned everything.

(The third music and movement passage ends the scene. Music fades. Transition to table to pick up red bowl and chopsticks.)

Everything is burnt. The battlefield. The canteen. His skin. Her diary. Everything has gone to char and ash, it seems, except this story—which burns with new intensity now. As Chị Tôi's voice plays on the tape, I take up a few ripped pieces of the ripped timeline. Clenching the paper tightly in my hands, I spread the still wet blood-paint until it streams down both of my arms from palm to elbow. Backing up from the destruction, I tear the paper pieces into even smaller crumbled bits, letting them drop silently to the floor.

Part 5: Heart

(Pick up chopsticks and bowl. With arms outstretched, speak the word "heart" and begin taking up the crumpled pieces of the timeline with the chopsticks. Place the paper pieces in the red bowl while speaking the narrative.)

The two final scenes honor loss and absence through images of gathering. Chị Tôi tells me her "heart is like a container" for pieces of remembered experiences, shreds of stories, and past lives. She moves beyond the trauma of her history by remembering what pieces of her past she does know and holds close. In telling, she scatters them. In recollecting, she gathers them up again.

I crouch lightly over the scraps of gold and red paper that now litter the stage. One at a time, I pick up the crumpled remains with chopsticks, placing them in a red and gold Asian bowl while speaking, almost to myself, what has become for me Chị Tôi's song—the summary refrain she tells herself as much as me:

CHỊ: And so [there] are [ ] pieces
I have been amassing in my life [pause]

and my heart is like a container for all those pieces.

. . .

People [pause]
and what they have left in me.
So the people,
the corporeal [pause] shell
has left me [pause]
they have left me
and all alone.
But, I have that piece of them in me [pause].
And the piece is,
a piece of their mind,
a piece of their soul,
a piece of their heart [pause]
that they have given me
in some time of life.
And that has remained intact.
All the other attributes,
they took with themselves [pause]
didn't leave me anything [pause]
but at least I have that small piece [pause].

(Leave the bowl and chopsticks at the altar downstage center. Transition back to the table for red veil in preparation for final scene.)

Part 6: Blood

This final scene continues the image of the heart and takes the performance full circle, returning to another version of Chị Tôi's birth story. I reach for the last prop. It is a sheer red cloth that has been covering the table. I hold it extended in each hand with two fingers slowly rippling it back and forth. *It pulses in the rhythm of a slow heartbeat.* I speak as myself, telling the audience that what they will hear next is Chị Tôi translating a passage of her father's diary from Vietnamese to English.

Chị Tôi told me that he wrote in his diary at night, over the course of many war-long years. He wrote by the light of a small alcohol lamp in the forests, or wherever else he found himself. And he would put blankets over his head so he would not be seen and shot at through the darkness.

As a tape of Chị Tôi's voice plays, I lean forward and slip under the fabric. Chị Tôi speaks her father's words. Lightly and barely audible at first, I underscore their voices with my own, while continuing to compress, expand, and drape the cloth to depict a heartbeat, blanket, swaddling cloth, and finally a shroud. In several places, the tape fades out as my own voice rises. We exchange and take turns with the passage, sometimes speaking alone, at other times together:

(Begin the tape of Chị Tôi translating her father's diary.)

CHỊ: "So many worries, so many hardships,
 running up and down, questions [pause]
 anxiety [pause]
 everything for your sake,
 my little child [pause].
 Your mother and I have been,
 [pause] so
 [pause] worried,
 [pause] for you
 even [pause] when you were not [pause] conceived yet."

I am being absorbed, deliberately and unexpectedly, into the dialogic continuum of Chị Tôi's stories and life. Instead of speaking for her, I speak with her, imagining her father thinking and writing these words:

(Tape of Chị Tôi's voice fades out. I speak.)

"You were born [pause] at the moment when, [pause]
 the Kilinski—my ship—pulled anchor.
 I bid farewell to you my child,
 I bid farewell to our beloved Southern land [pause]
 I bid farewell to your mother
 to go to the North.
 And you know why?
 My little child?
 It is for your future.
 You are now [pause] in life."

(Chị Tôi's recorded voice returns. We speak a few lines together before my voice fades out. Chị Tôi continues alone.)

"I will be back in a couple of years.
 I will embrace you, I will hug you, I will kiss you so much [pause]
 my most precious [pause] daughter.
 You are now on this earth to make us happy
 to make your mother [pause] happy
 while she is away from me, your father [pause].
 Be a good girl, little one [pause]
 and love your mother."

As Chị Tôi's father finally reassures her that "I will be back in a couple of years," I unfurl the transparent crimson cloth over the altar now fully accumulated on the floor directly in front of the audience. We hear Chị Tôi speaking the last lines alone: "I will embrace you . . . Be a good girl, little one [pause] and love your mother." While Chị Tôi speaks, as a final gesture, I carefully pick up her family photograph from its place at the center of the memorial, recalling that this was "the only time the three of us were 'ever' together," and then slowly return it to the place beneath my shirt. The picture is just one of the living fragments I now keep "in me."

(Turn to leave as lights fade. Performance ends. Lights out, then up.)

* * *

Like Chị Tôi, my body has become "a container" for "all those pieces" of "others and what they have left in me." Chị Tôi and I share a sense of connection about her past, and consequently, about her present. We know each other well enough that I feel I can—sometimes, with care—speak of her and on behalf of her to others. But I wanted to herald some of our principal differences in the performance and now, here. I cast myself as more of a shadow of her in my likeness, rather than in any way identical. I do not "channel" Chị Tôi, nor do I—following traditions of mimetic realism—"become" her. Growing out of Chị Tôi's experiences, the performance primarily embodies learning about her life. It is meant neither to capture nor to overtake, but to respond respectfully to Chị Tôi, and in doing so, to extend her narrative memory into others' awareness. Likewise, when I speak of feeling Chị Tôi's presence inhabiting my body, she does not claim or obscure my sense of self. The pieces she has left in me exist in the form of altered or heightened awareness of the struggle that has comprised my dear friend's life, of Vietnamese history in a global context, and of the elusive nature of memory and the challenge of life narrative. In performance, I wish neither to eclipse nor to dissolve into her, and yet, through performance, I am fundamentally changed by her. I am affected by Chị Tôi, in intimate and sometimes painful ways, which is why I often describe her lingering presence in my everyday experiences as a kind of "wounding."

In more direct and injurious ways, the past inflicts its presence and present absences on Chị Tôi's body. I inherit differently felt wounds from the impact of her stories. In the performance process, I was not claiming to feel her sadness or to know her past in any way that could be considered "the same." I would not presume to relive her trauma, although it often felt that, in the process of trying to understand hers, I was generating my own; and though I was not alive during the Vietnamese–American war, I nonetheless feel implicated in her, and her family's and country's, past suffering and current geopolitical inequities. What I have is a window into knowing that I cannot know the painful depth and breadth of her experience.

I am painfully aware of the limits of my knowledge. I cannot feel far enough beyond my own skin. Paradoxically, sensing the distance between us brings me closer to her.

In telling me her life stories, Chị Tôi does not expect that her wounds will simply heal, disappearing without a trace. This is not possible, nor is it desirable. Telling, for Chị Tôi, is not about forgetting. It is not exactly about reliving either. To just re-experience these inflictions would be a kind of recursive trauma. Together, we witness toward something more than repetition. We speak memory, experiences, and voices into renewed significance, moving into uncharted territories in the hopes of opening new spaces of learning and possible transformation. By performing witnessing in our respective ways, Chị Tôi and I seek to remember into the present and future, "rebuild[ing] [lives] so massively destroyed, without, however, denying the destruction or [their] wounds" (Bal, 23).

It would be wrong to use the performance of oral history to cover over the "wounds" of history, to try to fix them, or even simply to expose them to anything like sensational voyeurism. These would be acts of violence in their own right. Performing memory is more about bearing witness. Bearing witness, however, does not just entail carrying memory. Bearing the past is to allow it entry into bodily consciousness and continuing social experience, so that living with memory means giving residence to pieces of the past that in turn, even in their painfulness, sustain and charge one's own being. Witnessing is a necessarily unfinished and incomplete process of sensing and knowing, of reaching out with respect toward another's life. As much as witnessing is a double-act of seeing and not seeing, it is also a double act of seeing, telling, and asking the listener for radical openness: to allow these stories, these lives, into his or her own life without possessing them, without "knowing" them. I do not claim to call what I know of Chị Tôi to be anything akin to total understanding. Saying "I understand you" implies a sense of possession, where the "I" overtakes, or undertakes the "you," seemingly indicating that no continued explanation, dialogue or interaction is necessary.

The hope of witnessing lies in its endlessness. Witnessing charges understanding to become a practice of processual encounters, perhaps with points of concentrated attention, but with the effect of continually postponing ending. Accordingly, we witness each other into an ever receding space: into what is more and more unknown or less and less known. Instead of feeling I know Chị Tôi more with time, I increasingly realize just how much there is that I do not know—that the expanse of her life-story and storied life exists "beyond" anyone's ability to contain.

Witnessing in this sense is destabilizing. Hearing Chị Tôi's stories, whole worlds that I never knew about at least partially opened. And in their unfolding I became aware of the infinite magnitude of what I do not know. But this sense of increasing absence or receding knowledge that displaces the kind of contentment that might come from fullness or completion is no reason to abandon the project of doing and performing oral history. Paradoxically, it must be the impetus for continual remembering.

Sitting at Chị Tôi's kitchen table, I am eyewitness to her retelling, but not to the historical moments at which she was materially present. Chị Tôi performs eyewitness, or firsthand, memory as well as stories inherited from beyond her direct experience. In my retelling of Chị Tôi's narratives, the performance itself becomes an act of witnessing, a space in which I acknowledge, through echoing and interpreting, the extent and limits of my understanding. I hear pieces of stories and sense how experiences "might have felt" but I cannot claim to know them in any total sense. In "bearing witness" to Chị Tôi's life in performance, I acknowledge myself as an onlooker "to what is beyond [my] knowledge or recognition" (Oliver, 18).

Still, I cannot stop where absence begins. Performance draws me into active speculation: *What lies beyond the edges of this photograph? How did Chị Tôi understand her war-torn surroundings when she was four years old?* Knowing a few pieces from her past, I can *imagine into* the absence, into what is beyond my experience. Performatively moving "as if" I were there, within the tattered pieces of Chị Tôi's past, I think: *maybe this is how it felt to learn for the first time, at age twenty-one,* "that I have a father." *And* "by the way, he is dead."

Playing with imagined possibility enables me to gain awareness of what I do not and cannot know, what is "beyond [my] recognition" (Oliver). When working with or listening to Chị Tôi's stories, witnessing feels like an attuned, actively engaged *lean* into another's life. Performance helps me grapple with the paradoxes of witness and experience. It compels me, in relation to the audience for whom I am a witness, to imagine and to act just over the edge of our incompleteness.

The process of rehearsal became a place of discovery and intensive exploration of Chị Tôi's life and life narratives, even—or especially—when she was not present herself, except as a kind of witnessing ghost.[6] Sensing her possible responses to the developing performance helped keep me accountable and attentive to the numerous ethical and political choices involved in performing another's life stories. Rather than providing some kind of transparent testimony, this kind of witnessing entailed thinking and learning through *doing*, through the activity of engaged bodily sensing: asking, listening, experimenting, questioning, and imagining with Chị Tôi.[7]

What seems the most ephemeral and fragile may in fact be the most enduring. Flesh fades, diminishes and dies. On the breath and through the performing body, story keeps its airy lightness and flooding force, suggesting one possibility of life-beyond-death. In this sense, memory endures, paradoxically, because it moves. Only through movement can memory take up residence and build a dwelling place within us. As sites of accumulation we become shelters, or living archives, for memory. Our bodies hold a myriad of incomplete pieces, the presence of which we are sometimes unaware. Because our bodies "never stop [ ] accumulating" (Trinh, 123) doubled within "every gesture, every word" is "our past, present, and future." The past becomes us, doubles us and shadows us, and in so doing, it physically haunts the present with the hopes of actively witnessing and performing memory into possible futures.

It is not just our own pasts, futures and presents that we carry, and that sustain us in and as witness, but others' lives as well. In gathering others' story-pieces, "I carry with me everything—all those people, all those places, I carry them around with me until my shoulders bend" (Myerhoff, 74). And yet, while carrying these memory fragments *"in me"* is vital, it is only part of what is required.

In the end, preserving memory means giving it away. Together, Chị Tôi and I perform memory toward "disappearance" rather than "preservation" (Phelan, 148). We honor the "beauty in what is vanishing" in history and in the ephemeral transference to other bodies/witnesses in live performance (Benjamin, 87). To perform memory is thus to enter into vanishing and to embrace the loss that comes with each retelling.

Instead of keeping her memories safely bound, Chị Tôi knows knowledge "is not made for understanding; it is made for cutting" (Foucault, 88). What she knows, she received in pieces. In retelling, she reconfigures the fragments and cuts them again. Her history cuts her, wounds her. But her purposeful dissipation is not really a deterioration, but a regeneration and revitalization. Her memory charges her future with meaning. And in its release and reception, memory extends itself into others' lives and living. The number of years that have passed since I first asked Chị Tôi if she would tell me about her past has not diminished the impact of her stories on me. Her narrative slivers continue to cut through my skin. *I could not extract them if I wanted to try. Sometimes I find her in my breath. In fleeting dreams as I rub my eyes awake.* There is no denying Chị Tôi's lasting presence in my day-to-day life. Her voice whispers in my ear. *So what are these fragments of memory? What of the past endures?* A seed. A spark. An intentional or unknown gift. Tatters. Shards. Incomplete but vital pieces:

> a piece of their mind,
> a piece of their soul,
> a piece of their heart [pause]
> that they have given me
> in some time of life
> [. . .]

Notes

1. Throughout the chapter, the research collaborator is referred to as "Chị Tôi" for purposes of confidentiality. Chị Tôi is a respectful Vietnamese term of address meaning "my older sister." All other Vietnamese words, such as Viet Minh or Dien Bien Phu, are English transliterations.
2. The performance of *And So There Are Pieces . . .* was made possible through financial support from the University of North Carolina at Chapel Hill Office of Distinguished Scholarships and Intellectual Life, the Department of Communication Studies, and

Wordshed Productions. My sincere thanks and appreciation to these sponsors, as well as to Chị Tôi, my committee and family members, and all individuals who contributed so much time and energy to the event.

3. This study was given IRB approval on May 1, 2001, by the Academic Affairs Institutional Review Board (AA-IRB) of the University of North Carolina at Chapel Hill. I received written consent from Chị Tôi on May 12, 2001. Throughout the interview process, I also kept a journal to document thoughts before, between, and after interviews. The study is ongoing.

4. The performance text is composed of transcription pieces taken from interview tapes (appearing in the text in poetic transcription), my memory of Chị Tôi's words (appearing in the text in quotation), and my own affective and descriptive commentary, framing her stories. Chị Tôi's narratives include notation of pauses and silences, excess words, repetitions, rhythms of speech, and sounds such as laughter, breath, and sighs, what Anna Deavere Smith calls "bad grammar" (xxxi). Re: transcription methods, I generally relied on Smith (*Fires in the Mirror*), Madison ("My Occupation"), Pollock (*Telling Bodies*), Langellier and Peterson ("Politics of Personal Narrative"), and Fine (*The Folklore Text*).

5. Almost all of the props used in the performance were in full view of the audience at all times. Most of them, with the exception of the umbrella and photograph, initially resided on a table situated in the upper left corner of the performance space. The performance was divided into six basic parts, with each part focusing on specific transcribed narrative passages from our taped interviews. During each part, usually one and sometimes a few related objects are used to assist in telling the story.

It might be more accurate to call the props transformational objects because they are used to express multiple and layered meanings in literal and figurative ways. The props' meanings are fluid, not fixed. A shirt may be a shirt, a second skin, a mask, or an anchor at different moments. The shirt can also embody all or some of those meanings at the same time: the shirt may signify the comforts of a second skin while expressing the weight of an anchor.

6. Unfortunately, due to distance, Chị Tôi was unable to attend the performance. Nonetheless, in the final performance as in rehearsal, I felt that something of her was still very present. While rehearsing, Chị Tôi was my imaginary or "ghosted" audience. Despite her absence on the performance night, Chị Tôi had several close friends in the audience who acted as proxies, one of them being the Vietnamese friend who first introduced us over dinner two years earlier. Following the performance, attendees were invited to write down short messages to Chị Tôi. I later gave Chị Tôi the audiences' personal notes, as a small token of thanks and as an offering of recognition, to let her know that her stories had been heard and appreciated.

In addition, I also gave Chị Tôi copies of the written thesis. Talking with her months later, she told me about translating several passages for her mother (who lives in Vietnam) while they spoke over the phone. And the written thesis continues to travel (receiving more circulation than I ever imagined) as Chị Tôi apparently gave copies to close American and Vietnamese friends and family members living in the United States. Recently, Chị Tôi told me that the thesis had prompted conversations between her and several Vietnamese–American relatives. One relative who fled Vietnam as the war ended told Chị Tôi he felt he understood her experiences and perspectives much more fully after having read her words.

For more than four years, I have found myself retelling Chị Tôi's stories in an array of settings: to classes, community audiences, in essays and conference presentations, and in everyday conversations. As this project expands, Chị Tôi remains a consultant, collaborator and confidante in all resulting writing and performances. The performance that took place two years ago was the culmination of my M.A. work. But I soon realized, it also marked an important beginning in my desire for a continuing and deepening engagement with narrative, memory and performance, with Chị Tôi, and with the people and histories of Vietnam.

7. I was moved to think, following Oliver and others, that through joint acts of telling and witnessing, Chị Tôi and I can enable each other as "active agent[s]," being both "selves" and "subjects, hav[ing] subjectivity and agency by virtue of our dialogic relationship" (Oliver, 18). We became our selves (and strange to ourselves) in active relation to each other. I listen to Chị Tôi in the hope of being an "external witness," for without external witness, we cannot develop or sustain the internal witness necessary for the ability to interpret and represent our experience (88). The relationship between external witness and self-witnessing allows the recognition "necessary for subjectivity and more essentially for both individual and social transformation" (88).

Works Cited

Bal, Mieke, Jonathon Crewe, and Leo Spitzer, eds. *Acts of Memory: Cultural Recall in the Present.* Hanover, NH: University Press of New England, 1999.

Benjamin, Walter. *Illuminations.* Ed. Hannah Arendt. Trans. Harry Zohn. New York: Schocken Books, 1969.

Brecht, Bertolt. *Brecht on Theatre: The Development of an Aesthetic.* Ed. and trans. John Willett. New York: Hill and Wang, 1957.

Conquergood, Dwight. "Performing as a Moral Act: Ethical Dimensions of the Ethnography of Performance." *Literature in Performance* (1985): 1–11.

Fine, Elizabeth C. *The Folklore Text: From Performance to Print.* Bloomington: Indiana University Press, 1984.

Foucault, Michel. *The Foucault Reader.* Ed. Paul Rabinow. New York: Pantheon, 1984.

Karnow, Stanley. *Vietnam: A History.* New York: Viking, 1983.

Madison, D. Soyini. " 'That Was My Occupation': Oral Narrative, Performance, and Black Feminist Thought." *Text and Performance Quarterly* 13 (1993): 213–232.

Myerhoff, Barbara. *Number Our Days.* New York: Simon & Shuster, 1978.

Oliver, Kelly. *Witnessing: Beyond Recognition.* Minneapolis: University of Minnesota Press, 2001.

Peterson, Eric E. and Kristin M. Langellier. "The Politics of Personal Narrative Methodology." *Text and Performance Quarterly* 17 (1997): 135–152.

Phelan, Peggy. *Unmarked: The Politics of Performance.* New York: Routledge, 1993.

Pollock, Della. *Telling Bodies, Performing Birth.* New York: Columbia University Press, 1999.

Smith, Anna Deavere. *Fires in the Mirror: Crown Heights, Brooklyn and Other Identities.* New York: Doubleday, 1993.

Trinh, Minh-ha T. *Woman, Native, Other: Writing Postcoloniality and Feminism.* Bloomington: Indiana University Press, 1989.

"Tic(k)": A Performance of Time and Memory

Gretchen A. Case

For Mark F.

Gretchen Case offers the script of her performance, "Tic(k)," framed by a reflection that locates history in the body and performance as consequently a premiere mode of knowing history—knowing it differently, of course: knowing it as replete with the quirks and contingencies, the feelings and failings, and the sensual delirium of bodily life itself. Case gives us performance as not only an alternative but a preferred epistemology. For Case, as for so many of the other authors in this volume, what we can know about the histories our bodies carry and move expands with the possibilities for the embodied work of staged performance.

I am an oral historian, a performer, a teacher, a student, and—sometimes—a mourner. I often bring my grief onstage on me. While the personal narratives that I write and tell as part of larger performances concerned with health, illness, dying, and death serve as public lamentations, they are also theoretically grounded reflections on the ways in which my academic and professional lives intersect with my (supposedly separate) personal life.

I approach performance as a means of reflecting on the choices I face constantly in my research. By re-presenting fragments of thought and memory from my research process in a framework defined by my voice and the aesthetics of the stage, I am able to make space for introspection. Performance offers room for reflexivity, for questioning the environment in which I do my research as well as my motivations for pursuing it. For instance, in 1998 and 1999, I performed two versions of "Hx," a show I titled after the common medical abbreviation for "history," meaning, of course, a certain kind of medical history. Among other things, "Hx" focused the ironies implicit in what it means to "take a history." My inspiration for this script was itself a script: a list of questions given to medical students to be memorized and asked in precise order when taking a medical history from a patient. I was fascinated by the rigidity of this system and wondered how successful these questions were in gathering necessary information. Soon I saw the connection to the way I ordered questions in the interviews I conducted, including interviews with doctors. So I began to write about doctors, but also about the passing of my grandmother and her siblings, about their childhood home far up in a mountain hollow, and my mother's serious illness. As the script expanded, I found myself including more about the living than the dead, history still in the making alongside the made. My own medical history slipped into view, and I moved from interviewing doctors to being interviewed by them. A white jacket turned front-to-back became a hospital gown. A list of questions in a medical textbook became a list of questions on an interviewer's notepad, the responses to those and other questions eventually became the realization that I was interweaving the categories of family history and medical history, and that was as it should be. There is no history of just one body.

In a 2002 script, "Sound," I returned to the final oral history interview I conducted with my mother before her death from cancer. Writing this script was a symptom of the primary reaction I had to my mother's death sentence: I became obsessed with documentation. I had been conducting oral history interviews with both my parents, in an unhurried sort of way, certainly spurred on by my mother's illness and my father's own brush with cancer. Once it was clear that my mother's final appeals were denied and the temporary reprieves were lifted, I stepped up the speed of those interviews, pulling out the tape recorder whenever she felt well enough to talk. I took endless photographs of her alone, of her with her grandchildren, with me, and with my father. This was often distressing to her. She didn't feel well or think she looked well, and the camera was an intrusion on her body, her privacy, and her vanity. Whenever she said something I found particularly wise, I would scribble it down. I found myself taking notes on our phone calls, saving her emails and sorting them into folders by topic. At that time I lived 3,500 miles away from her; I flew home every weekend during those months, and spent my time with her trying to fix her into place: on film, on paper, on tape. A year after her death, I tried to fix her into place on stage—ironically, the least likely space for anything to stay still—by writing a script that attempted to capture the experience of interviewing her, both of us knowing it would be the last time.

My performances ask questions that answer themselves in part by blurring boundaries between public and private, intimacy and distance, life and sex and death. My work sometimes unsettles audience members who expect a linear narrative progression and a demure attitude toward troubled and dying bodies. Two audience members at a performance of "Hx" vehemently objected to the parallel I drew between a medical examination and an erotic encounter. An audience member at my single performance of "Sound" forcefully accused me of hiding shameful secrets rather than pointing to indescribable moments of revelation. My work is neither linear nor demure; my grief is messy and my mourning untidy.

"Tic(k)," the script I offer here, is a contemplation of the deaths of my maternal grandfather and of three men I interviewed for an oral history project for the U.S. National Cancer Institute between 1997 and 2000. I could have chosen to author a brief memoir of my sadness or an academic treatise on the interviewer's relationship with her narrator and either might have been appropriate—and perhaps more cogent to readers for whom these genres of historical representation are familiar territory. But I understand performance to be a peculiarly powerful form of historical documentation. It records the confluence of what may seem disparate events that culminates in historical time on stage. The performance itself is also a historical document, in which I establish a series of events through the authority of witness and re-presentation, and reflect on their respective and combined significance in dynamic engagement with an audience.

The text-in-script and the text-in-performance are also theoretical documents, informed by my tussle with ideas about history, memory, and the performance of each. My use of a clock face as an organizing metaphor for the staging of my script comes from reading philosopher Paul Ricouer. In *Time and Narrative*, Ricouer establishes an intriguing hermeneutical circle: "time becomes human time to the extent that it is organized after the manner of a narrative; narrative, in turn, is meaningful to the extent that it portrays the features of temporal experience."[1] We humans need time to make narrative and narrative to make time, writes Ricouer, and I find this ticking 'round the clock a comforting reminder that I am constantly *telling time*: telling stories to make time human, and making those stories meaningful by portraying some of the fundamental "features of temporal experience." The deaths of my grandfather and my NCI narrators evoked a longing in me for times and narratives passed and past: for times that have fallen into the past and for narratives that seem to have passed away with them. In "Tic(k)," I am concerned with time passing, even as it does so here and now. I borrow on the "here and now" of performance, moreover, to dramatize the incoherence of untold time. Time needs narrative, and narrative needs time. Time does not "naturally" follow a narrative sequence. Dying itself acquires meaning through the narrative arc and continuity we attribute to living.

Onstage in this performance, I move through time with the narratives of my grandfather and narrators only to find that time is treacherous: it repeats itself and changes shape and meaning before the repetition can be secured. Each stop on the "clock" in "Tic(k)" represents a moment that does not necessarily flow into chronology. Unlike the linear order of the chronicle or chronology, or the sequential logic of the classical argument, my work favors the unstable logics of simultaneity, circularity, and chronic repetition. Even the title, "Tic(k)," with its quirky little parentheses, is meant to honor the repetitions to which clocks and human bodies bind us.

Quid est enim tempus? What, then, is time? I appreciate Ricouer's struggle with this, St. Augustine's, question. For Ricouer: "The skeptical argument is well-known: time has no being since the future is not yet, the past is no longer, and the present does not remain. And yet we do speak of time as having being. We say that things to come *will be*, that things past *were*, and that things present *are passing away*. Even passing away is not nothing" (Ricouer, 7). Accordingly, for me, performance combines the *will be, were,* and *passing away* of history. It puts us always somewhere between a past, a present, and a future, none of which fall in a straight line or stay in the same place for long, and yet with people and stories that we touch as they *pass*.

I first presented "Tic(k)" to audiences in Berkeley, California, in February 2000, many months after my three narrators from the National Cancer Institute died and more than seven years after my grandfather passed away. Until that point, I had not written anything about the intense grief I had felt at the death of my grandfather—the first death I experienced as an adult—or about the surprising mourning into which I entered after the deaths of each of the three men I had interviewed. The complicated emotions that wound through and around all of these losses were difficult to sort out and to put down in anything like an organized fashion on paper. My grief for my grandfather, certainly "due" and conventionally authorized, became confused in relation to what seemed the unauthorized, unritualized, and unplaceable grief I felt for the scientists I had met only on the "excuse" of interviewing them. Certainly I am not the first to be bewildered by how to grieve for those known only in a professional or otherwise limited capacity. I am often reminded of Theodore Roethke's poem, "Elegy for Jane," in which he urgently mourns a student but concludes, "I, with no rights in the matter, / Neither father nor lover."[2] I, the interviewer, with no rights in the matter. No sanctioned way to show what I feel. And so, it seemed, no sanction for my feelings.

Memories of my grandfather's death offered me stable ground from which to explore this unfamiliar grief. I readily understood the occasion of a beloved relative's death and I recognized my prescribed role as mourner. The vivid ceremonies that marked his passing provided further contrast to the absence of ritual (for me) accompanying the news that my narrators had died. I imagined, rather than attended, those funerals and wakes, feeling unwelcome at gatherings of family and friends when I was neither. That all three of these narrators were men of my grandfather's age is important, for it allowed me to connect their lives. In telling stories of my grandfather's life and death, I created a space for mourning my lost narrators. In turn, by opening this space for mourning, I was able to grieve more deeply for my lost grandfather.

"Tic(k)" is a performance *about* oral history rather than a performance *of* oral history. In this text, I do not perform the stories that my narrators have told me but rather the stories I have told and continue to tell about them. I perform, rather than write, these stories because performance, like life itself and unlike papers in an archive, is mutable and temporary. I do not fix my narrators' lives on the page, but move them on the stage with me, choosing activity over artifact. I offer this performance as a response to the weary claim that history is about dead people: oral history is about dying. It is about people needing, wanting, to make their time human in stories that "portray the features of temporal experience" before their libraries of life stories vanish with them. It is about *making time* in the act of telling and retelling stories, not "saving" lives exactly but re-creating—through the peculiar repetitions of narratives in the highly charged, unpredictable space of performance—something of their narrative work. It is consequently, then, about loss, about what is irretrievable in the passage of time, and about lives dignified by the "tic(k)s" of living grief.

For me, the interview setting is a place of intimacy, a solemn exchange of gifts in a sacred grove. Yet my professional and personal respect for the narrators' privacy insists that I maintain certain conventions of distance: release forms and other legal paperwork, control of my own emotions and responses, properly constrained channels of communication. The narrators and I subtly negotiate these conventions over the course of our relationships; some eventually become friends and correspondents while others remain one-time acquaintances whose shadows are tucked into my file cabinets. I am always aware that I am interviewing narrators who wish to leave records of the memories they carry lest those memories go with them to their graves. Oral history pivots on mortality; it hovers on the edge of death, reaches for the disappearing. More than fixing a life in place or saving a story from being forgotten, oral history profoundly honors ephemerality and loss by acknowledging the slipping-away. The professional dimensions of my role as a keeper of history—as scribe, as witness, sometimes as confessor—have not muted the pain of these performances of oral history, which, like any other performance, are fated to leave only traces. Performance, at its core, is loss. The performed text dissolves as it goes, leaving behind only ghosts disguised as records.

I have worked as an oral historian since 1988, having trained at least as much in the field as in the classroom. And yet neither seemed to be of particular help to me in sorting out my responses to the deaths of three of my narrators. I turned to performance as a way to understand and to share the knowledge of life, death, and grief I seemed to be gaining despite myself. In early 2000, when offered the chance to develop a solo performance on a topic of my choosing, I entered an empty rehearsal space to see what might happen. I was surprised when my confused grief surfaced immediately, filling not only my thoughts and body but, it seemed, that entire room. I started with an image that has been with me since my grandfather's funeral: the rhythmic sway of crimson capes as the Knights of Columbus marched down the church aisle in his honor. This ritual movement quickly became associated with other acts, more deeply ingrained, exhumed from many hours as a child jumping rope on a concrete playground behind a parochial school. The bodily memories of swaying and jumping led to the text. Rather than beginning with words that I would then block or choreograph, I began with simple rhythms. A gracious friend transcribed movement and words for me as I felt my way through what I wanted, needed to say.

The show's development from that point on is a mystery even to me. I cannot report on either a logical progression toward a finished script or even a consistent rehearsal process.

Truth be told, the show won't stay still: it changes each time I perform it. In the version of the script published here, I have removed several sections that consistently edited themselves out in the moment of performance as I realized that they skewed the emerging pattern. Gone is a story of a colleague, another historian, who inherited a stamp collection and proceeded to remove them from their albums and use them for postage. Her pragmatism erased all possibility of sentiment and flustered her preservation-minded co-workers, but I knew the story only second-hand, years after it had happened. I realized quickly that I had included this tale in an embarrassingly selfish play for shock or laughter, and it did not serve the greater narrative. Gone too, are a few didactic moments that similarly coerced response from the audience. One of the reasons I choose so often to work solo on stage is this possibility of changing lines without disturbing other performers. For the same reason, I keep my solo performances as technically simple as possible and prefer non-traditional perform-ance spaces. I would rather adapt a black box theater or bare classroom than bridge the distance from a proscenium stage to an audience bank. Still, I remain the bane of light board operators and other stage technicians, who are doomed to chase after me as I change cue lines.

In Berkeley, I performed the show on three consecutive nights and listened as the words came precisely as they chose. These were minor variations on the same theme, but each change seemed crucial as it took its turn on stage. The next time I performed "Tic(k)," at a meeting of the Oral History Association in Durham, North Carolina, in October 2000, the changes were more radical. Midway through the performance, I stopped dead. Perhaps I stopped with the dead. Suddenly I was overwhelmed as I spoke and my mind clicked in place, over and over, like the pendulum of the metronome I'd used as a prop. I hesitated: barefoot, blank, and vulnerable. The dis-tance I had maintained from the words—as any good performer does—shrank, and I was standing too close to my memories. I looked around for help out of this actor's nightmare and saw only faces, waiting. I smiled and asked my audience to *give me a minute*, to wait. Perhaps I just needed a moment of quiet with them, or they with me; they waited patiently. Eventually, I gathered myself and plunged back into the pre-scripted words. I had never before suffered a break like that and have not since. There are rules and conventions for performers just as there are for interviewers, and I had violated a key precept by losing command of my emotions. Something powerful pulled me aside, whispered to me, distracted me from my task.

Performance is, in many ways, defined by the presence of an audience. Whether imagined in rehearsal or embodied in chairs in a performance hall, the audience sets up a condition of *address*. Whatever is said is not only *to* but in anticipation of response *from* audience members. Thus performance describes a reflexive relationship between the performer(s) and audience members who mirror and prick each other's consciousness, even when the audience remains conventionally silent. Not all performances take advantage of this relationship. Indeed, many refuse it. I tend to make myself as vulnerable to the reflexivity of performance as possible, largely because of the riches waiting in store: the possibilities for new realizations, shared discoveries, stronger affiliation, and even something like ritual re-seeing. The changes I make during performance depend on my audiences. Their varied responses are immediate and persuasive and shift the performance itself as I integrate their sighs and laughs and questioning looks into my body, words, movement, and looks. In this sense, the performance site becomes another grave—carved into a forest dense with fleeting and surging emotions, sudden recognition, rising realization, and the pleasures and dangers of exchange.

I welcome audience responses after performances, and am frequently asked whether anyone other than me could perform this script. This is a question I ponder again as I consider that all the "stage directions" here are written in the first person. I can't envision another body offering these words, but then again, might that not be exactly why someone else should perform them? I share with many other performers the well-founded fear that autobiographical narrative will descend into stories that serve only the authorial/performing self. However, I think and hope that "Tic(k)" offers something of value beyond my individual experience, that it takes up a topic that is not often discussed yet is of critical concern to anyone who conducts interviews as part of her life's work.

We interviewers often enter into communion with those we suspect are dying and so feel threatened by the extinction of their embodied histories. We do not recognize this as a last rite, however, and in some ways that may be best: already the interview threatens privacy and compromises boundaries. The act of asking someone to perform a life history for the tape recorder suggests that the narrator might be reaching life's end. To declare this a sacrament between interviewer and narrator also asks for a commitment and recognition of mortality that many do not wish to give. Yet we must acknowledge that a bond is forged in the telling of stories and that when death separates us from the teller, we respond to that new absence. Though I read my narrators through their narratives, the loss of the teller affects the tale. Upon each death, I am elevated from keeper of a story to keeper of a story never to be told again. This responsibility intensifies my grief, but I still have no idea how to grieve properly. In presenting "Tic(k)" as a public performance, I hope to have started a productive conversation with other interviewers on the topic of the strange and intimate loss of a narrator.

In his 1940 essay, "Theses on the Philosophy of History," German philosopher Walter Benjamin famously describes artist Paul Klee's painting "Angelus Novus." The painting, Benjamin tells us:

> shows an angel looking as though he is about to move away from something he is fixedly contemplating. His eyes are staring, his mouth is open, his wings are spread.

This is how one pictures the angel of history. His face is turned toward the past. Where we perceive a chain of events, he sees one single catastrophe which keeps piling wreckage upon wreckage and hurls it in front of his feet. The angel would like to stay, awaken the dead, and make whole what has been smashed. But a storm is blowing from Paradise; it has got caught in his wings with such violence that the angel can no longer close them. This storm irresistibly propels him into the future to which his back is turned, while the pile of debris before him grows skyward. This storm is what we call progress.[3]

Benjamin's interpretation of Klee's painting has memorialized it as an image of modern history and yet, at the same time, has to some extent eclipsed it. Many of us have read and appreciated Benjamin's infamous "Theses" without ever having seen the painting (or even a copy). In the painting, Klee's angel is little more than a sketch, yet Benjamin found in it the basis for exegesis on the whole of history. For many contemporary readers, Benjamin's words have moved in front of Klee's brushstrokes, not only lending import to but becoming more important than the painting that inspired them. This eclipse haunts me now as I try to write a companionable interpretation of a script that I wish I could just perform for anyone who asks. I fear my that my descriptions and theorizing will cover over the script—let alone the performance event, "losing" once again the lives and living they invoke.

In "The Storyteller," Benjamin tells us that the story with the least explanation is often the most powerful and persistent because it allows later readers to find relevance through their own acts of interpretation. Recalling an account from the ancient historian Herodotus, Benjamin writes: "it resembles the seeds of grain which have lain for centuries in the chambers of the pyramids shut up air-tight and have retained their germinative power to this day" (Benjamin, 90). Unlike a book or a seed, a performance cannot be cloistered, stored safely away from the ravages of history. It is history—ideally not in the image of an angel propelled by heaping catastrophe backwards into "progress," but something smaller, more mundane, something more akin to the beautiful and difficult work entailed in making a life that becomes a story. Even so, I want to protect the performance I recount here from interpretive eclipse by its creator. My hope is that this introduction and the script that follows still hold the germinative power of live performance and will lead to your own fruitful understanding of this text's brief history, even insofar as that history contains an unpredictable future.

"Tic(k)"

© Gretchen A. Case, 2000

Stage is set with small wooden step-ladder downstage center and a wooden chair upstage directly behind it. The ladder and chair are connected by Chinese jump-rope, which is

looped around the front two legs of the chair and all four legs of the ladder. Lighting is a general wash, with one special high above the ladder to light my face.
Enter in very low light from stage right, come to chair, then pace a circle clockwise, ending up at chair again. Lights begin a slow fade-in as I walk, singing, heels clicking in time.

(*Singing*) My grandfather's clock was too large for the shelf, so it stood ninety years on the floor. It was taller by half than the old man himself, though it weighed not a pennyweight more. It was bought on the morn of the day that he was born, and was always his treasure and pride. But it stopped short never to go again when the old man died.

Lights up to full. Jump into Chinese jumprope and do Regular, Snapsies, Clapsies, Walksies while chanting the song's refrain.

Ninety years without slumbering, tick tock, tick tock. His life seconds numbering, tick tock, tick tock. It stopped short never to go again when the old man died.

End on out. Climb up the ladder, stand on top.

My grandfather fell from a great height. At his funeral, I watched from up in the choir loft in the back of the church he and his brothers had built.

I wore pink and green and purple; my pantyhose were the only speck of black in my clothes. No one in the family wore black, in fact: for one thing, San Diego in July is awfully hot.

He was a lifelong Roman Catholic and a lifelong Knight of Columbus, and they sent him out in style, dozens of his fellow Knights in full regalia. At the beginning of the service, a double line of men in red capes and wide black hats marched solemnly down the aisle. Their swords and capes swung with their cadence, and the church itself seemed to sway with their heaviness.

My grandfather's body waited at the front, already returned to its ashes.

We sang, the singing members of his family, from up above, we sang over the swish of the red capes and the clank of the swords and the click of the heels. And the readings were read, and the priest spoke at length, and the songs began and they ended. And the sorrow built and built until I heard a slowly building shriek and I looked around to see who it was.

And then I remembered: we were in the Church of the Immaculata at the University of San Diego, one of my grandfather's earliest construction projects. He and his brothers had sited the church on a hill above the athletic fields. There was a cheerleading camp on campus—we had seen their buses when we drove in. The shrieking was hundreds of hopeful high school students! The words to their cheers were suddenly clear in the air, louder than we could ever hope to sing.

"Ohhhh!" I heard my mother gasp, standing beside me. "Oh!" I turned, expecting to see anger on her face mirroring my own. "Oh," she said again, and smiled. "He loved young people. He would love to hear their voices here."

Climb off the back of the ladder, go to the chair, move chair to 2 o'clock.

(*Singing*) In watching its pendulum swing to and fro,
Many hours he had spent when a boy

And through childhood and manhood, the clock seemed to know
And to share both his grief and his joy

Chinese jumprope was an obsession at my elementary school. With the circular, elastic jumprope around the ankles of two girls, we would leap in and out, performing endless variations. The basic pattern was simple: "In-Out-Side-Side-On-In-Out."

Do Runsies quickly, then come downstage toward audience.

Once you mastered (*counting off on fingers, tapping foot*) Regular, Snapsies, Clapsies, Walksies, Runsies, Sideways, Backwards, Turnsies, and Blindsies, you moved up the body from the ankles to Calvesies, Kneesies, Thighsies, Hipsies, Waistsies, Chesties, Shoulders, and Necksies. Yep, Necksies. We had elastic ropes and elastic bodies.

My childhood was full of rhythms like this that have stayed with me. I can't look down at my body now without taking a mental inventory: Kneesies, Thighsies, Hipsies. Maybe that's why I was so attracted to history—I love patterns.

Move chair to 4 o'clock.

(*Singing*): For it struck 24 when he entered at the door
With a blooming and beautiful bride,
But it stopped, short, never to go again
When the old man died

Do Sideways.

So now I'm a grownup, and my job is to interview people. I'm very, very, very lucky. Several times a year I get to sit in a room with my tape recorder and a notepad and talk to geniuses about their life's work. Sometimes they tell me what I already know. Other times, they tell me things they never included in their memos, or bills to Congress, or scientific journal articles. Those are the very best days.

I met him at his office high up in New York City, at a prestigious address in a mahogany paneled room overlooking St. Patrick Cathedral. His business associate had warned me that time had not been kind to this great man's mind; things were not as clear as they used to be. So I interviewed him over lunch, to put him more at ease. Lunch. Oh, how they pampered me— I felt like a royal guest. Five courses served by a uniformed waiter in a private dining room. I was so nervous I flipped my fork—full of food, of course—off my plate and into my briefcase. The waiter rescued the fork before I even had a chance to pretend it didn't happen. Several weeks later, when I got the tape and transcript back, there was no amount of editing I could do to make that conversation into a historical document. What he knew would stay with him. So why do I feel like I took so much with me?

I met him at his home, tucked into the crook of two tree-lined streets in a very nice neighborhood in Washington, D.C. I'd been caught in a snowstorm the day before, so he had very kindly rescheduled. Still, I arrived that morning feeling guilty and disheveled. I had already been told that he was one of the great scientific minds of our time, so I had done my homework. Good thing, because he quizzed me. I suppose I passed his test, because he went on to tell me about his work in great detail. I got it all on tape, took notes on all of it. I could look it up for you, if you want to know what we talked about. But do you know what I remember? He told me the secret of taking blood from a crocodile. He's one of the few people in the world who knew this trick. And now me. He gave it to me. And I'm not telling.

I met him in a high rise retirement community in a wealthy suburb. Everything was beautiful and well-planned, from the lobby to the view out of his apartment window. But I could tell his life had really ended when his wife had left him for a nursing home. The only decoration in the apartment was a painting of their beloved summer home in Maine. He met me at the door with copious notes handwritten on a yellow legal pad and gave me an organized, chronological account of his work. He didn't give me the notes. I wanted those notes. I wanted something of his to keep, something in his handwriting. A few months later, I received a package in the mail. In it was a note from him, saying how much he had enjoyed our talk, and a book. It was his autobiography, self-published, distributed only to his family and close friends.

Move chair to 6 o'clock.

(*Singing*) My grandfather said that of those he could hire
Not a servant so faithful he'd found
For it kept perfect time and it had one desire
At the close of each day to be wound

Do Backwards.

How do you know if you're—a historian? Does someone notice and tell you? Is it the way that you walk? I have it engraved on a business card, does that make it so?

Pull business card out of dress and offer it to audience.

Can you tell someone is a historian just by talking to her? I don't know . . .

Move chair to 8 o'clock.

(*Singing*) And it kept to its place, not a frown upon its face
And its hands never hung by its side
But it stopped, short, never to go again
When the old man died

Do Turnsies. Spin around dizzy and sit down.

They're gone.

Gesture to 3 o'clock.

It took me a long time to write the condolence letters. I wrote them all at once, late one night when I couldn't bear to have it on me anymore. I couldn't decide—handwrite or type? Personal stationery or business stationery? Polite sympathy or heartfelt sorrow?

This pain doesn't seem like it should be mine. They weren't my family, my friends, my loves. I got the first message a year ago January. I heard about it by email, which I received while up at school. I burst into sobs, the kind where you can't catch your breath long enough to explain what's going on. Even when I did, it sounded kind of pathetic. To say that "someone I interviewed died"—what does that mean? So people patted me on the shoulder and said they were sorry, walked me out of the building as I left to go home.

I got two more emails this past fall, within a few days of each other. I had just sent out letters to update them on the oral history project. I wonder who opened those letters.

I knew them each for a few hours, a few phone calls, a few letters. But they're still with me, on tapes, each in a little box, tucked in a drawer. Saved.

I feel like a reliquary. Like I have their bones inside me. It's not their spirits, or their memories, or even their voices. It's something hard, solid. Something I can feel. Something at my center.

Walking upstage with back to audience, drag chair to 10 o'clock.

(*Singing*) It rang an alarm in the still of the night,
An alarm that for years had been dumb
And we knew that his spirit was pluming for flight
That his hour of departure had come

Do Blindsies.

Did I get it? You lose your turn if you miss.

Step up on chair and put arms out.

There was always a statue in my grandfather's gardens, either St. Francis or the Virgin Mary, arms outstretched to the flowers around them. Little shrines. He always seemed to live in a house on the edge of a small canyon, which he would fill with all the gorgeous plants that grow in Southern California.

As kids coming from back East to visit him, we were dazzled. Fruit on trees? Was that possible? Goldfish ponds surrounded by hibiscus? Were we in paradise? We chased his many cats and kittens up and down the hills and marveled at the land where my mother and her brothers and sisters had grown up. When the cats got on my grandfather's nerves, he would tell them, "Go poona poona!" which was some half-German slang that my mother also used on us when she wanted us to leave her alone.

I live in this strange land now. I call it home.

Jump off chair.

I knew my grandfather for 21 years. In the end, that doesn't seem like much time. He came to visit just after I graduated from college. He asked me what I would like for graduation, and I told him I wanted a big, beautiful book called "North Carolina Architecture." He was so pleased. Construction and architecture had been his life. He had always built things. The evening he bought the book, he and my mother sat at the kitchen table, going through it page by page, her arm around her Daddy's shoulders. I was busy doing something else.

The next day, I left to go to a high school reunion in another part of the state. I could have stayed and visited longer. They went to the Transportation Museum that day, looking at history. I went to my old high school that day.

He died a few days after returning to California. Within a week of his death, a package arrived at my parents' house for me. In it were a book on architecture and a copy of Architectural Digest. There was no note, but the address label was in his handwriting, the post-mark was the day of his death.

I had been busy with something else.

Move chair back to 12 o'clock.

(*Singing*) Still the clock kept the time
With a soft and muffled chime
As we silently stood by his side
But it stopped, short, never to go again
When the old man died

Climb back on ladder.

My grandfather fell from a great height. We will never know whether he died because he fell or he fell because he died. He was up on the ladder in his orchard, working on those gorgeous fruit trees. He was just 2 months away from 90 years old when his friend found him, lying at the foot of the ladder.

Jump off ladder, come down center.

Gesture left and right throughout this next section. Like a pendulum.

Hours (*left*), years (*right*), they are all with me, in me, around me. In-out-side-side-on-in-out. Sometimes the rhythm and the weight of our histories threatens to crush me. Other times that's all that holds me up.

Back up to the ladder, lean against it.

I'll tell you a story. I read about it in The Chronicle, so you know it's true. (*Smile*) There's this clock in North Beach, in San Francisco, built into the façade of a building that houses a clock shop. The man who owned this clock shop loved that clock more than anything. It was his treasure. The day he died, in 1959, the clock stopped working. His right-hand man, who took over the shop, worked on that clock for 10 days, but nothing happened. On the tenth day, he told the clock it just had to start working—he didn't know what else to do. He gave the pendulum a final swing and the clock started again. This clock became his pride. Last October, a truck accidentally backed into the clock, shattering it. Two days later, the clock's new owner passed away.

(*Singing*) It stopped. Short. Never to go again when the old man died. Ninety years without slumbering, tick tock, tick tock, his life seconds numbering, tick tock, tick tock, it stopped (*stop singing abruptly*)

> *Exit by walking counter-clockwise around the circle, singing softly, as lights do a slow fade-out. Then walk off SR, shoes clicking. Lights go to black before I reach the edge of the stage.*

Notes

1. Paul Ricouer, *Time and Narrative*, trans. Kathleen Blarney and David Pellauer, 3 vols. (Chicago: University of Chicago Press, 1990), p. 3.
2. Theodore Roethke, *The Collected Poems of Theodore Roethke* (New York: Anchor Books, 1975), p. 98.
3. Walter Benjamin, *Illuminations: Essays and Reflections*, ed. Hannah Arendt, trans. Harry Vohn (New York: Schocken Books, 1968), pp. 257–258.

EIGHT

"My Desire is for the Poor to Speak Well of Me"

D. Soyini Madison

Soyini Madison has written a montage-essay that is a performance in its own right. Anticipating the star-filled night on which her students would finally present their collaborative performance, Is it a Human Being or a Girl?, *the essay constellates disparate parts of Madison's life in Ghana as a Fulbright scholar: her experience teaching literature through performance at the University of Ghana at Legon; the students' ready sense of the relevance of that literature to the problems of poverty, sustainability, and "free trade" in Ghana; the stories they offer about the effects of global banking and investment on domestic economies; Madison's own turn toward field research into the hotly contested "Trokosi" tradition of sacrificing young girls to shrine priests; and finally:* Is it a Human Being or a Girl?, *the performance she developed with her students that brought all of these aspects together in a critical investigation of the place of the Trokosi ritual in a human rights agenda.*

This chapter consists of two, complementary parts—an interview and essay. The interview took place between Della Pollock ("DP") and scholar and director Soyini Madison ("SM"), in her home in Durham, North Carolina on May 14, 2002. It is included here as a preface to the essay in order to establish some of the logistical, ethical, political, and aesthetic contexts that informed the production at the heart of that essay.

Interview with D. Soyini Madison

DP: You spent almost two years in Ghana, teaching literature in and through performance. While there, you began researching the controversial practice of *Trokosi*: the ritual sacrifice of young girls to shrines usually in reparation for a sexual crime committed by a male member of the girl's family. This culminated in a performance that joined your fieldwork and teaching, *Is It a Human Being or a Girl?* But why Ghana in the first place? I know you got the Fulbright, but why Ghana?

SM: Ghana was the first African country to win its independence, and it holds the dynamic legacy of Kwame Nkrumah. I don't know if it carried through in the stories my father told me about what it meant to be an African person who was transported to America making me an African American person, but Ghana was always the specific site that I thought of when I thought of Africa and when I thought of my own history.

DP: And you were teaching American or African literature?

SM: With the Fulbright you can either teach or do research, or you can choose to do both. I chose to do both. I couldn't imagine doing research without teaching in Ghana or teaching without doing research. They're always conjoined for me. It was just a no-brainer that I would do both. I taught African American literature, literary theory, and a course on literature of the black diaspora. In my research and teaching, I was particularly concerned with contemporary Ghanaian novelists and their intersections with oral traditions.

DP: And for people that would have no idea of what that classroom would consist, what was it that you were actually doing?

SM: We would start off by talking about what the literature meant, but then we would talk about ideas. Ama Ata Aidoo's novel *Sister Killjoy*, for instance, is about a Ghanaian woman who goes to London, and she's very surprised by the literal bodies of Europeans. What she describes was a big deal for many of my students who can't get visas to go abroad.

Okay? So discussion started around issues of mobility. And what it means when your mobility is restricted and then you finally move, and you discover yourself in a world where people don't look like the human beings that have always been around you. So, the discussions always circled beyond the literature to its implications, which often related to the day-to-day economic and material constraints the students face in their lives. In the example of the novel *Sister Killjoy*, after discussions around meaning and implications inherent in the text, we did a lot of improvisational work on mobility and foreignness and made various stage pictures. We sculpted our bodies to create specific images—making these ideas into something three-dimensional and embodied. We would then go back to the literature and enact selected passages.

DP: And what did it mean for your role as the teacher, even insofar as you were talking about issues of foreignness and mobility? I mean, you were "foreign"—and yet mobile enough to come there and, in effect, teach the students there about some of the literatures from their own traditions.

SM: That was the most stunning experience, because I was always aware of myself as a teacher in front of the classroom and having a certain amount of authority as an American. I could never quite let go of my own sense of privilege. Because it was such a striking difference to be in a space where most of the people there didn't have the kind of freedom of movement that my citizenship allows, yet, ironically, a space where almost all of my students spoke four different languages. This freedom of movement means something altogether different to me now than it *ever* meant before. Too many of my Ghanaian students will never be granted visas to travel with the freedom one can experience with an U.S. passport.

DP: And what are the particular constraints on that?

SM: Well, there are concerns around foreigners, particular foreigners, with certain kinds of bodies and living in certain kinds of developing countries coming into this country or Europe and not going back home.

DP: Immigration anxiety.

SM: Yeah. Immigration anxiety. But, the other level of foreignness, for me, was experiencing poverty in the global South. Most of my students were the first generation to attend college. They knew the stakes were high for them to be there. And this combination of constrained mobility and dire poverty makes you very much aware that the world is uneven. I have never lived this reality before Ghana. Although I *knew* the politics and the unevenness of the world, to *live* it on a daily basis is such a profound awakening. The discrepancy between my country and their country in terms of political and economic power is something my students in Ghana live and know. And as a result, when I come into the classroom, I represent not an African American person but an American person. I am *abruni*, I am a foreigner; I am white. They know I'm *black* American, but I live in a white "advanced" country. This fact often eclipsed my blackness. I couldn't rationalize or theorize this "foreign-ness" away. It was a point of deep reflection for me, but it also motivated me to work harder at wanting my students to . . . how can I say it? . . . wanting my students to enjoy every minute in the classroom.

DP: In trying to ensure students some pleasure there . . . one of the great gifts was performance. Can you just talk a little bit about what you hoped for, for them, in the process of engaging them in performance?

SM: I wanted them to relate. I wanted to give them something they would really remember. I wanted them to remember the classroom as a community. I wanted them to remember each other. I wanted them to remember what it was like to talk about some of the most amazing and profound questions that literature provides. In Ghana, I was reminded again of the power and beauty of literature. And how literature can help us understand in such beautiful, beautiful, and sometimes sad and tragic ways, who we are and *why* we are. And I wanted them to remember how we worked through talking about all this in our class. Not just talking about those ideas, but taking them into our bodies; placing ourselves in space and in motion, and very deliberately contemplating the kind of choices we make in crafting performances—these stage pictures and these sounds and these moving images. Even if the performance is five minutes, in every second within those five minutes we ask: What are we doing? How are we capturing these wonderful, important, formative moments the literature provides? How are we living the language that makes the text's meanings more beautiful, that makes it even more than what it is? Yes, to conjoin literature with bodies in order to make something that's ultimately communicative . . . that possibility is what I was really reaching for with my students and wanted them to remember.

DP: And it was through that process that you became involved in the issues of *Trokosi* . . .

SM: Actually, I didn't think about the issue of *Trokosi* until I was reading a newspaper, and I read about this debate between Ghanaians over tradition and religion. On one side, the debaters were set on honoring, preserving, and sustaining tradition or, in this case, the *Trokosi* practice; and, on the other side, the debaters argued for change, development, and human rights. Reading about this controversy just swept me away, because it was a debate about dignity, and geography, and history, and the tensions between morality and modernity. But at another level, it was a debate about a fundamental reassessment . . . a reflection on all that you know— all that you were taught and understand yourself to be—that now may have to undergo radical change. That was profound to me. It shook me—it shook me. So, I wanted to understand the nature of that debate in the most soulful kind of way.

DP: You move from bringing performance to the study of literature in the classroom to involving those students in the performance of your fieldwork in this broader and deeply connected debate that is appearing in the vernacular press. How did that happen?

SM: Performing in the classroom is more of a turning inward. Of looking at ourselves in a way that we otherwise might not be able to do so pointedly, or poignantly. But performance also involves seeing ourselves and showing ourselves to ourselves in a way that allows you to understand something new about who you are in *relation* to your outer environment. It is a doubling. So that performance is very much a kind of meta-narrative—performing performances of our inner and outer lives.

And then, for the fieldwork performances on *Trokosi*, there is another kind of performance going on as a result of invoking the nonfiction of other people's stories and vulnerabilities. This dimension of performance is highly communicative, marked by an investment in an identifiable change.

DP: Can you talk, then, about what it means to craft the final performance that came out of that study, which was very much a staged work.

SM: I wanted to make a performance that I hoped would get at what's ultimately earth-shattering about this debate . . . what ultimately is its essence, if you will.

I wanted to get to the point where, if we don't get this element of it, we're not going to get it at all. So I began asking: what are the nuggets, the golden pieces, that one must discern amongst all of this talk and all this flux and anger? I started listening to my field tapes again, hearing the voices again, remembering what surrounded them, and then began to render them for the stage: scripting field notes for performance, and then, finally, putting all the layers of word, context, and meaning into symbolic motion as a starting point for beauty. You know, in Yoruba, beauty is truth. It is what *feels* true in a particular moment, at a particular time. Truth is not foundational or immutable, nor is it merely relative; it is deeply felt.

So I hope we reached that. I think we did. I think we did . . . The audience became engaged with the act and the aesthetic and the form and the politics of this performance. There was something about things moving and being seen and being heard in the alchemy of performance that seemed to compel or to create the potential in audience members to imagine with us. I'm not sure what you call that thing but beauty. There is this big, big present moment . . . and we live in it fully.

The debate about *Trokosi* was the beginning point, but it was not the end point. The nugget, the "truth," was truly about *poverty*. I *saw* it. I was *there* up close and personal to inexplicable poverty. And I saw that the level of human rights abuse was in direct correlation to the level of poverty. I witnessed villages that had little access to water. No access to electricity. Hardly any access to books . . . the women would travel very, very far to fetch water. The whole notion of possibility and potential on which performance relies means that you're open to certain questions and challenges beyond where you are at this point. The ground on which you stand is but a stepping off to somewhere beyond where you are. But that requires access to certain things and experiences. If it's not water, if it's not electricity, if it's not books, then it has to be new stories, at least new stories. But where do these new stories come from under duress of the most fundamental requirements of existence? So, in those villages where food, water, and books were accessible and where children were going to school, new stories were being imagined and created and, and even critically contested—in those villages, *Trokosi* was practiced very differently. The extreme unevenness of the global economy is the underlying evil of the *Trokosi* practice . . . that some people are so extremely rich and others are so extremely poor, on such a vast scale of difference, is the greatest evil of all.

And I didn't know what to do about that other than to make the performance. That was the only thing that I knew to do about it.

DP: As a space for new stories . . .

SM: Absolutely. Absolutely, a space for new stories. A space for new stories that would turn stories into action and turn action into change . . . Then we could go from the beauty of narrative to the very fundamental and practical notion of public policy. That was my concern.

DP: And do you feel you achieved that?

SM: I think so. I have to say that with some humility. But, I think so. Because if I didn't feel that I did, I wouldn't be finished with it. I wouldn't have staged it in Ghana and I wouldn't have tried to stage it here in North Carolina . . . The thing about this notion of undeniable truth, that I really really believe in, is that it has to be understood not as a form of tyranny; it's not that. It doesn't mean that it excludes something else. It means that what it is, amongst other truths, is undeniably what it is.

Della, when you sit with somebody and they entrust you with what's important to them, they trust that you're not going to make a fool of them. You have an obligation; I think it's a sacred one. It is also this obligation that keeps you from saying the performance is ready and it's over, when it really is not.

DP: What else do you take to be the successes of this work? What worked well?

SM: (*laughing*) That I did it. That it happened. That it really happened. You know, that there were people who had stories to tell, that they just told me, and now hundreds of people have heard their stories. And that students who spent some time with me—I'm speaking specifically about Ghana—students who spent some time with me have a memory of that performance. And their families and their friends have a memory of doing that performance that was for a good purpose and that in some corners made people talk about *Trokosi* differently. The everlastingness of all this is a success.

And that you have this vision, based on a certain level of training, and that you must be generous and caring and delicate about the way you train and communicate that vision to your performers. But, I think that, in addition to everything else, it is the knowledge that you start with an audiotape, and then you make a performance, and there are all kinds of philosophical, aesthetic, political, and important moral reasons that you do this, but you must also have the skills! You must have the heart, but it is not only the heart. You must know what you're doing technically. Can I make a two and a half hour performance based on what I think I'm skilled and trained to do? So, I strive to make these audiotapes more beautiful, because I'm offering their contents to a group of people who will come to see the show for not just my interpretations of them but also my hope for them, for their possibilities. That is always the daunting task for me.

DP: Given how many people working with audiotapes are becoming keen to the power and importance of performance, but who may not have your training and experience or sense of craft, performance may seem daunting. It is difficult. And maybe it should be, in some ways. That difficulty is connected to the sense of beauty and possibility you talk about. But it can't be so difficult that people can't do it.

SM: Because performance isn't one thing. Performance can mean that you do a transcription of your tapes where you, or your student, or your performers sit in chairs before a group of people and read with profound empathy what those words mean. When well done, this can be as moving, and as significant, and as complex as all the props and lights and costumes and movement . . . Sometimes it's a matter of deciding in the performance process just how much layering of points of view and contextual aspects you feel comfortable imparting. But, performance can take on so many shapes and forms and representations. It's a communicative act in which you have people basically saying: I want to connect my voice and body to this story that is not mine, or yet that could be, in this very distinct moment in time and space. And, I want to make this communicative connection before and with others because I think what I have to say is just that important. And to read it silently does not do it justice, in the biggest sense. It has to be enlivened through sound, imagery, emotion, and a kind heart.

The Classroom: First Encounters

The man watched the bus go all the way up the road and then turn and disappear around the town boundary curve. Behind it, the green paint was brightened with an inscription carefully lettered to form an oval shape:

> The Beautiful Ones
> Are Not Yet Born

In the center of the oval was a single flower, solitary, unexplainable, and very beautiful.

As he got up to go back into the town he had left in the night, the man was unable to shake off the imprint of the painted words. In his mind he could see them flowing up, down and round again. After a while the image itself of the flower in the middle disappeared, to be replaced by a single, melodious note.

Ayi Kwi Armah, *The Beautiful Ones Are Not Yet Born*

A poem isn't finished unless the reader reads it aloud . . . language is not only physical, it's a living thing, a living organism . . . it's informed by the physical environment, by how we breathe . . . Metaphors are alive. When they come into being, they are informed by the politics and the sociology and economy of now . . . language—the written word and the spoken word, but especially the spoken word—is so evocative that there's a constant recreation going on. It's ritualistic. The sounds themselves evoke feelings; that's the way you are touched.

Etheridge Knight, *On the Oral Nature of Poetry*

Performance opens the secrets of a literary text. As the reader opens a book, the performer opens its secrets. The details—sometimes small and obscure, ambiguous or polemical—are brought into *form*. They are opened up for broader questions and deeper reckonings through the guiding frame of performance. The performer, beyond bringing movement and sound to words and flesh to feeling, opens literature to the possibility of the hidden. And, within this possibility lies the potential for political *investment*. This political investment is of a very particular kind. It is a politics of the *near*. It is intimate and close because it circles from the boundaries of the text into our inner world. It moreover brings into focus the regulating factors governing our day-to-day lives and our personal destinies. It puts our lives and destinies into question. Performance opens the secrets of literature because it invites embodied comparisons between undercurrents that constitute operations of power in the literary imagination and undercurrents that constitute operations of power in our lived experience. The read but unnamed and the lived but unnamed are present in the text and in life, but are often only tenuously or partially realized. Performance promises engagement with what is otherwise hidden, oblique, or secret. This is a political enterprise. It involves unearthing the subtext in literature and the unearthing of subtext in experience. But the archeology of unearthing is never neat. Felt-sensing and embodiment of the imagined world offered by a literary text invite an impassioned and critical *resurfacing* of appearances in our lived world. This resurfacing invites us to imagine differently and deeply. We are invited (even implored) in turn to pursue extended political insight and to entertain a sense of possibility for our life, home, neighborhood, nation, and world: a vision of how different it could look, how different it could be. It is a promise of unveiling.

"There you go again, Sissie, you are so serious."

But how can I help being serious? Eh, My Love, what positive is there to be, when I cannot give voice to my soul and still have her heard? Since so far, I have only been able to use a language that enslaved me, and therefore, the messengers of my mind always come shackled?

Ama Ata Aidoo, *Our Sister Killjoy*

What is "(un)seen" in our experiences before we dis/un-covered it through living in a literary world, performance makes manifest. Other (re)visions are now played out on the very surface of our skin, voice, and gesture. The body is charged with recognition, will, and action through allegorical (per)*form*(ance).

The students in Ghana read and entered literature through performance, and they taught me a poignant lesson about the political investment of performed literature. The political intimacy and depth of their encounters with the assigned literature emerged in myriad personal narratives and critical oral histories that accompanied their short performances for class.

It was Thursday, March 18, 1999. As I walked to the University of Ghana at Legon, the rain was pouring down providing a refreshing respite from the usual blazing dry heat. When I arrived, the students in my course on "Literature and Performance of the Black Diaspora" were busy talking among themselves in a restrained panic about the exam I had scheduled for Tuesday. The students at Legon take learning with the seriousness of religion. They know the world too well to be flippant. The cool breeze from the rain circulated through the open windows of the classroom. The students quieted down and settled in their seats. My entrance signaled to them that I was the lecturer, the professor, but most important, the elder. They would give me the respect granted by my age, my status, and, above all, by their tradition. They took out their study sheets for the upcoming exam. I wrote on the board "hidden abode." I turned to the rows of intense faces staring at me. I thought: I am in the "Third World" where reading a novel is often a luxury and a blessing for many, and because it is, they will tell me about "hidden abode" on this day and remember it.

I turned to them and said: "In a work of literature, we want to go beyond 'appearances,' beyond what is clearly visible. We want to locate those hidden forces beneath the surface—beneath what's immediately apparent—to those forces that cause the characters to do what they do, be who they are, desire what they desire. Let's take Karl Marx out of his chair and perform him today, like you performed Ayi Kwei Armah's novel, *The Beautiful Ones Are Not Yet Born*, last week. What did your performances reveal about what was operating below the surface of the novel? Remember, the hidden abode is powerful because it is both motivation and disguise."

Kwame raised his hand and said, "Karl Marx and Ayi Kwei Armah are both talking about remote control!"

Everyone laughed. We laughed because we knew exactly what he meant.

I feigned innocence, and, of course, the students knew it: "What do you mean Kwame?"

We proceeded with workshop performances that were as much about excavation as they were about embodiment. The undercurrents that rose through the temperature of their performing bodies penetrated appearances, evoking deeper and more abiding possibilities. Possibilities that performance in the flesh made intimate and life experience made near. I did not know that on that day the students would take another step, from the performance of literature to memorable and provocative performances of personal, oral narratives. Through the performance process, literature ironically sparked orality: other stories—personal stories, social histories. Stories about the politics regulating the students' daily lives. About the corruption, greed, and local suffering in Ghana under the ominous and determining power of global forces and economic injustice. Inspired by the power and alchemy of performance and literature, they narrated their excavations of what was now not so "hidden" anymore. This poetic trajectory from literature to orality was a call and response between life and art and art and life—calling and responding, living and creating—re-marking the ground where they stood.

* * *

What follows are two illustrations of in-class performances based on students' exploration of the "hidden abode" in Armah's *The Beautiful Ones Are Not Yet Born*. These take the form of symbolic acts, stage pictures and "image theatre" reflecting passages from the novel (transcribed in italics below) and followed by the students' framing, reflexive narratives (transcribed in ethnopoetic dialogue):

Workshop Performance 1

(A circle of performers are surrounding an old man and young girl. The old man is trying to give the young girl a sip of water but his hand is shaking as the girl strains to drink from the cup. As this action continues, the circle of performers reach for imaginary strings from their very large pockets. They break the circle and wrap the strings around the girl and the old man. The performers now return to the circle holding the ends of their strings while speaking passages from the novel in an ironic tone. The passages all represent moments of bribery and corruption. The performers speak in repetitive and cacophonous voices. The old man continues with great effort to give the young girl water but he can hardly balance himself and the frantic pull of all the strings prevent the young girl from moving her mouth. Each pull on the strings force the old man and girl into distorted motions, which the student-actors exaggerate. They eventually lose their balance, only to help each other up again. In the final beat of the performance, the old man and girl hold on to each other very tightly. They are now turning in circles. They repeat passages by the protagonist of the novel who refuses to succumb to the corruption and greed around him and who envisions a different future. The old man and the girl spin until the invisible string breaks and the circle of performers collapse.

Kwame and Kofi, students who had participated in the performance, took the lead in discussion, offering their own critical narratives.)

KWAME: Right now in Ghana, and all over Africa,

what you see on the surface is poor people,

people who are suffering and dying—tribal wars and corruption.

But what you don't see is the connection between the U.S. and Europe and the conditions here.

It is hidden, because American and Europe control Africa by remote.

The colonial masters and America are running Ghana by remote control.

These advanced countries

dump their products and sell them at a lower price than our

local farmers can charge in our own local markets, so the farmers suffer.

The farmer will make a day journey from the village to the market praying that he will sell his goods that day.

He sells nothing that day because poor people can only afford the imports from rich countries.

If he lowers his prices he will lose money.

The farmer and his family suffer. This is a way of life here.

This is all some of us know.

It is almost accepted as . . . well . . . as the way things are.

But it shouldn't be like that. It makes me very angry.

We are Africans, Ghanaians, but we are not stupid people.

KOFI: I am from Burkino Faso and my grandfather was a rice farmer . . .

A hungry country will export its food grains, because that's all it really has to export.

The country sells the grains as cheap as possible to as many other countries as possible to pay for the loan debts.

But the world prices have fallen,

so the prices drop even lower leaving

the country with less profit than before,

and with food grains the local people cannot afford to buy.

So the local people starve while rich countries get fat off our grain

and pay nothing for it.

As a little boy in the village,

I watched my grandfather work on his land everyday in the hot sun.

He was old and should have been resting, enjoying his grandchildren.

But he would work so hard and then go to market always hoping

he could sell more rice this time.

My grandfather is gone now. But nothing has changed. I am at the University.

We are here to make a change.

This is what we wanted our performance to tell you.

Workshop Performance 2

(Three performers are trying to reach a human wall. They are running in slow motion. Other performers enter the scene one by one to join them. But none is able to go forward; they are running in place, going nowhere. They cannot move because each performer is pulling the other back . The human wall backs up as the runners work harder and harder in their efforts to reach it. Behind the wall are performers who appear to be picking something. Each is miming a picking motion in multiple directions. After picking their objects they place them in the "cracks" in the wall, that is: in the spaces between the actors who form the human wall. Eventually, the wall can no longer hold all of the objects placed upon it. One of the "pickers" bumps into the wall while trying to place one more object on it. The wall begins to tremble. The runners freeze while the pickers continue to work, speaking relevant passages from the novel.

The performance prompted several of the students to make deeply felt, direct political commentary. Akosua was one.)

AKOSUA: Ghanaian currency is worth almost nothing anymore. It is losing value day by day.

What are people going to do? Eh, too much suffering in this country.

Speculation should be stopped, eh?

These rich people trade money by the minute and make profits

as our money loses its value. How does this happen?

The world prices fall because poor countries are all increasing their exports

at the same time in order to pay for their loans,

so there is an overabundance of goods.

The poor countries are also competing with each other
for the lowest prices to sell on the market.
They are competing for poverty.
Our goods have fallen in market prices
while manufactured goods processed by rich countries have risen.
We can hardly pay the tariffs of the rich countries and
we cannot charge tariffs in our poor country—tariffs the rich countries could easily pay
if trade was fair.
In our performance, the wall was the global market, we were running toward the wall,
 pushing each other back, just as African countries are competing with each other
 and losing the way to economic independence.
Dr. Madison, we don't make the rules.

The Field

Although as researchers, we may not be interested in global capitalism, we can be
sure that global capitalism is interested in us . . . In this context we envision important new developments of Marxist ethnographic practices that both complement
and extend many of the exciting new approaches that we are witnessing within the
precincts of postmodern, and post-colonial ethnography.

> Joe L. Kincheloe and Peter Mclaren,
> *Rethinking Critical Theory and Qualitative Research*

The human face is the epiphany of the nakedness of the Other, a visitation, a meeting, a saying which comes in the passivity of the face, not threatening, but obliging.
My world is ruptured, my contentment interrupted. I am already obligated. Here is
an appeal from which there is not escape, a responsibility, a state of being hostage. It
is looking into the face of the Other that reveals the call to a responsibility that is
before any beginning, decision or initiative on my part.

> Emanuel Levinas, *Ethics and Infinity*

I remember those first days in Ghana as I tried to note the details: the blazing heat;
the colors and smells of the market; the fumes from old cars and stand-still traffic; the
quick animated sounds of local languages; the young girls selling water to passing
cars; the Mobil and Shell stations alongside kiosks and worn down buildings; the
enormous baskets women balanced on their heads as they carried their babies on their
backs; the school children with their natural hair and brown uniforms. The details are
endless and the feeling I am coming to recognize is that of being both inside and outside an unaccustomed reality—inside the space of it, yet outside the animation and
complexities of its meanings. In those first days reality became intensely surreal,

larger than usual. Unfamiliar as it was, I felt I had to pay even closer attention to it and to enfold its nearness.

I was now here with Levinas' "Others," both inside and outside borders of geography and culture, in an unfamiliar yet shared space. Now I meet and witness strangers on their land. My initial feeling that there was something familiar residing in the unfamiliar is now face to face with the humbling certainty that there is much here that is strange, but that the real stranger in this land is me.

I am only one in a long procession of seekers wanting to know the worlds of Others. But as I join the paths of these seekers, I remember that their effects have been as variously harmful and useful as their intentions: to invade, liberate, colonize, discover, venture, misname, rename, civilize, save, and add to the chronicles of specialized knowledge—to develop a discourse on the Other for illumination and for publication. Recalling the history of colonial ethnography is a substantial reminder of my location and obligations, but what is most pressing, whether I like it or not, is how I *feel* here, now. I feel strange. I am now meeting the Other in myself. It is me who is the unknown and the unknowing. I am in a *position*. It is this position that I must consider, unless I am to succumb to gratuitous narcissism on the one hand or the pose of invisible omniscience on the other. Ethnographic positionality is always already embedded in layers of (un)knowing even as it is embedded in layers of power and privilege. Positionality is charged.

Because ethnographers are the unknown and the unknowing, all that we don't know and all that doesn't know us forms a chasm that becomes the allegorical grounds of our investigations. This is the paradox of being someone who is paid and culturally understood to be a knower, a professor, and a teacher nonetheless embedded in an environment of internal and external unknowing. However, the greater paradox of being in the unknown and being unknown is that you *do* know. Indeed, you know something. You have done your reading; you have experience in the field. It is because of what you do know—what you are trained to do and be and see—that you are in the midst of this unknowing in the first place. Accordingly, I felt myself performing a self-reflexive passage from the unknown to the known, and from there to the purposeful interpretation of what it means to be present in body, feeling, and thought in *both* the unknown and the knowing. From the beginning to the end, we are never exclusively in either domain but are always traveling across borders we carry within ourselves as Others.

When people do fieldwork they are refracted: passing from home to field, from one prismatic surface to another, practicing an immense doubling. *Experience is always conjunctural, located in the backwardness and forwardness of the historical present.* The ethnographer lives in dual time zones and dual temperatures. When you first arrive the doubling is acute. But, the double time of our double lives begins to fade— still with us, always already with us—but fading with the body's certainty that it can be only in one place at one time. The place in which it listens, and breathes, and lives is the place it holds the body *in* place and *in* attention. I am yielding my own doubleness, my own past, to memory and forgetting because the pulse of this new life, here, now—the sights, the sounds, the rhythms—are claiming me; because I am beginning to do what the Ghanaians do, but more importantly, I am learning to hear what they hear; and because this is becoming my life now and, at least for now, I truly want to be *here*. I came here to teach literature and have found that that very literature has carried me into the politics of the near which I hoped to ignite in my students. Through their performances, and their subsequent stories, questions, and commentary, I have become deeply, affectively invested in the intimacies of politics of this place.

I am in a village outside the capital city of Accra, wearing the garments of a researcher: sunglasses, shoes, a notebook, a tape recorder and a pen. I feel silly. The children circle around me; they want the pen. I feel silly and undeserving. Damn. I should have brought extra pens. Stupid. I look down at my hands; they are so dirty. My feet, my hair, my clothes are covered with the red dirt of Ghana. I am dirty and everything smells of poverty. I look at the children around me and I look over at the women pounding fufu. They have walked miles for water: buckets on their head and children on their backs, and they come back home and pound fufu. About 1.2 billion people worldwide do not have access to fresh water. And I am sitting here with some of them right now—mother and babies, red dirt under our feet, and I have a newfound reverence for rain and well water.

We look on dirty people in dirty places with disgust. Mary Douglas said, "holiness and impurity are at opposite poles" (38).

We are told, *cleanliness is next to godliness*. Dirt is demonized. Dirt offends against order. How many times have I heard renditions of *those dirty Africans* in my lifetime? I watched the sneers of disgust on the faces of those whose sense of purity and order are affronted by the sights and smells of what poverty and inaccessibility to water *caused*. They were disgusted not by the cause but by the human forms of its consequences.

The human body is indeed a wonder. In its beauty it is a miracle. The beautiful body is our divine experience of pain and pleasure. It is both a blessing and an object of desire. The Other bodies, the loathsome bodies—the dirty body, the disfigured body, the sick body, the body that smells of refuse, the body that oozes, excretes and cannot shelter its waste, the body whose matter is grotesquely "out of place"—are the bodies that wrenching poverty breeds in its abominable lack. Disgust encircles these bodies with visceral loathing and fear—fear of nearness and the threat of contamination; loathing for spoiled appearances and the failure of these bodies to keep themselves out of sight and out of mind. This encircling is Kristeva's abjection, the untouchable and unthinkable nearness between the outside of the Other's grotesque appearance to the inside of our vulnerable and ordered being. But the body lives in space and time. And it is the political arrangements of space and time that secure the visceral power of disgust.

For much of the global south, specifically Africa, dirt is a fact and a symbol. Blackness, dirt, and disgust are perennially linked. Some areas are filled with disgust because they seem to be filled with "blackness." Literally and figuratively: dirty people having dirty children with dirty faces wearing dirty clothes. We know that dirt is to be gotten rid of, but we tend to forget that dirt dwells where water is inaccessible. Nor do we remember that when sanitation systems are ineffectual or nonexistent, dirt braces disease. Dirt is a stigma *and* an effect for many of the world's poor. It is both imagined and real. Dirt resides where poverty annuls the time and resources to attend to it, and when global machinations neglect its relief. Dirt and political economy are insidious partners. Dirt is an effect of material and political conditions but, as a tactical deflection, is generally cast as a *moral flaw.*

And while there are poor people who are noble, there is no nobility in *being* poor—not when it is forced upon you, not like this. In this village, in Ghana, among the 2,800 million people who live on less than $2 a day and comprise 46 percent of the world's population are 2,800 million stories of epic injustice. *This* is both urgent and disgusting.

The heat is blazing . . . I look over at Patience sitting beside me. I ask her to take a photograph of the village women with whom we have been talking all day before we leave to go back to the city. Comfort is a human rights activist. She is Ewe, a tall striking woman with large eyes and high cheekbones. On this long drive back from the village to Accra, I am thinking about the children, the red dirt, disgust, and the fact that these women may never have piped water. Comfort asks my why I'm so quiet. I tell her I'm just thinking.

Comfort turns to me:

People from the outside, mostly tourists, get off the bus and walk about
    the village.
They stay together because they seem to be afraid of the people here
Like they will eat them or kidnap them or something
They act like they are afraid but they still seem sad for the people here
It is still all very strange to me
They get off the bus and they look like they have stepped into a different world.
And they have.
Most of them have never experienced people living like this.
People living in huts with no flowing water, no electricity
Nothing but the hot sun and each other and the land they're standing on.
I mean the foreigners act like they can hardly believe that people still live
Like this
Some of them act like they are afraid of the people here
Like if one of them touches them or breaths on them too close
It will hurt them/like they will die or something.
It is always the women in these villages who suffer the most.
They work all day and night trying to sell their tomatoes or garden eggs

Or melons or bananas . . .

Who buys them?

Can they sell enough to buy flowing water, or electricity, or a house to shelter them from the
heat?

Women. . . . Women. . . .

What is the future for these women?

Comfort looked at me without flinching for a response. I did not speak, not because
the question was too enormous, but because I felt so completely that to speak would
be unworthy. What I felt, and what I felt Comfort wanted was the kind of engaging
silence that only comes with the humbling quality of genuine listening. But what I
could have said, and perhaps what I wanted to say and did not was, "You are the
future for these women."

It was with these concerns in mind that I began to listen more closely to particular stories of injustice: stories of the *Trokosi*, of the girls sacrificed as brides to shrine
priests as a ritual means of repairing an actual, criminal flaw within a family structure,
usually a crime committed by a father, uncle or brother. I listened to the often contradictory stories the *Trokosi* brides told and to the intense debates swirling around
them. I began to interview human rights workers, traditionalists, journalists, artists,
intellectuals, and activists—people who were variously invested in human rights and
who had a stake in this debate. I interviewed over sixty people in all. In a circular turn
from literature to the students' life stories to my field research and back to the
classroom, I then involved students from the University of Ghana in the preparation
of a public performance based on those interviews and field study. I engaged the
students in many of the same kinds of workshops we used to connect the inner worlds
of literature with the outer worlds in which the students lived. Again, we worked
with symbolic representation, movement sequences, and body-images, this time
combined with verbatim interview narratives, news reports, and field notes to create
what would become the two and a half hour public performance, *Is It a Human Being
or a Girl?* funded by the American Embassy and the Fulbright Foundation and presented at the University of Ghana and The W. E. B. Dubois Outdoor Theatre. While
Comfort's words and my analysis led me toward a strong polemic, the performance
remained open—to the night air in which it was presented and to the global human
rights/local traditionalist controversies in which it was embedded. I was still learning.
And listening to the Trokosi women who took pride in their role and duty made it
especially difficult to make a judgment on their behalf. Instead, I made the dual-zone,
affectively charged ethnographer that I have discussed here, a central character in the
performance. Her queries, analytical process, constant upturnings, and de-tourings
were the connective tissue of a performance otherwise filled with the voices and
bodies of the Ghanaian student-performers telling the stories interviewees told me,
telling their own stories, and making a space for new stories that might break through
the cruel logics of "disgust" and at least clarify the grounds for questioning the

dereliction/sacrifice of young girls' bodies in the traditional ritual practice of *Trokosi.*

The Final Performance

From Fieldwork Journal, entry for June 25, 2000, reflections on the culminating performance of Is It a Human Being or a Girl?, *at the Outdoor Theatre at the home and final resting place of W. E. B. Dubois:*

On this Ghanaian night, I stand far in the back of the Outdoor Theatre at the home that once belonged to the American ex-patriot W. E. B. Dubois. I am looking out over the audience as they sit and watch the performance. I'm watching the performance too but as a director with that overwrought intensity and vulnerability that never seems to ease up for some of us. Our watching is always more than watching: it is obsessive. We are hostage to every sight, sound, and movement within the performance frame. Our hearts jump at the possibility of some wayward slip-up; natural breathing is suspended until the show is over and we can exhale, finally, in the greetings and chatter, the congratulations and small talk that comes after the End. So, I stand here now knowing this is the final scene and the End is soon approaching, knowing that this End means our last performance, forever gone, disappeared. I stand here now knowing that my life in Ghana will soon end, and I will leave this performance, this theatre, this country and go back to the U.S. And, now, suddenly I feel the weight of too many endings. I will hang on to this moment like time has no force. I wish I could put this moment in a box, wrapped in forever-and-ever, then pull it out, once in a while, when I really need to live inside it again—exactly as it is right now—when I'm back in the States, or next week, or when I'm 99. It is Sunday, June 25, 2000 at 10:13 P.M. and I am standing watching this audience of Ghanaians watching my show, our show, and I am going to pay attention to every detail of this moment because there is no such thing as a box wrapped in forever-and-ever. There is only memory. I will remember this moment in its complete, specific, detailed, and utter fullness; most of all I will remember how it feels—the breeze and the stars and the smells of this night, the feel of the ground under my feet, the sound of the drum. I will remember it in my skin. I stand here holding my breath in the presence of this performance. The stage is a dreamscape of blue, green, and red batik draped around dark skinned bodies moving with nervous resolve in a dark skinned country that nestles the beauty of its darkness in hope and contradictions. When Ghanaians speak, the quality of their voices, their pitch and intonation, are more foreign to me than their words. I never realized the magnitude of the human voice—the assorted sounds of words spoken—before I came to this country. When I leave Ghana I will miss the sounds of her voices. The stage is more alive because it is filled to bursting with this particular un/familiarity. The performers are speaking stories handed down to them. Stories I gave them. Stories that were given to me. A collection of stories, arguments, and sounds, rhythms, and resounding phrases that reflect histories of bodies of women and bodies of belief. It is said that ethnography is an art and a science, but I know it is more about presence. Presence in the living immediacy of stories being made and remade in the act of telling. I listened, I lived, I recorded. I felt. I did. And the doing is this performance right here and now.

* * *

Is It A Human Bring or A Girl?

Performed June 25, 2000

From Scene One

(Actors are scattered throughout the stage weaving in and out and between each other)

#1: Trokosi/Troxovi/Faishidi

#2: Troxovi—Troxovi

#3: Trokosi—Trokosi

#4: Faishidi

#5: Trokosi

#1: Toxovi

#2: Trokosi

#3: Troxovi

#4: Faishidi

#5: Trosi

#3: Troxovi

#2: Trokosi

#4: Trosi

(Performers remain in place as #1 and #2 come downstage and stand with their backs against each other.)

#2: Mama. Grandmother. Queens fit for kings.
   The only, among women, who can reprimand the Chief.
   The Faishidi attends the sacred stools.
   The Faishidi selects who should be ga, hanua, or hlofia:
   headmen, youth leaders and chiefs.

#3: Troxovi—A divinity which adopts children.
   A divinity of justice, morality, public security, education and social welfare.
   Afegame—Great House.

(Performers #1 and #2 now begin to take steps away from each other as they perform their lines.)

#2: Trosi—Tro/God Asi/wife—Wife of God.

#1: Tokosi—Tro/God—Kosi/Slave, Virgin, Wife

#2: Trokosi—Wife of God

#1: Trokosi—Slave of God!

#2: Trokosi—Wife of God!

#1: Trokosi—Slave of God!

#2: Trokosi—Wife! / #1:Trokosi—Slave! / #2: Trokosi—Wife! / #1: Trokosi—Slave!

#1: Slave/Wife (*Repeat*)

(Actors #1 and #2 are on opposite ends of the stage now speaking out to the audience as the other performers remain upstage in position looking on at the two downstage.)

#1: The Trokosi system demands that young girls be sent to a shrine by force

> As reparation
>
> As atonement
>
> For a crime committed by a member of their family
>
> Many of whom she does not even know
>
> She is sent to the shrine where she must serve the priest
>
> She must serve his every need
>
> She labours in the shrine
>
> She labours on the farm
>
> She must have sexual intercourse with the priest
>
> She is a virtual slave to the shrine and the priest in atonement for
>
> An offence committed by someone else!
>
> She must be sent to the shrine to satisfy God
>
> Or tragedy will befall her family, befall the community
>
> If a Trokosi dies she must be replaced by another young, virgin, girl from her family.
>
> Trokosi are in bondage
>
> The Trokosi have no freedom
>
> The Trokosi are denied an education
>
> The Trokosi are denied the fruits of their own hard labour
>
> They are denied the protection and dignity of their own bodies
>
> They are denied the freedom to choose their own destiny
>
> The Trokosi girl has committed no offence, no crime.

(Each performer from their position repeats "lies" turning in all directions with focus on each other, offstage, and to the audience. Performers do not move out of place. Throughout the performance the word "lies" is NOT spoken together but individually and chaotically.)

LIES/LIES/LIES (*Repeat*)

(#1 and #2 still at a distance; they remain in place and again speak their lines from opposite ends. #3, #5, and # 4 move upstage left facing each other and speak their lines looking out beyond each other's gaze.)

#2: The Trokosi system is a system of training
And education
Young women are sent to the shrines to learn valuable lessons of
Social, cultural, spiritual, and moral behavior
The young girls are honored and distinguished
For they are trained to be wives of the God
Their children are most ennobled and glorified
For they are children of the God
They are NOT sent to the shrine in Atonement
But sent for training to lead a righteous path because
Their families can no longer teach them and lead them
To serve as role models in the society.
These queens will lead us!
"If you educate a man, you educate an individual
if you educate a woman, you educate a whole nation"
There are break-away shrines—quack shrines
These shrines do NOT adhere to the proper training
These shrines do NOT honour and protect the girls
These shrines do no NOT practice Traditional African Religion
Genuine troxovi shrines are Afegame [great houses]
To train these girls as leaders—to be great women of
Moral and spritual character
The Trokosi are honored
The Trokosi are protected
The Trokosi are trained
The Trokosi are loved

(Performers begin moving in a weave-like pattern—in and out and between one another. They repeat "Lies" and speak their lines, again in multi-directions.)

LIES/LIES/LIES *(Repeat)*

#3: Christian Chauvinists!
#4: Human Rights Activist!
#5: Traditionalist!
#3: Offenders of human rights!
#4: Religion!
#5: Bondage!
#3: Training!
#4: Slavery!
#5: Training!
#3: Slavery!
#4: Religion!
#5: Bondage!

From Scene Two

(Performers form a small circle downstage center. Their palms are touching in various patterns to suggest symbolically a matrix of intricate connections. They will change positions periodically but they maintain the motif of the "matrix." Another performer, who has been in the background, hardly noticeable, comes forward to observe the web of human connections. She examines it carefully and thoughtfully. She sits on the platform and begins writing. She reads her fieldnotes aloud to herself.)
(Lights dim. Spot on Recorder.)

#3/Recorder: Truth is elusive.
    It is becoming too difficult to disentangle.
    I cannot find it.
    It is not neat and clear, not anymore.
    Not as I travel further, look deeper, and hear more.
    Am I looking in the wrong places?
    I am only stumbling past a million half-truths.
    Yet, all of them are partial and powerful.
    I've met so many people here who are telling their side of the truth:
    the women and girls known as Trokosi *do* live in servitude.
    Yes, I've seen them; I've listened to their stories.
    I've been to those places . . . servitude, it is true.
    But there is another truth.
    There are women who are called Trokosi who live honorably within the rituals of
        an ancient tradition.
    There is a truth somewhere between servitude and honor.
    I need to ask more questions.

(Lights dim on the Recorder and slow fade to black.)

From Scene Three

(#5 performs the two different Trokosi women. She holds a basket of various items from the two different Trokosi shrines. She pulls various items and symbolic wraps out of the basket as she "dresses" and "undresses" herself to represent the vastly different experiences of what it means to be Trokosi.)

#5: My name is Efua and I am a Trokosi from the shrine in Klikor.
    I am very proud and happy to be a Trokosi because it is a special honour.
    I am the great, great, great-granddaughter of a Trokosi—my great grandmother, my grandmother, my mother, and now me—all Trokosi!
    I come from a long line of Trokosi queens, and I am very proud.
    My great, great, great grandmother became a Trokosi because
    her brother did a terrible, terrible thing.
    A slave girl became pregnant.
    When the elders asked her who was the man who made her pregnant,

she pointed to my great, great, great grandmother's brother.
When he was identified, he then became very angry because
he did not want to be disgraced before the whole village,
so he stabbed the slave girl to death.
The family of the slave girl demanded justice,
so my great, great, great grandmother was sent to the shrine.
When she died, all my mothers after her and now me—
all Trokosi; and, when I die, my daughter will become Trokosi.
My life here in the shrine is a good life.
It is a very good life.
I have learned so much.
The Trokosi here are trained to be women deserving of respect.
We are taught lessons in morality and religion.
We are taught how to cook and clean and manage our affairs.
We are taught how to take care of ourselves
and how to keep our body, mind, and spirit pure and uplifted.
We are trained here, and it is this training that guides us through our life
and makes all of us walk with dignity and knowledge.
We Trokosi are powerful women,
for we are the only women that can reprimand the priest and the chief! These men must listen to what we say,
because we are Trokosi!

(The performer now goes back to the basket and begins "undressing" herself placing items in the basket to now re-dress herself to become the second Trokosi.)

My name is Abena.
When I was seven years old, my grandfather came to my school
and told me I had to leave my class because
I was going away to visit a friend of the family.
But that was not true. I was taken to a shrine.
I was taken here because my uncle became very sick.
He could not move his legs.
The day I was sent to the shrine,
my mother gave me a mat to take with me for sleeping.
I remember there was a crowd of people that walked with my mother and me
    to the shrine.
At that time, I didn't know why they were singing and I didn't know where I was
    going.
When I got to the shrine, a woman was there.
It seemed like she had been waiting for me to come.
She took me inside the shrine.
Her hands were hard and quick.

They were not like my mother's hands.

The woman began taking off my clothes; she took off my panties.

She wrapped me in a cloth and placed a cord necklace around my neck.

I began to cry. I wanted my mother to take me away from that place.

But mother left me at the shrine. I was very confused and frightened.

I was at the shrine for ten years. I was unhappy there. I missed school.

I wanted to go back to school and I wanted to go back home with my mother.

I wanted to read and write like children who were free.

But at the shrine, all I did was clean, work on the farm, and fetch water.

When I started bleeding,

I knew that soon the Priest would come and make me sleep with him.

I was so scared because I didn't want him to touch me.

He was too old and I didn't like him. But what I feared so much was soon to come.

One night he came to me and he made me take off my clothes.

He entered me. He entered me and I remember everything started turning in my head

and all around me because it hurt so much.

He didn't care that it hurt. He didn't care at all.

When it was over, he left. I felt like I had been broken. I had been broken into pieces.

I now have two children by the Priest.

He doesn't care for my children—sometimes there wasn't enough food to eat.

All my work—on the farm, cleaning the shrine, and carrying water—all my work

. . . and still there wasn't enough money or food for me and my children.

(black out)

The Classroom: Return

"Is he a stranger then?"

"He is one of us all right. Only nobody knows much about him. They say he does not go talking about himself. Only the work we have to do."

"He is another fool, then" Etse said. "Just like the others, talking to men without jobs about the work we have to do."

Ayi Kwi Armah, *The Beautiful Ones Are Not Yet Born*

The class was almost over and the rain was still pouring down. I had just enough time for one last question: "You have given me a lecture on the unfairness of free trade in Ghana, but what does this hidden abode of your remote control economy have to do with literature and Armah's novel?"

Efua spoke:

The characters in the novel are motivated by greed, corruption, and material
  wealth.

We tried to show in our performances that some of these rulers are but puppets
  of American and British foreign policy and rich businessmen from the
  West

who rape our land, steal our labor, and gamble for sport and profit on our future.

There are Ghanaians who want to dress like Westerners, look like Westerners,
  drive big cars, and have lots of money.

They have turned their backs on their own people who are suffering and need
  their help. The poor do not speak well of them.

It is the protagonist who withstands the temptations of corruption, material
  wealth,

and selfish greed.

He is scorned for his honesty, but he keeps his integrity.

We performed the big monkey on our back
  and how that monkey will run and hide if you dare to speak its name.

When you lift your back straight, the monkey falls down
  and there is strength now for you to hold your brother's hand
  and lead each other out of the forest of
  monkeys.

The class was going past time and my colleague in the English Department, Kari
Dako, was patiently waiting outside the door to set up the room for her next class.
I was about to dismiss the students when Kofi spoke, as if for all of us:

My desire is not to have big cars, but for the poor to speak well of me.

Works Cited

Aidoo, Ama Ata. *Our Sister Killjoy*. New York: Longman, 1977.

Armah, Ayi Kwei. *The Beautiful Ones Are Not Yet Born*. Oxford: Heineman, 1969.

Douglas, Mary. *Purity and Danger: An Analysis of the Concepts of Pollution and Taboo*. London:
  Routledge, 1966.

Kincheloe, Joe L. and Peter McLaren. "Rethinking Critical Theory and Qualitative research."
  Handbook of Qualitative Research. Thousand Oaks, CA: Sage, 2002.

Knight, Etheridge. "On the Oral Nature of Poetry." *Painted Bride Quarterly* 32/33 (1988):
  13–17.

Kristeva, Julia. *Powers of Horror: An Essay on Abjection*. Trans. Leon S. Roudiez. New York:
  Columbia University Press, 1982.

Levinas, Emanuel. *Otherwise than Being or Essence*. Trans. A. Lingis. The Hague: Martinus
  Nijhoff, 1981. Qtd. In J. Olthius, "Face-to-face: Ethical Asymmetry or The Synergy of
  Mutuality?" *Knowing Otherwise*. Ed. J. Olthius. New York: Fordham Press, 1997,
  pp. 143–160.

NINE

Experiencing History: A Journey from Oral History to Performance

Natalie M. Fousekis

Natalie Fousekis's essay is the story of a daughter becoming a scholar and teacher who faces and embraces the vagaries of remembering. Fousekis recounts finding her way through the maze of her mother's degenerating memory and her first encounters with "others" in oral history fieldwork, finally—much to her surprise—turning toward performance as a treasured pedagogy. Reflecting on the naivete of the first-time interviewer who is surprised to discover that she shares concerns and history with people apparently very unlike her, Fousekis also invites us to remember the difficulties of performing our respective class positionalities in fieldwork—even as her own reflections on difference take her headlong into oral history performance. Overcoming an anti-theatrical prejudice that has long marginalized performance in Western thinking, Fousekis finds—with increasing enthusiasm—that performance is an effective means for studying memory, for igniting passionate interests in history, for building and transforming social relations, and for engendering unique historical insight.

I discovered oral history and Alzheimer's disease at the same time. Ironically, just as I began to see the value of preserving people's memories on tape, I learned that my mother was losing her memory to Alzheimer's. I started to dream about her almost every night. Each time the nightmare was different. Sometimes, I would just be crying and telling a friend about my mom. She or he would try to comfort me and convince me that everything would be all right. Other nights I watched my mom crying from a distance, but I could not reach her and could not help her. A few times she even died in my dreams. For over a month, Alzheimer's crept into my mind this way—during each evening when I hoped to rest and forget about reality. (Every night I wished I could wake up the next morning and find out that the doctors had made a mistake, but instead I woke up feeling drained and scared about the future.) This disease incensed me—because of my mother's age, because of my age. On June 5, 1994, a few weeks before the diagnosis, we celebrated her fifty-fifth birthday. I had just turned twenty-six. We still had so many things to do as mother and daughter. I had imagined us going places and doing things together as we always had—hiking, shopping, and visiting museums. For many years we were still able to do these things, but gradually I became a constant observer, watching for clues and signs of her weakness—in her and in me. As I write this a decade later, my mother still has a physical presence in my life, but now her memory has deserted her. There are only flickers of her former self in an occasional smile or a knowing look. Her disease and the multiple losses my family faced have made me confront basic issues of memory, identity, and history.

I conducted my first oral history interview for the Southern Oral History Program (SOHP) at the University of North Carolina, Chapel Hill (UNC-CH) two weeks after I learned of my mother's illness. I had accepted a job at the SOHP as an interviewer and research assistant because my Master's thesis committee suggested that I incorporate oral history into my research. It was its closeness to my mother's diagnosis, however, that made my interview with L. C. Bruce, a "Carolina" alumnus and a man who had dedicated his life to community service, stand out so vividly in my mind. As I sat talking with this eighty-year-old man, I could not help but compare his memories to my mother's. Mr. Bruce spoke clearly and in much detail about growing up in Old Salem, North Carolina and about his days as a student at UNC or at "Carolina" as he, like so many others, called it. As he spoke into the microphone his stories and experiences were becoming part of the historical record, while many of my mother's recollections were already gone forever. My mother's fading memories gave me a sense of urgency about oral history. It secured my belief that historians must preserve memories, not just to inform and transform the way we view and write history, but also to remind us about the importance of individual lives and histories. For while my mother's life may have little meaning in the grand historical narrative, her thoughts and experiences are irreplaceable to my family and our friends.

The following year, I encountered performance as a way of presenting oral histories and the stories embedded within them to a wider audience. Unlike my quick embrace of oral history, however, I did not immediately grasp the cogency of performance and did not see its value to historians. Rather, my conversion was slow and painful. In fact, performance seemed antithetical to my definition of what it meant to be a historian—someone reading, writing, and analyzing historical evidence and definitely not acting. I certainly did not expect it to be a method that would reveal new historical insights, heighten the power of each narrator's story, suggest a new way of thinking about how memory is stored and conveyed, and eventually transform the way I teach oral history.

My traditional historical training had limited the way I understood learning about and presenting history. Historical research and presentation meant document-based research in the archives, historiography, and the ultimate goal of a written text. These methods were very familiar, comfortable, and straightforward. What has always grabbed my attention in the archives, however, is what larger historical trends meant for individuals and how individuals interpreted their own lives and experiences. History, for me, came alive in the voices of those far removed from the centers of power. Oral history, and then performance, unlocked a part of history that was hard to find in government documents or the papers of prominent men and women. What I discovered in the ten years since my introduction to these new methodologies is the importance of oral history and performance both for historians and our students. Each can allow those outside academia to experience history, with all of its complexities, as well. Originally, I had assumed that performance lacked the depth of written histories. I soon realized that performance speaks with as much or more authority about the past. The authority comes not from the pen and written word of the historian, but directly from the voices of our interviewees as performers embody and recreate their pasts. In this case, sophisticated historical analysis emerges from the weaving of words, memories, and histories of individuals into a performance. Furthermore, as a teacher I see performance's unique ability to help my students create original narratives and tackle the large thematic questions those narratives raise.

My Conversion to Oral History

As I have continued to record individuals' lives and experiences through oral history, my thoughts have often turned to the exchanges that take place between interviewer and interviewee. Because we ask the questions and reveal little about ourselves, oral historians are often in a position of power in relation to those we interview. What has continued to interest me, however, is the impact each interview had on me, on the way I see myself and the way I approach history. After most interviews, a flood of emotions overtake me—compassion, anger, admiration, or guilt. Often I have to wait several hours before I am ready to interact with other people. I have a difficult time articulating and explaining my experience to those unfamiliar with oral history. Frequently I leave these interviews reminded that I should never assume anything about other people's lives.

Oral history also compelled me to reflect on my place in the process of writing history. Strangers invited me into their homes or their communities for a few hours or a few days. For a short time, we managed to find some common ground as they shared their memories with me. They have comprised a very diverse group: older white men, white, middle-class women day care activists in Durham, North Carolina, black and white teachers in California child care centers, working mothers, a black woman law professor and activist, and men and women who lived on the

North Carolina coast during World War II. Each interview compelled me to confront the differences as well as the commonalities between my interviewees and myself. Although I conducted every interview in the United States, each has seemed like a "border crossing" (Behar, 15–16).[1] As a result, I have thought intensely about what it means to be a historian writing about and interviewing subjects whose experiences seem so removed from my own.

My interview with Carol Watts, a law professor and advocate for poor women and children, was the first instance in which I had to confront the distance imposed by ostensible difference. At the same time, I saw little that we would have in common. She is a black woman who has raised four children—much of the time as a single mother. She went on Aid to Families with Dependent Children (AFDC) for a short time and worked her way through law school. My own experience seemed completely unlike hers; I was a childless white woman who grew up with many privileges. For the first time in an interview I confronted my whiteness. I have been conscious of color many other times in my life, but at that moment I contemplated what it meant for me as a white woman to be recording Carol's story. I could no longer just theorize about color differences. Our encounter embodied them, and challenged each of us to talk across deeply ingrained "firewalls" and prohibitions. The striking contrasts between my life and Carol's emerged in her descriptions of racial discrimination and her work as a civil rights organizer (Brown, 85). Around 1968, for example, the year I was born, Carol and her husband were under investigation by the FBI for being members of the Black Peoples' Unity Movement, a black power organization in New Jersey. My parents bought their first home in 1971, about the time Carol's husband, who had been shot at by federal agents during a raid of their home, fled the country to escape the possibility of a life in prison. I was at the time enthralled and overwhelmed by these apparently very different trajectories, trajectories that gained their respective momentum by differences in class, access to mobility, and political convictions. In this way, what I felt was respect for the emerging clarity of another's life freely given in personal and historical narrative.

Carol Watts shared many very personal stories with me that day, but what seemed our key differences crystallized in a few moments that stood out above the others. As the interview came to a close, Carol turned to her involvement with Planned Parenthood and NARAL and her belief in a woman's right to an abortion. Suddenly her descriptions shifted back to her childhood:

> I think that my two early pregnancies were not of choice. Between my first two kids and my last two I had gotten pregnant again and my father took me . . . to this guy. I don't remember his name now, but it began with a C. He would do abortions for girls. He eventually went to jail for it. My father took me to this guy's office one evening and I had this abortion. I remember I was crying. It's like seared in my memory . . . . It wasn't in his regular office, but it was in some office that had been set up in some sort of business office building. It was all secretive, scary, and dark.

My father said to me, "Why are you crying? You weren't crying when you got pregnant. Why are you crying now?" I would never want to have a young teenage girl to have to go through that. To have their father stand there while they have an abortion and tell them they shouldn't cry. (Fousekis)

I was stunned. As Carol recounted this terrible experience I could almost feel the pain it must have caused her as a sixteen-year-old girl. Before I realized it, I had tears in my eyes. I found myself imagining my own father taking me to have an abortion. The thought horrified me. This story not only emerged unexpectedly, but it was the first time I had talked with a woman about terminating a pregnancy. The interview with Carol drew me into a level of personal reflexivity I had never before experienced in the course of studying history. In turn, I grew increasingly agitated and angry at the injustice Carol recounted.[2]

Carol's story and poignant spoken memories dominated my thoughts for weeks afterward. I kept thinking: how can I convey this story of individual will and strength to other people? How can a scholar communicate the kind of experiences Carol shared with me in a way that will allow others to understand her struggles? Is it even possible to move others through the written word on the same level? While I was, and still am, looking to answer these questions, my interview with Carol had forced me to confront the relationship between myself and my subjects, even insofar as my sense of my own privilege had kept me from interacting with an unpredictably wide range of people. Could it be that, even as I contrasted myself to Carol, painfully aware as I was of my whiteness, I was performing the white-other? As Carol narrated her life and her experiences to me in the heightened, face-to-face context of the interview, she initiated a lifelong review of how I think about my place in the world and my own history.

Moreover, in this interview, someone else's history not only came "alive" but became part of my life, my memory in an entirely new way. Carol remembers every word her father said to her. The office, her tears, his words are "seared" in her memory. I do not assume to share her primary memories. What feels equally seared in my own memory, however, is the pain and courage she showed in the act of remembering, and her coursing rise through her personal narrative to political conclusion: "I would never want a young teenage girl to have to go through that." Carol's stories not only had personal meaning for Carol and me; they revealed larger historical insights into the world of terminating pregnancies before *Roe v. Wade*, and also made strong claims for race and gender justice in a contemporary context still fraught with debates over reproductive rights.

A month after my interview with Carol, I took my first weekend trip devoted to fieldwork. It entailed a different kind of border-crossing. The distance between Chapel Hill, where I was pursuing graduate work, and Holly Ridge, a North Carolina rural farming and fishing community, is only 180 miles, yet it seemed like a foreign country. Holly Ridge is one of those towns you could drive through without realizing it. The only noteworthy building at the main intersection is an Exxon gas station/mini mart. The only visible sign of the 25,000 person army base constructed in Holly Ridge during World War II is a faded yellow sign on Route 50 that says: "Historic Camp Davis Restaurant next left." It probably shouldn't have been surprising (although of course it was) that in my two days in Holly Ridge I learned as much about myself as I did about the impact of World War II on coastal North Carolina.

When I walked into the Camp Davis Restaurant with Lena Ritter, a community leader, oysterer, and lifetime resident of Holly Ridge, I realized I had truly left my world behind, and the distance between my subjects and myself seemed unbridgeable. The dining room was dark and smoky and full of elderly men. As I followed Lena to a table, I thought to myself: everyone is staring at me; I am the only outsider here. Desperately wanting to fit in, I ordered exactly what Lena did for breakfast, a ham biscuit. I hoped my diffidence would fade with a little food in my stomach. When Lena proposed that I leave my car at the restaurant so she could drive me around, my uneasiness began to subside. My Volvo station wagon had seemed very out of place in Holly Ridge. Driving around in my foreign automobile was like advertising that I was a rich girl from California. It was just a car but it projected me into a position of difference and privilege from which it would have been difficult to conduct a hearty, reciprocal interview. This initial encounter foreshadowed much of my weekend in Holly Ridge—a series of "cross-cultural" interactions calling up contradictory reactions, from unease to a relaxed sense of feeling at home.[3]

Most important, my conversations with the residents of Holly Ridge challenged many of the assumptions I had made about class. Walking into a mobile home that morning for the first time in my life, I encountered the warm smile of ninety-year-old Bertie Mills. When Lena introduced us, Bertie walked right over and gave me a big hug. It took me by surprise but made me feel welcome. Immediately my shoulders relaxed, my breathing got easier, and my discomfort began to melt away. Lena left me with Bertie for over an hour. While Lena was gone, Bertie told me about growing up poor and what it had been like to be a sharecropper and tenant farmer all her life. Her memories about specific events were not always clear or easy to follow but her big heart and sense of no regrets let me know how fortunate I was to have met her. She constantly repeated a phrase "we had a pretty poor life, but it was a good life" (Millis). As I packed up to leave, Bertie offered me one of the crocheted dish towels she was making as Christmas presents and insisted I accept it as a gift. At first I would not accept it, but I was touched by her insistence that I take it, so I did.

At the end of the weekend I drove home to Chapel Hill west on Highway 50, this time in the dark, passing occasional groups of homes displaying bright and colorful Christmas lights that broke up the blackness surrounding me. Driving alone in the darkness, suspended between my world and Holly Ridge, I replayed the entire weekend in my head—the wonderful people I had met and how they had welcomed me into their homes and into their community. Before this trip, I had always assumed that people who worked for low wages and struggled to get by must be miserable.

That was a very naive and elitist assumption for me to make, but one consistent with larger discourses of "noble suffering" among the poor. Lena and her friends measured their lives by different standards. They cared more about the trust between members of their community and the value of hard work than how much they earned. Those who had lived all their lives in Holly Ridge looked out for each other and used their community networks to support each other financially when one member of the community was down on her luck. Whether it was my class privilege or my anxiety about it, I had remained distant from the beauty and gift of these values.

My conversations with Lena as we drove around Holly Ridge and Onslow County that weekend not only shattered many of my preconceived notions about the working-class, but they also helped me become more comfortable with my privileged background. At one point Lena shared a couple stories about staying in "fancy" hotels. Describing her experience at the Omni Hotel in Charlotte, Lena explained how uneasy it made her to let a strange man take her bags out of the car and how she hated not knowing where the valet had parked her car. Checking into the Washington Duke Hotel, when she went to speak at a seminar at Duke University, also made her uncomfortable. Because she felt out of place in the hotel's fancy and stiff interior, rather than stay the night, she drove the three hours back to Holly Ridge. While this might not be the response of every person from Lena's background, I had always assumed that someone who could not afford a hotel room at a place like the Washington-Duke would jump at the chance to revel in its "fanciness." Lena best summarized her perspective. "See," she said, "I wouldn't want to live your life, and you wouldn't want to live mine." "But," she continued, "we both share a desire to preserve and record the stories of those who saw the transformation that took place when Camp Davis came to Holly Ridge."[4] In these two sentences, Lena had accomplished three things: she acknowledged our differences, validated our differences, and, in turn, accepted them. In this exchange with Lena, I slowly traveled to a new sense of myself, and I drove back to Chapel Hill with a new outlook, one that included not just a fuller acceptance of who I am, but a better understanding of others.

As I sat at home in my Chapel Hill apartment, mulling over the weekend, I thought back three years to when I arrived at UNC in 1992, and of the distance between my present and my former self. Then, I had tried to hide all of the privileges I had grown up with from other graduate students and professors as well as from myself. In those first years, I struggled over how I would place myself. I did not want to be "an upper class white woman." Graduate seminars had reinforced what I already knew—that those in positions of power in this country often exploited and oppressed those with less money and no power. Over the years, however, it took more energy to mask how I grew up than to tell the truth. While I am sometimes still uncomfortable with my background, I am perhaps more skeptical of the cultural discourses around wealth that led me to deny my upper class background. In fact, despite all my efforts to mask a fortunate upbringing infused with goals of kindness and social justice, I had ultimately failed to preserve a neutral subject position. Race theory had taught me

I could not hide my whiteness. These first interviews, however, helped me move past theorizing and toward accepting my whiteness and realizing that my class privilege is neither fixed nor invisible. My many years of graduate school, almost a decade of conducting oral interviews, and especially my conversations with Lena Ritter and Carol Watts helped me to realize that where I come from does not have to dictate the history I write.

These experiences have all influenced the kind of historian I have become. My mother's memory loss has reminded me of the obvious—that individuals matter to history and that recording their lives is one way to ensure their importance. Moreover, watching my mother's memory fade and experiencing the power of stories retold in an interview prompted me to shift the way I approached my own research. I first approached child care issues with a Master's thesis that was, in effect, a top–down study of the legislative battles for a child care licensing law in North Carolina. My emphasis shifted as I continued to conduct oral histories and observed my mother's losing battle with Alzheimer's. Now in my research on the legislative campaigns and grassroots political battles over day care in California, I am committed to letting women tell their own stories about their struggles to find affordable quality child care. In doing so, I have added the voices of those far removed from the official realm of power to legislative and gubernatorial discussions of policy. Oral history has allowed me to trace the critical role of political actions and claims for child care made by women at the grassroots level in shaping the public debate in the state capital. This new perspective on political activism would not have emerged had I not encountered oral history.

Watching my mother as she lost her memory and identity to Alzheimer's disease also made me aware of the importance of telling and retelling our interviewees' stories. Now that my mother's memory is gone, the effect has been to erase many of my own memories of our relationship and our own history. Alzheimer's has slowly stripped the layers of my mother's personality and memory away and, in turn, has peeled away our conventional means of communication as mother and daughter. I have been reminded, as many scholars have argued, that memory and history are created and solidified by the interaction between people, by the telling and retelling of experiences shared (Hall, 464–465). Our strongest memories are those we can reinforce. I remained unaware of my own memory loss until I had a phone conversation with a friend a few years back. She has barely seen my mother since Alzheimer's claimed her and she recalled to me in exhaustive detail her memories of my mom before the disease—my mother's spirit, her intelligence, her sharp wit, and her talent as a photographer. It's not that these images of my mother seemed totally foreign, but they aren't memories I can easily recollect. Now when I'm with my mom, I can't revert to the person I used to be with her—the daughter and friend who shared everything with her and looked to her for sage advice and guidance. Our interactions are completely different. When I pick her up at the Alzheimer's facility, where she lives with others suffering from this tragic disease, and we spend an afternoon together,

I desperately hope to evoke the most basic emotions from her, a smile or a laugh, some recognition that what I'm saying has been heard. I search for some reaction that seems familiar, that harkens back to our past. Occasionally, we connect through a smile or a touch of the hand, but the moment is fleeting and then she is gone again. As a result, I have become a historian of my own life, trying to re-construct and re-remember my friendship and connection with my mother. Every time I return to my childhood home, I mine the closets, cabinets, nooks, and crannies for "our history"—that of us as mother and daughter before her illness. As my mother has forgotten what our relationship was like, I too have lost many of my memories of my mother. My memory loss reminds me that what we remember and understand about the past comes from sustained relationships between tellers and listeners. The work of oral history is to keep those relationships alive and so to keep memory alive and active.

My interview with Carol Watts and my discussions with Lena Ritter provided me with a new sense of self and a different view of my place in the historical process. As a historian trained to recognize and highlight difference, I assumed when I met these women that we would be unable to relate to each other. Through my interaction with them and many other interviewees, I found some common ground. It was in these moments of connection that I realized that my background did not have to be a barrier to studying women whose lives and experiences were ostensibly far removed from my own. While there is little I can do to change the inherited differences between myself and the women I interview and write about, I have come to appreciate our shared view that women's lives and stories, particularly the voices of those previously overlooked, must be preserved and retold because these stories not only memorialize the past but mitigate the fixity of untenable boundaries.

Furthermore, these interviews inspired me to search for new methods of transmitting the power of these stories to others, long after the interviews had themselves become things of the past. I wanted others to experience the force of these historical encounters and to feel their relevance as I had during my interviews. For as Lucie White says, "language does not gain the force to convey psychic pain through the formal features of its rhetoric, but rather it gains such power when it is used by two people to bridge the distance between them" (White, 1998). White suggests, however, that even if we cannot replicate the power of face-to-face interactions, scholars can use women's testimonies to tell new stories that can have an impact on the policy process. In my own research this means centering my history of child care policy in the lives and words of working mothers. By focusing on these women's stories, my work illustrates how women's personal needs for child care translated into political action. The result is a history that shows how ordinary women with children in California's child care centers took their own definitions of their day care needs and directly challenged the interpretations of women's needs held by the state's policymakers. Since these early interviews I have also discovered another method that comes close to replicating the power of face-to-face interactions—oral-history-based performance.

The Reluctant Performer

In 1995, the same year I met Carol Watts and Lena Ritter, I encountered performance for the first time. It was not a way of doing or thinking about oral history that
I embraced or even considered valid. One of my classmates suggested that we do a
performance as part of a final research presentation in Jacquelyn Hall's "Women's
Leadership and Oral History" course at UNC-Chapel Hill that spring. From the
moment we learned of the group presentation requirement, Kathy Newfont excitedly
declared, "we must do a performance."[5] With a little convincing, another student,
Will Jones, agreed. I, on the other hand, dug in my heels and stubbornly resisted. The
respective work of the members of our group (Kathy, Will, and myself), unlike the
others, did not seem to share a strong enough thread to hold a presentation together.
We seemed to have nothing in common. Kathy had interviewed environmental
educators, Will had interviewed women in the North Carolina NAACP, and I had
interviewed two women who fought for quality day care services in Durham.

My resistance operated on many levels. The thought of standing in front of the
class "acting" made me very uncomfortable.[6] I didn't have the required training;
I didn't understand the relevance of performance as a means of presentation much
less of historical inquiry; and, frankly, the whole thing seemed a little silly. I did not
see or understand the point of performance. I had never seen an oral history-based
performance and had only read a little bit about performance in general. Everything
in my scholarly training suggested that performing our interviewees' stories would be
trivializing them: putting them "on show," using them for our spectacular advantage.
Performance was a foreign medium, one I saw as detracting from the power of my
interviews rather than heightening their importance. I could not imagine how we
could say something meaningful about women's leadership and activism through performance. Finally, it was unclear to me how this kind of presentation could bring our
diverse interviews together. It was only Kathy's persistence and our close friendship
that convinced me grudgingly to give performance a try.

Initially, the process of crafting our performance did not persuade me that I had
made the right decision. I felt it was right to resist. Kathy, Will, and I met early one
April evening in my small, Chapel Hill apartment. We sat around the kitchen table
wondering how we could find connections among the lives of the women we had
interviewed. Although all activists, they differed in age, race, region, and style. For
the first hour we made very few connections. We tried discussing the themes that
emerged from our interviews, but the conversation just kept traveling in circles,
locating little that these women shared. What kept us on task, and me from giving
up, was one shared belief—each of us knew our interviewees spoke eloquently and
that each interview included pointed, inspiring segments about women's leadership
and activism. We could easily convey to each other the wonderfully perceptive things
our interviewees said about women, activism, and leadership, but we still could not
find a way to pull them together.

After numerous false starts, we tried a new approach. Each of us pulled out our tape logs/transcripts and began highlighting the narratives and stories that we found most moving and revealing, not worrying about connections with the others. We sat there, scissors in hand, literally cutting up our tape logs. When we finished, each of us had a pile of our favorite passages from the interviews. Then we started reading. As we spoke—making public to each other these powerful stories—I got the chills. The minute I uttered my interviewee's words, they took on new meaning. I had experienced the power of oral testimony before—in the interview itself and as I listened to the tape while transcribing, but this was different. What actually happened still remains something of a mystery to me but somehow having these women's words come out of my mouth accomplished exactly what Della Pollock argues can happen in live performance. I was experiencing "the power and responsibility of making public what had been told in private" (Pollock, 15). These women no longer seemed like individuals talking about their particular experiences. Rather they became more like a group of women whose descriptions linked their lives, who were speaking together about their struggles and triumphs as leaders and activists.

Slowly, the structure and form of our performance began to emerge. As I shared a narrative about one of my interviewee's struggles to raise children and be an activist, Will responded "my interviewee said something similar." As they each read aloud, Kathy and Will soon discovered that the women they interviewed had both discussed how, as dedicated activists, they had negotiated problems in ethnic differences. This process continued for a few hours or more, as we struggled to put our narratives side by side, in conversation with one another. What we realized as we created our script was the power of performance to demonstrate how seemingly different types of women activists shared similar views and perspectives. Only as we sat together cutting and pasting our tape logs did these important themes appear. Suddenly these women were connected in ways that we had not seen before and in ways we would not have discovered had we not elected to create a performance. It changed our understanding of women's leadership and activism from that point forward.

Performing the words of the activists we interviewed, moreover, made me feel that I had a keen responsibility not to be the interviewees per se but to be myself, the person who, because I anticipated representing these women's stories to an audience, had gained a clearer understanding of the larger meaning of their lives. As a performer, I realized that I was indeed being a historian as I spoke before the other students in my oral history course. To the extent that we were acting, *we were acting like historians.* Our performance communicated the experiences of these individuals to a miniature and captive public, broadening this groups' understanding of leadership and activism while we simultaneously celebrated and validated the important contributions these women had made to all our lives. Through public performance, we were bringing a new group of historical actors into our collective understanding of the past and its implications for our shared present.

Our performance was so well-received (much to my surprise) that we were encouraged to present it to a larger audience. We took it informally on the road—to the Oral History Association meeting in 1996, to Della Pollock's "Performance and Oral History" class in 1997, and to the North Carolina Teacher's Institute in 2001. In each retelling at least three things happened. First, we shared the experiences and histories of our interviewees as well as our insights about women's leadership and activism with a new public. Second, new meanings emerged—about oral history, about women activists, and about performance as a means to express, to explore, and vicariously to experience history. Third, at the same time, some dimensions of the stories we told and retold became more solid, less pliable, more "the way things were." It's only with the benefit of "historical" perspective that I came to comprehend the significance of what we were doing. At the time, I did not appreciate these some-times paradoxical values and the unique contributions of performance. I still had more to learn.

Reluctant Performer Becomes Enthusiastic Teacher

Even as I performed and re-performed our composition of these activists' stories, I did not imagine incorporating performance into my future as a historian and teacher. How, then, did I make the final leap from reluctant performer to a perform-ance advocate, one who encouraged and now requires students in oral history courses to present final projects as performance? It was not until I sat in the audience watch-ing oral history-based performances by two of Della Pollock's "Oral History and Performance" classes at UNC-Chapel Hill that my final transformation took place.[7] I realized then what it was like to be a witness-observer learning about people's lives and experiences as they were acted out before me. My understanding of the power of performance to transform both witnesses and history was solidified once and for all in April 2001 when I attended a public presentation by Jacquelyn Hall and Della Pollock's students, "Oral Histories of Desegregation and the Inner Life of Schools." These presentations highlighted student research in oral history and performance in two separate courses in the hope of expanding public dialogue about desegregation. Sitting in the James M. Johnston Center for Undergraduate Excellence on the UNC campus where the presentations took place, I found myself immediately transported by the performances into consideration of the distinct but similar issues raised by each. Again, I was experiencing the power, authority, and immediacy of history through performance.

Pollock's students explored everything from the surprising lack of racial tension they discovered at West Charlotte High School to what it meant to be a white, Catholic, Northern college woman interviewing a black, working-class, Southern woman to one student's quest to explore the racism within her own family. As I watched this last person perform her interview with her uncle, who had been a Klan member and an overt racist for most of his life until he met the black man who would become his best friend and business partner, I was struck by the multiple levels of meaning in this one story. The "story," such as it was, included the student's reflections on how impossible it had been to get her closest family members to accept her black fiancé. The performance revealed as much about the student's life as it did about her uncle's. It embodied the reflexive struggles of a niece and uncle trying their damndest to understand and discuss racism—and was so compelling that I found myself trying to stop the tears—of recognition, identification, empathy, admiration, and support— from rolling down my cheeks. I could see and feel her pain and tried to comprehend the courage it took for her to perform this experience publicly. I reacted emotionally to the complex emotional landscape of her story, but also to the layers of under- standing about racism and race it seemed to reveal in a flash. Her performance, osten- sibly about one family's experience, showed the complicated ways race operates across American society.

As I sat there watching each piece presented by Pollock's students, all whom had approached oral history through performance that semester, the authority of their voices immediately struck me. Again, I was reminded of the power of spoken narra- tives and how this power can sometimes be lost when we only write about historical events (Pollock, 4–5; White, 1998–1999). Such stories are meaningful in their own right, but it was the public, collective retelling of them that engaged audiences in heated discussion of both the difficulties and benefits of desegregation as well as the complexities of race and racism, issues that historians of the United States continue to explore.

The students who signed up for my oral history course in the spring of 2002, unlike Pollock's, enrolled because they wanted to be introduced to a new historical methodology, one that allowed them to explore the perspective of the average American. Most were attracted to the idea of hearing history first hand and compar- ing oral and written sources. Being introduced to oral history, said one of my stu- dents, "reinforced in an exciting way what [I] already loved and believed about history"—that it was about individual lives and stories.[8] Her views were shared by many of her classmates. Even though these students enthusiastically embraced oral history, they did not expect to experience history through performance.

In the spring of 2002, I was a newly minted Ph.D. and an experienced oral historian enjoying my first full-time teaching position at Whitman College in Walla Walla, Washington—where I had received my undergraduate degree. Now the pro- fessor, I hoped to open my students' eyes to the pleasures of oral history, the value of collaborative work (challenging the myth of the lone historian), and the possibility of presenting history in a non-traditional venue. Furthermore, I hoped the experience of creating a performance would help them to tackle larger historical questions.

The topical theme of the oral history course was war, a subject that was uppermost in the minds of my students and the nation in the wake of September 11, 2001.[9] The class provided a unique venue in which to explore war from an inevitably new perspective. Americans were now re-remembering their wartime experiences through the lens of the "War on Terror." The students viewed their interviews as a way to engage actively the questions they were all asking as young Americans after the attacks in New York, Pennsylvania, and at the Pentagon the previous fall. For one student, this meant exploring the history of Whitman in order to understand how students in the past, on her own campus, had experienced war in such an isolated location. For others, it was about looking at how their parents' generation, either those who fought in or those who protested against the Vietnam War, viewed war and their wartime experiences. Another student, whose friends and family had been in New York City on September 11, 2001, wanted to talk with those who had opposed the Vietnam War, but were now parents with children in New York the day the Twin Towers came crashing down. All expressed a sense that as young college students, studying history at a small liberal arts college in remote eastern Washington, that they could only talk about war in the abstract. They were eager to speak with people who had "real" wartime experience.

My goal in this course was not to have my students create a performance, grounded in the complex theories and meanings of performance studies. Rather I intended to use performance as a pedagogical tool to help students think about what it meant to be the interpreter of their interviewees' histories and to think out-side of their own individual projects. I only suggested they see performance as a use-ful way of sharing their interviewees' stories and thinking comparatively. Finally, I hoped their final presentations would engage the class as a whole in a historical dialogue, one grounded in their interviewees' memories reinterpreted by their group performance.

While my students embraced the theme of the course and were excited about reading, theorizing, and practicing the methodology of oral history, they appeared less enthusiastic when I announced on the first day that I was encouraging them to do their final projects as performances.[10] As I looked around the room that first night, there were many quizzical expressions on their faces (the two with some theater training were the only ones who seemed less apprehensive). I remember one asking immediately, "what do you mean by performance?" Another responded, "we don't *have* to do a performance, right?" Not wanting to force performance on them (still feeling uncertain about its pedagogical value), I elected to make per-formance just one option for my students for their final group projects. The initial group meetings revealed that there were many who opposed doing a performance because as one student put it, "I am not a performer and get extremely nervous talk-ing in front of people."[11] A second said that she saw it as "having the potential to be really cheesy and 5th grade." Similarly, another wrote that her "gut reaction was of elementary school group projects."[12] This was not the level of enthusiasm I had hoped for. My students' reactions, of course, were very much like my own in 1995— not seeing the value of performance, viewing performance as acting and, therefore, something I was not good at, and having the potential to be not only pointless, but degrading.

I hoped that once my students understood what I meant by performance, they might be more willing to give it a try. Not an expert in performance studies myself, I had to teach them the only way I knew how—by example, drawing on my limited personal experience. I candidly shared with them my own resistance to performance. I solicited the assistance of my more willing students to help me recreate the presentation Kathy Newfont, Will Jones, and I had put together for Hall's class and we performed it for my class. I described in detail how Kathy had put friendly pressure on me to try performance, how exasperating the process of coming up with the performance had been at first, and what I ultimately learned from the process about oral history, women's leadership, and women's activism.

The reading assignments on performance were short and few, with the hope of focusing students on the practical work of developing interviews and performances. To acquaint them with the process I had them read one scholarly article about oral history and performance—Della Pollock's "Telling the Told: Performing Like a Family," and one short piece on the creation of *The Laramie Project*, the play based on the horrific murder of Matthew Shepard in Laramie, Wyoming in 1998. I had seen *The Laramie Project* at Berkeley Repertory Theatre in the summer of 2001 and had been struck by its use of oral history to retell this disturbing story. Written by Moisés Kaufman in collaboration with the Tectonic Theater Project, the play uses the oral histories conducted by the theater company with the residents of Laramie to explore how this community struggled to understand this tragic event and how it could take place in their peaceful, small city. The Tectonic Theater Company had asked themselves this question: "what can theatre contribute to the national dialogue of current events?" In response they claimed that theater is "a very human form of communication" and that, accordingly, they designed *The Laramie Project* in such a way that "a community could talk to itself" (Kelley, 3). I instructed the students that they were to ask a similar question and to use performance to put their specific projects into a larger context.

Apparently, the readings, our recreation of my 1995 performance, and our discussions in seminar, convinced the resisters in the class to give performance a try. But even though the students were now enthusiastic, I still had questions about how it would all turn out. In my few years of teaching, I have discovered that even the most well-conceived classroom activity can go awry. My sense of unease also reflected my lingering feeling of inexperience as a historian who uses performance. The students performed just for our class and not in a public setting, although they invited a few outside guests to attend and, in the end, I wished we had opened it up to the campus. The performances took place on the last day of class. As we had all semester, we met at my apartment, this time for an end-of-the-year pot luck/party and an evening of performances. As I sat on my brown speckled carpet, anxiously waiting for the first group to perform, I felt a sense of nervous excitement. It would soon become clear that my untested experiment worked.

The first performance, which focused on World War II, included the voices of a female student at Whitman College during the war, two Japanese Americans who had been interned, two men who had worked for the War Relocation Authority and carried out the federal government's internment policy, and a chaplain in the European front. Here the students juxtaposed the chaplain's memories of being among the first troops to arrive at a concentration camp in Germany with a Japanese American's detailed description of packing his two suitcases to go to an internment camp in Lone Pine, California. Three years separated these events but, by putting them side by side, the students made a powerful comparison between American soldiers freeing Jews from the Nazi concentration camps and America rounding up its Japanese Americans and placing them in camps of their own earlier in the war. After this segment, the students juxtaposed the words of a War Relocation officer saying what a terrible mistake FDR made in 1942 by signing the Executive Order 9066, which authorized interning Japanese Americans living on the west coast into camps, with the recollections of a former Whitman College student, whose life was altered only by rationing, no heat in the classrooms, and very few men on campus. We were all struck by the divergence of these wartime experiences, but also by what such comparisons revealed—that even on the homefront on the west coast, the government's preparation for war meant very different things to different groups of its citizens.

The most memorable moment was an exchange on internment between students performing a Japanese American and an administrator in the War Relocation Authority. We were all amazed to learn that the War Relocation administrators and Japanese American internees shared similar views of FDR. Both admired the man as a leader but believed he had made an enormous mistake in signing the executive order for internment. Teacher and students alike, we had assumed that these men would have nothing in common. But when their voices were put side by side and the students spoke the interviewees' words, they opened up a dialogue about what it meant to be patriotic during World War II. They moreover concluded by comparing World War II and George W. Bush's "War on Terror," focusing on the internment of Japanese Americans and the way Americans have treated people of Arab descent since September 11.[13] Beyond this fruitful dialogue, new historical insight about FDR and the relocation of Japanese Americans emerged, revealing the complex set of emotions American citizens felt toward this popular president and his policies. In this case, two men separated by ethnicity and access to power, one administering the nation's internment politics and the other interned under these policies, shared similar emotions.

Since I had illustrated the only version of oral history performance I knew—following the process Kathy, Will, and I had dreamed up—to the class, I worried that each presentation would follow the same model. My fears were shared by at least one of my students, who later wrote, "As we created our presentation I thought it was pretty straightforward and would be similar to the other groups' . . . but each presentation turned out completely different."[14] One group took a distinctly theatrical approach, providing a more ample sense of scene by projecting images of the Vietnam War on the wall while they spoke their interviewees' war memories.

They took us on a trip back to "Nam," drawing us into the pretense that we were all sitting in an airplane flying from the United States to Saigon, Vietnam. Once we arrived, we were bombarded with more visual images of soldiers, nurses, and officers in Vietnam overlaid with the students' performance of the narrative images that comprised their interviewees' reflections on the war. This group had decided that since Vietnam was the first "television" war, they wanted to provide media images to complement their interviewees' words. Here they presented us with the contrasting voices of the combat veteran who recalled, "I thought it was pretty bad . . . The whole thing was evil" with an officer whose experience was characterized by playing tennis and embassy parties. They hit on many important and somewhat familiar themes as well—questions about why American soldiers went to Vietnam, the jobs they did there, the lack of racial tension in platoons, the interaction between the Vietnamese and the soldiers, and the return home to an America where they "knew [the war] was unpopular."[15] Again, I found the contrasts among the combat veterans', officers', and female nurses' voices and the sense of a new, more bracing and embracing narrative emerging from these comparisons, a narrative that encompassed intimate reflections, contradictions, and unresolved issues and that proved extraordinarily revealing about the diversity of experience, the range of emotional responses, and the shared history of those who fought and served in Vietnam.

The final group ended up (by accident) representing a turbulent exchange between antiwar activists, conscientious objectors, 1960s radicals, and still very angry and bitter Vietnam Vets.[16] Initially, I formed this group because all three students intended to explore antiwar-related topics. One student's interviewees changed when he discovered that he could interview his uncle and his uncle's good friend about their experiences as Vietnam era veterans. Both are still hard core military men and were passionately outspoken about the military in their interviews. One had spent the war on a submarine and the other in intelligence. The performance became a lively and instructive exchange between the ardently antiwar/peace activists and these two very pro-war Vietnam vets. You could literally see why America seemed to be "coming apart" by the end of the 1960s. In fact, as members of the audience we were experiencing this fracturing right before our eyes as students retold their interviewees' stories, creating a more comprehensive and yet also more fraught narrative about the divisions in America in the 1960s than might have been told from any one perspective. They also made very insightful comparisons between the past and the present with a segment connecting accounts of the terrorist attacks on September 11, 2001 and the Gulf of Tonkin incident in 1964. Motivated by hearing one interviewee draw a direct comparison, stating that "watching the twin towers fall on CNN is a lot different than hearing about the Gulf of Tonkin on the radio," the students positioned each event as the catalyst for U.S.-led war, in the first case, a war allegedly begun to roust the terrorists who plotted and organized the attacks on September 11 and, in the second case, to prevent a small nation in Southeast Asia from falling to communism. The interviewee saw the former as a valid, understandable call to military action, the latter as a fabricated incident that gave President Lyndon Johnson a blank check to escalate the Vietnam War. In this performance, the students used the past to engage the present by interpreting current events through a historical framework anchored in the tangible memories of war, a war that took place almost forty years earlier.

For the students, the process of creating the performances offered many challenges and rewards. First, for two of my students the public telling of stories had been extremely difficult because the words they spoke were so painful. One had to relay the disturbing and gruesome descriptions of what the chaplain witnessed as part of the first regiment to happen upon a German concentration camp in 1945. For the other, the challenge was more personal. As a devoted pacifist, this student had to put aside his own view both during the interviews with his uncle and his uncle's friend and during the performance. He said that to embody these men's words, "to try to take their feelings as my own during the reading was absolutely exhausting and sickening."[17] The performance had forced him to confront difference in its most painful way, by having to speak and momentarily to claim viewpoints that radically diverged from his own.

Second, in the end, the students saw the performance as a powerful extension of their role as interviewers and historians. One student wrote that "oral history is the interaction between interviewer and interviewee, between historian and society, [this interaction] was a continuing dialogue and could be well represented by audience and performer." She saw making the interviewees' stories public through retelling as the best way to capture the true "spirit and humanity" of history.[18] Finally, many shared with me that both participating in and watching the performances gave even more traction, more historical significance, and more vitality to their interviewees' words. One said she was "impressed with how much each voice gained by being with all the others." They saw the adaptation and performance of individual voices in social relation to the world and each as adding "complexity" and giving them a "more full-flavored taste of what it was like during a certain time."[19] By developing the performance and speaking their interviewees' words, my students realized they were creating powerful, new interpretations about war and American society. Their interviewees' memories were no longer private, ephemeral and forgotten, but public, alive, and sustained.

Looking back I have been reminded of where this journey has taken me: from a daughter grappling with the pain of losing a mother to a historian revived and energized by the pleasures and challenges of the face-to-face exchange and intimacy of an interview to the reluctant performer hesitant to speak publicly and finally to the historian/teacher who appreciates and values the power of oral history-based performance. I began this slow, reluctant embrace of performance as a participant, recreating the past through the embodied memory of performance. As an observer, I shared and felt deeply the pain and joys of the multiple pasts recreated before me. Now I am the proud teacher watching and listening to the memories and stories my students creatively join in their performances. In each of my experiences with performance a deeper historical understanding has emerged—about women's leadership and activism, about race and racism, and about war and society. These moments of public retelling keep historical memory alive beyond the confines of a written text and help historians and our students advance new narratives and new knowledge about the past.

Notes

1. Ruth Behar and other ethnographers describe journeys back and forth across the border from Mexico to the United States as "border crossings" in order to indicate crossing both literal and cultural borders. To her, it means entering a world very different from her own (Behar).
2. This also became quite apparent to me during the Mellon Seminar at Duke University in the spring of 1996 when Lucie White brought one of her interviewees with her. Through her descriptions about domestic violence and her own experience with it, I will never forget the violence committed against her. It was not until I re-read Lucie White's "No Exit" article for the third time that I realized that Barbara Sutton, a woman in Lucie White's article (under a pseudonym), whose personal experience with violence I had forgotten when I only read about it, was the same woman she brought to the Mellon Seminar.
3. Michela Di Leonardo in "Oral History as Ethnographic Encounter" outlines the differences between ethnography and oral history. She argues that ethnography by definition is "cross cultural" and that oral history is only different in the way scholars label their work. Based on my encounters in Holly Ridge, I would argue that work within the United States can also be called intercultural rather than intracultural. I knew little about my subjects' lives and they knew little about me.
4. Conversations with Lena Ritter in her car and at the Riverview Cafe & Restaurant in Sneads Ferry, NC, December 9–10, 1995.
5. Kathy Newfont was already a performance convert, having taken a course co-taught by Jacquelyn Hall and Della Pollock on oral history and performance the year before.
6. Clearly, I had not yet thought about lecturing as a performance, a notion with which I'm now extremely comfortable.
7. The other performance was "In a House of Open Passage: Performing Women's Leadership and Activism," which I saw in the s.e.e.d.S. Phoenix Garden in Durham, NC, April 1997.
8. Author's correspondence with Claire Novotny, April 4, 2003.
9. Credit must be given to Jacquelyn Hall for suggesting this topic over coffee in Chapel Hill, NC, in November 2001.
10. I now require a group performance at the end of my oral history courses.
11. Author's correspondence with Erin Gettling, March 25, 2003.
12. Author's correspondence with Annelise Heinz, April 20, 2003.
13. "World War II," Performance by Annelise Heinz, Allison Clark, Marie Hoguet, and Katie Billings, History 378-A, Whitman College, Walla Walla, WA, May 1, 2002.
14. Author's correspondence with Katie Billings, April 25, 2003.

15. "Vietnam a Journey," Performance by Nicholas Braus, Claire Novotny, Travis Jo Cufley, and Heather Fife, History 378-A, Whitman College, Walla Walla, WA, May 1, 2002.
16. "War: Abroad and at Home," Performance by Isaac Grody-Patinkin, Erin Gettling, and Jeff Chubb, History 378-A, Whitman College, Walla Walla, WA, May 1, 2002.
17. Jeff Chubb "Evaluation of Group Performance" (in author's possession), May 2002.
18. Author's correspondence with Travis Jo Cufley, June 9, 2003.
19. Author's correspondence with Marie Hoguet, April 24, 2003 and Claire Novotny, April 4, 2003.

Works Cited

Behar, Ruth. *Translated Woman: Crossing the Border with Esperanza's Story*. Boston: Beacon Press, 1993.

Brown, Elsa Barkley. "Polyrhythms and Improvisation: Lessons for Women's History." *History Workshop Journal* 31 (1991): 85–90.

Di Leonardo, Michela. "Oral History as Ethnographic Encounter." *Oral History Review* 15 (1987): 1–20.

Fousekis, Natalie. Interview with Carol Watts [pseudonym]. Southern Historical Collection, November 18, 1995.

Hall, Jacquelyn Dowd. " 'You Must Remember This': Autobiography as Social Critique." *Journal of American History* 85 (1998): 439–465.

Kelley, Laura. "Chronicling Impressions of a Town Murder." *Performing Arts Magazine: Berkeley Repertory Theatre* (2001): 3–7.

Millis, Bertie. Personal Interview. December 9, 1995.

Pollock, Della. "Telling the Told: Performing Like a Family." *Oral History Review* 18 (1990): 1–36.

Spacks, Patricia Meyer. *Gossip*. Chicago: Chicago University Press, 1985.

White, Lucie. "No Exit: Rethinking 'Welfare Dependency' from Different Ground." *The Georgetown Law Journal* 81 (1993): 1961–2002.

Afterword: Reverberations

Jacquelyn D. Hall

Oral history and performance, inflected by feminism and mediated through friendship, have reverberated through my work as a historian in ways both profound and evanescent. Even when I am writing in tones and about topics that seem far removed from either, I find myself preoccupied with what I take to be some of this book's central themes: the challenge of speaking for others; the dialectic of identity and difference; the danger of dualisms that create fictitious unities and secure power relations; the conviction that meaning emerges from dialogue, that identity itself is performative—cocreated, coproduced in relationship to others; the ethical imperative to "pass it on," to make the stories entrusted to you a part of public memory; the desire for a history that explodes into the present, for a way of writing/telling history that makes something happen, that registers in the body and has material, ethical, political, emotional effects.

Indeed, I cannot imagine how different every aspect of my life and work would have been if I had not met Della Pollock in 1987 and found myself learning from her and with her through intimate conversations and elaborate collaborations ever since. Here, I can do no more than describe one of those collaborations and hope, through that description, to suggest some of those reverberations. In so doing, I speak mostly in the first person, cognizant both of the impossibility of separating what I felt and experienced from our interaction with one another and of the danger of collapsing our goals and motives into a false "we."[1]

In the spring of 2001, Della and I decided to link our respective courses—my oral history seminar and her course in performance studies—in a common research project on the process of school desegregation and then bring the two courses together at the end of the semester to share what we learned with one another and with our interviewees. I was motivated in part by a sense that the civil rights revolution was receding into a past that was all too safely closed off from the present. The mass demonstrations that are stamped on my generation's collective memory seem more and more distant to my students. Yet the parents, teachers, and students who pioneered school desegregation did so for the most part not during the turbulent years from "Montgomery to Memphis," but in the late 1960s and early 1970s, after the television cameras had shifted away from the South and the civil rights movement was supposedly at an end. Many of my students belong to a critical third generation in this saga—they are, of course, not the activists who fought for and against integration, nor their children, the *crossover generation*, the first to attend desegregated schools, but their children's children, the first to grow up with no memory of legal segregation and no memory of what we might call the "integrationist dream." By amplifying the voices of the crossover generation of the late 1960s and early 1970s, especially those of the students who made history simply by getting up every day and going to school, I hoped to open the past into the present and connect my student to the integrationist dream.[2]

I also wanted to expose my students to the synergy between oral history and performance. I knew from our earlier experiences in team-teaching oral history and performance courses what a powerful heuristic method oral-history-based performances can be. I had seen students, under Della's inspired guidance, learn through performance how to understand oral historical materials from the inside out. I had also witnessed, time and again, the power of such performances as a representational practice—a way of bringing both the act of remembering, the "occasion of the interview," and the "storied experience" of the uncelebrated into public conversation and debate.[3]

With this broad agenda—to document a largely undocumented history; contest the false closure of the civil rights story; cultivate in students a sense of themselves as agents of history and as participants in an ongoing struggle; experiment with oral history-based performance as an analytic and representational practice; and mobilize both oral history and performance to affect public memory and discussion—we launched what turned out to be one of the most fraught and energizing and transcendent teaching experiences I have ever had.

The plan was as follows: students in Della's performance class would interview individuals from a wide range of communities. They would be especially attuned to the performative nature of oral history. And, in a practice that Della Pollock evocatively calls "listening out loud," they would take the risk of representing, through their own bodies and voices, both that engagement and the stories they would be privileged to hear.[4]

My course, on the other hand, would work collaboratively toward an understanding of the "ordeal of desegregation" in Chapel Hill, North Carolina, home to the University of North Carolina where Della and I teach, and a town proud—then and now—of its reputation as a bastion of liberalism in the South.[5] I did not aspire to writing the story of desegregation in Chapel Hill, but I did hope to tap into the competing narratives about that process and arrive at a complex, layered understanding in which many witnesses would have a say.

I also wanted my students to grapple both with written and with oral sources, using each to illuminate and critique the other. Finally, I wanted to introduce students to the work of archive building, in part because the task of preservation is so central to the mission of the Southern Oral History Program, which I direct, and in part because I wanted to demystify the archives, to demonstrate their fragility, their dependence on active, vigilant *labor*. Like textbooks, archives often seem *finished* and therefore impenetrable and bloodless. I wanted students to see that an archive—with its letters written in a wavering hand, its voices painstakingly preserved—can also thrill, can set history alight.

As soon as we began to lay the groundwork for our projects, we realized that a local effort at historical reclamation was already in progress, centered around a reunion at Chapel Hill's Lincoln High School, which, like other such cherished and hard-won black institutions across the South, had been summarily shut down in the late 1960s, when Chapel Hill's schools merged. One of the leaders of this effort, Edwin Caldwell Jr., let us know immediately that we should *not even think about* appropriating this history and giving nothing in return. What Ed Caldwell told us, in essence, was that these stories were too urgent to be buried in the archives of a university with which the lives of black Chapel Hillians have been so entwined and about which they felt so much ambivalence, a university that in some ways sheltered them from the worst that the South had to offer and, at the same time, exploited their labor and failed to acknowledge their contributions.[6]

Our first meeting with Ed Caldwell was a moment that I will not soon forget. It confronted us at once with the barriers we faced. It raised the stakes. And it called forth a frank, searching dialogue that I came to think of as an example of the kind of truth-telling that we, in this country, desperately need.

I have in mind the process of "truth and reconciliation" that has become a kind of civil religion in the new South Africa. But over the course of the semester, I also found myself returning to the metaphor of "clearburning," which I came across in a wonderful book entitled *God's Long Summer* (1997) by Charles Marsh—about Mississippi in 1964. "Clearburning" is a farming term for the practice of burning the land in late winter when it is cleared for plowing. Clearburning allows the farmer to "see the ground for what it is . . . to prepare for a new planting and harvest." By writing with all the honesty and empathy he could muster about the religious ideas that animated *both* the civil rights movement and the opposition to it, Marsh tried to clear the ground, as he put it, "for a time when whites and blacks together will reckon with their common humanity."[7]

We answered Ed Caldwell's challenge by acknowledging the failures of our institution, expressing our desire to contribute to the black community's history-making project, and asking for the community's help with the ongoing task of teaching the young. By the end, we had come to a meeting of the minds. We would go forward with an awareness of risk and responsibility that charged the whole semester with a kind of urgency that I have never quite felt in a course before.

Then came the proverbial "first day of class," and I found myself facing a roomful of random enrollees who had a vague interest in oral history but no idea what this course was going to be about. The students who signed up for Della

Pollock's class were a diverse lot. Mine, to my dismay, were almost entirely white. The more I tried to impress upon them the importance of what we were going to do, the more they seemed to shrink in their seats, gazing out at me with that all too familiar deer in the headlights look. Their response came in part from the fear that talking to strangers inspires, especially when it entails talking about race across racial lines. But it also came from the topic of school desegregation itself. The words, I think, had an antiquated ring. Far from seeing school desegregation as we and Ed Caldwell and others in the community saw it—as a story that wanted urgently to be told—they could not imagine what, of interest, there was to study. Weren't the schools "desegregated" a long time ago, causing, as one student said, "some tension . . . somewhere in the Deep South—you know, Mississippi and Alabama, those *racist* Southern states."[8]

A few weeks later—with the kind of generosity that cradled this project all the way through—Ed Caldwell came to my class. We set up a tape-recorder, and I let the students interview him about his family, which has been entwined with the university since its founding, when his great, great, great grandfather labored as a slave in the household of its first president, and about his own life in the struggle. The students were mesmerized by his stories, but, as an irrepressible student named Melissa Froemming made clear, they had something else on their minds.

> "I have a question," Melissa broke in to say.
>
> This is a very sensitive topic and we've already talked a little bit about how definitely during this period of time there was a lack of trust, and definitely a lack of trust between the races. . . . One thing that I've thought very much about is that I don't want to make somebody feel uncomfortable, coming in as this high flown white college student and assuming that they're just going to tell me about their private life. How can I—I think you know what kind of a question I'm asking. I don't really know how to word it correctly. But to develop this kind of trust and make it a comfortable situation, when I don't know what kind of a history yet that they've had, and I don't know how to make them feel comfortable. . . . I know I'm not the only one who's thought about this. And it goes both ways.

Melissa looked around at her nodding classmates. It was obvious that they had been talking to each other about their fears, fears they had not been willing to bring up with me. Ed Caldwell answered,

> I know exactly what you're saying. . . . Okay, let me tell you this. I'm looking you in the eye. Pretty much I feel very comfortable with you. I feel you struggling. I don't listen to words, I read body languages. I have the advantage over you because if you're uncomfortable, man, you're going to get crimson (she does blush and everyone laughs). . . . Sometimes you're going to be uncomfortable or whatever, and that might be the key that makes them sort of feel, well, she's struggling, let me be nice

to her. I don't *know* what they're going to do. But all you have to do is be honest. Know what it is that you want to get. Stop, and don't worry about being white, female, or whatever.

Let me say one [more] thing. You've got to believe that what you're doing is important. All right? . . . it's important because Afro-Americans—blacks—have systematically been omitted from history. . . . I really believe . . . that all these tapes and so forth are going to be very important to us, because they are capturing our history. So what you're going to be doing is extremely important. . . . If you are in this course, I want you to take this very seriously. Because you are not just in here to get an A. You're in here [be]cause you're going to be doing a great public service.

Here I was thinking, "Ed Caldwell, thank you. Would you just teach this course for me?" But what I said was, "What would you ideally like to see come out of this class? What would you like to see us achieve?" "Okay" he said,

number one, I want [you] to get the information. . . . I also want you to gain a sensitivity to learning our culture, because you just haven't had the opportunity. You grew up in pretty much an isolated environment. . . . I hope that you'll be open and you will absorb things that you haven't had the opportunity to absorb before. . . . I'm not worried about you not being expert interviewers. . . . I hope this is a great experience for you. Great experience in that, number one, you gain some skills in being able to get from others things you feel are important. I think the other thing that you're going to get that's going to help you most is that you're going to see people in a different light.[9]

Over the course of the semester, we returned over and over to the themes Ed Caldwell had put in motion, themes that are beautifully amplified in a poem that a student named Lesley Williams wrote:

> It's worth risking
> uncovering hidden prejudices
> to give ourselves permission to think.
> It's worth risking
> stuttering and stumbling and offending
> to give ourselves permission to speak
> It's worth risking
> everything we think we believe
> to give ourselves permission to listen.[10]

What both Ed Caldwell and Lesley Williams were pointing toward is the necessity of close listening and the risk that listening entails. Deep listening. Listening through transcribing. Listening beyond and beneath words. Listening for layers of meaning, for the cacophony of voices embedded in every story. Listening to the rhythm, tone, inflection of words (the many meanings of laughter, the catch in the voice, the ironies that are lost on the printed page). Listening for the scripted stories, the ones that have been well honed through conversation, told and retold, or shaped by the media or by the overarching cultural narratives that emplot all our lives. But listening too for the unscripted, for the memories that hurtle to the surface for the first time, with a force that can make you rage or weep. Listening for the "stuttering and stumbling"—what we sometimes call, more clumsily, "communicative blunders"—the gaps, silences, misrememberings, false starts, and awkward, uncomfortable interactions that are so disconcerting to interviewers but so often comprise the rifts that allow new meanings to break through. And finally, "listening out loud," the unique melding of oral history and performance that Della Pollock's work exemplifies and from which I have and am learning so much.

When I say that such listening entails risk, I don't mean the risk students initially feared: the risk of not being "expert interviewers." In fact, what struck me over the course of the semester was how their interviewees—through the very force of their stories—made it almost impossible for the students to fail, or, to put it another way, how the *frame* of the interview became a safe place in which to fail. The risk that Ed Caldwell and Lesley Williams were pointing to, rather, is the risk of seeing yourself and others "in a different light." A student in the performance class expressed it this way: oral history takes us to the core of "our insecurities and fears. . . . it makes us question where we are, who we are, and where, as individuals and socially, we are willing to go."[11]

Over the course of the semester many of the students traced a common arc. They began in fear (based often on unexamined assumptions about themselves—as white, "high-flown college students," on the one hand, and as inept interviewers, on the other, as well as about others—as victims, heroes, or villains from a vanished past); then moved into relationships that simultaneously broke down barriers and clarified differences; and finally came back to a new awareness of self and others that contained unexpected possibilities for change.

The history they reconstructed began in 1961—seven years after the Brown decision, when Chapel Hill became one of the first communities in the South "voluntarily" (i.e., in the absence of a court order) to admit a handful of black students to its all-white schools. In 1966, the town closed both Lincoln High School and the white high school on Franklin Street and sent all the students to a new building on the outskirts of town. This occurred, as one of our interviewees put it, without "fights, without having to call on the National Guard, without having the police."[12] There were no problems; it all went smoothly, according to some of the white officials we interviewed.

It did not take long for the students to find the fault lines in this narrative. In fact, the school board obfuscated and dragged its feet. When the school systems did merge, they did so, as one black interviewee put it "on our backs." Black teachers and administrators were demoted or fired. All the symbols of Lincoln High School's life—the mascots, the colors, the names of the teams and the yearbook and the newspaper—were overridden and displaced. The trophies of its championship football team were left behind and lost; its fantastic band was heard no more. In effect, after long years of delaying tactics, the town dumped the children of janitors and professors, Klansmen and civil rights activists, mill workers and businessmen into a fortress-like building and wished them good luck.[13] To many of the black children who crossed over from one world to another the journey felt like a cultural one-way street.

Steve Scroggs, a white student in that first integrated class, told us what happened in an interview that vividly reveals memory at work. As he talked, he conjured up his viewpoint both as a teenage boy and as the man he has since become—a man who has studied and thought deeply about the social upheaval that shrouded his boyhood in a confusing fog. His testimony constitutes a kind of "clearburning"—a determined effort to reckon with the past.

> Even at Chapel Hill High School, brand new to all the kids from Franklin Street as well as all the kids from Lincoln, there was a feeling among some of the white kids, "What are you doing at my school?" . . . .We didn't realize what the kids from Lincoln had *lost* . . . didn't realize . . . that they . . . left behind a heritage that was so awe-inspiring when you really look at it and study it well. But in the first two years, in '66 and '67 . . . a quiet peace held. It was almost like the beginning of a boxing match when two boxers are just feeling each other out.

He then went on to talk about what some people call a riot and he called a protest mounted by black students in 1969.[14]

A black student named Keith Edwards remembered the quiet before the storm. She had been among the tiny handful of what she called "trial pupils" who had been admitted to the junior high school earlier, and she told harrowing stories of her experiences there, including an incident in which she found a dissected frog in her sandwich. She felt tremendous relief when all of the town's black students entered the new, integrated high school in 1966 and she was no longer alone. She spoke both for herself and for others, shifting from "I" to "they" to "you," implicating her white interviewer and beyond that a broader white audience in what occurred.

> That was really the only time that I really truly could *breathe*. It's like all the other years . . . I was holding my breath. . . . And when the blacks came along, all of them, they realized they were going to have to share a whole lot of things. And that these kids were not going to let you spit on them, hit them, trip them down the stairs, tamper with their lunch. . . . all of these little things that you had been doing all those years, they were not going to tolerate it. And they were not going to tolerate the teachers' behavior either.[15]

"You look back on it," Steve Scroggs concluded, "you realize that if somebody had spoken about it and spoken about the issues of pride and white privilege and the issues of what we give up in this world to accomplish [our other ends], I think we could have avoided what happened in '69. . . . I think the other issue is that when they decided to integrate the high schools, the people they didn't talk to were kids. . . . Lincoln High School was the heart and soul of the African American community." We didn't grieve over it appropriately or close it appropriately. "You can look back on it and say we did it wrong and we probably did."[16]

Worse things happened in other places. But like other communities throughout the South and the nation, Chapel Hill failed to meet the challenge before it: the merging of two very different educational cultures, each with its own symbols, traditions, and points of pride, into a new, democratic, equitable and excellent whole. That failure left a reservoir of bitterness among the town's African American citizens. It also left them with a "rage to explain," to set the record straight, to break a silence that left unquestioned the belief that black schools were categorically inferior and ignored both the pain and the dignity of those "trial pupils" who paved the way.[17] No wonder we ran into a counter-narrative wanting to be told.

Counter-narrative, however, is not quite the right word. It implies that there were two coherent, unitary versions—one white and official, one black and underground. In fact, the students quickly began to question such dichotomies. They met white activists, teachers, and students who had lived through those turbulent years and had grappled with their experiences—either in real time or, like Steve Scroggs, later, in a kind of retrospective anguish that made them perceptive witnesses to the past and engaged citizens today. The students also met African Americans who complicated the notion of an undifferentiated, united "black community," blocked any tendency to romanticize the Jim Crow past, and distinguished carefully between "rebbish" whites and allies in the classroom, on the school board, and in the town.[18]

The stories that emerged from Della's performance class added further complexities. Fewer of her students had grown up in the South, and they carried with them images they had gleaned from textbooks and documentaries—images of rock-throwing rednecks and ongoing racial tensions, which—to the white and Hispanic students especially—seemed to have nothing to do with them. But once they began to do interviews, to borrow Della Pollock's words again, "the weight of humanity" burned away layer after layer of stereotype and distancing simplification.[19] They heard stories of loss and pain. But they also met southerners from both sides of the racial divide who had slowly, miraculously inched forward on the road to "true integration," leveraging the gifts of forbearance and civility to overcome centuries of white cruelty, condescension and self-protective not-knowing, and of black exclusion and deprivation.[20] The students came to see "integration" not as a series of Little Rocks but as a process that took place—and is still taking place—person by person, place by place, encounter by encounter not just in the South but throughout the country. And they came to see oral history and performance as a means of pursuing this not yet realized ideal.

As the students in both courses traced the arc from fear to engagement to self-reflection, they found themselves crossing boundaries between present and past, black and white, South and North, self and other, that they had not even known were there. In so doing, they began to re-imagine the pioneers' first crossings of the racial divide. Exploring such metaphorical parallels, they spoke of their interviews as "little integrations," small, safe worlds in which they could model the equal interaction and dialogue that true integration demands. They began to speak of the complex interaction of storytelling as both a "model for and a mode for . . . integration, which was more a coming together as caring than coming together as the same."[21] They mourned the lack—in their own schooling, in the culture—of a "common, just and inclusive narrative." As one student said, "What integration needs in order to happen is a shared history, one that . . . includes rather than excludes."[22]

Retelling their interviews through performance—throughout the semester, in the case of Della Pollock's students, and, for all of us, in a culminating all-day event—opened up other prefigurative spaces, spaces for equal exchange between the students and the audiences they engaged. What struck me and, at first, unsettled my students, who were encountering this performative practice for the first time, were the communality and physicality of "listening out loud"—the way in which that practice overcomes isolation and engages both the body and mind. As one student wrote, "engaging an audience" has "connotations as disparate as betrothal and mortal combat, but all [involve] coming into direct relationship."[23] That directness overcame reticence, sparked a relay of storytelling, evoked laughter and tears.

The interviewee, as one student put it, "speaks the past to life . . . an act of trust that charged our time together with energy, feeling, and emotion."[24] The students retold those spoken memories, not by pretending to *be* the interviewee, not in stagy, stilted mimicry, but through a performative practice that involves a kind of "doubling . . . the simultaneous presence of the performer and the performed."[25] In some cases, that meant that the students "spoke to life" the interview scene, the interaction between themselves and their interviewees—and in so doing highlighted one of the unique aspects of oral history sources: their status as *cocreations*, brought into being by the interviewer's questions as well as by the interviewee's response. In other cases, it meant simply and profoundly that the students "performed" not only the stories they had heard but the insights and emotions the stories had evoked in them. In all of these ways, the students, like their interviewees, became, as one student wrote, "the locus for the past coming to existence in the present moment."[26]

Taken together, the vivid documents that comprised the Chapel Hill story's paper trail, our conversations with historical actors who turned out to be complicated, struggling human beings, and the risky act of performance—all seemed to evaporate distance, to bring history into the present, to drive home the fact that it is really there, invisible but affecting our every thought and emotion. Abstractions became what the poet Allen Tate called "knowledge carried to the heart."[27] Like Keith Edwards when the isolation of being a "trial pupil" gave way to integration, we all began to breath more freely, to see clearly and far. Jolted into a visceral awareness of our own historical agency, we shared the burden and elation of being protagonists in an unfinished revolution.

By the end, the students and their interviewees were pronouncing the project a "fantastic failure." A failure in the impossibilities it revealed. The impossibility of erasing the boundaries sedimented by slavery, segregation, and the ordeal of integration—even as we blundered across them, glimpsing what life would be like if they weren't there. The impossibility of doing justice to the story, with all its individual and local complexities and its state, regional, and national ramifications. And more than that: the impossibility of *representing*, through writing or performance, the full meaning of the stories we heard, in all their particularity and troubled, transcendent humanity. "A piece of the body torn out by the roots might be more to the point," as James Agee said. And yet "fantastic" precisely because of what the project dared and what limits daring will always reveal.[28]

In similar fashion, school systems across the nation failed to answer the call of the Brown decision, and yet, in many cases, they have reckoned with that failure and never stopped trying to create new, truly integrated institutions. The generation of students and teachers that first crossed the racial divide could not, by themselves, overcome what centuries of injustice had wrought, and yet many emerged from that experience dedicated to the ongoing pursuit of the integrationist dream. Just so, these courses called forth in our students what Della described as an "astounding dignity," the dignity of "hoping beyond failure and acting on that hope."[29] A student named Gwen Bell put it this way:

> So, in the end of this class, after all of the writing and talking and crying and learning, one important ideal piece of knowledge remains with me. That is, that we should not give up. Even if at times we do not give the complete story, as we never can . . . we must start somewhere. . . . We can look up at the sky for guidance, and we can bring an empty bowl with us wherever we go to be filled. And it will be filled: with the stories, the living history all around us, the truths people are, quite literally at times, dying to tell. . . .

Notes

1. For some of those collaborations, see Jacquelyn Hall and Della Pollock, "History, Story, and Performance: The Making and Remaking of a Southern Cotton Mill World," in *Reconstructing American Literary and Historical Studies*, ed. Günter H. Lenz, Hartmut Keil, and Sabine Bröck-Sallah (New York, 1990), pp. 324–344; Della Pollock, "Telling the

Told: Performing Like a Family," *The Oral History Review* 18.2 (1990): 1–36; and Pollock, "(Un)Becoming Voices: Representing Sexual Harassment in Performance," in *Conceptualizing Sexual Harassment as Discourse*, ed. Shereen G. Bingham (Westport, CT: Praeger, 1994), pp. 107–125.

2. Parts of this paragraph are drawn from Jacquelyn Dowd Hall, "Mobilizing Memory: Broadening Our View of the Civil Rights Movement," *Chronicle of Higher Education*, (July 27, 2001); B8. For subsequent thoughts on "the long civil rights movement," see Hall, "The Long Civil Rights Movement and the Political Uses of the Past," *Journal of American History* (March 2005): 1233–1263. We benefited especially from the work of Pamela Grundy, who had conducted an oral history project on West Charlotte High School in Charlotte, North Carolina, for the Southern Oral History Program and was teaching a similar course at Davidson College. For Grundy's project, see *Charlotte Observer* (October 9, 1999): 19A. For the Charlotte interviews, see series K, Southern Oral History Program Collection, Southern Historical Collection (Wilson Library, University of North Carolina at Chapel Hill). <http://www.lib.unc.edu/mss/inv/htm/04007.html> September 2004.

3. As per the introduction to this volume.

4. For "listening out loud," see Della Pollock, "Memory, Remembering, and Histories of Change: A Performance Praxis," in *Handbook of Performance Studies*, ed. Judith Hamera and Soyini Madison (Thousand Oaks, CA: Sage, 2005).

5. Orlando Patterson, *The Ordeal of Integration: Progress and Resentment in America's "racial" Crisis* (Washington DC: Civitas/Counterpoint, 1997).

6. Angela Hornsby and Molly P. Rozum, "An Ironic Jim Crow: The Experiences of Two Generations of Southern African American Men," *Southern Cultures* 8.3 (Fall 2002), 97–105. Edwin Caldwell died a year and a half after this project began: *Chapel Hill News*, October 21, 2003.

7. Charles Marsh, *God's Long Summer: Stories of Faith and Civil Rights* (Princeton, NJ: Princeton University Press, 1997), pp. 8–9. Parts of this paragraph are drawn from Hall, "Mobilizing Memory," p. B9.

8. Lesley Duggins Williams, student paper (in Della Pollock's possession). All student papers quoted with permission.

9. Tape-recording of class discussion (in Jacquelyn Hall's possession).

10. Williams paper.

11. Gwen Bell, student paper (in Della Pollock's possession).

12. Stephen Scroggs Interview by Elizabeth Hamilton, April 9, 2001, series K, Southern Oral History Program Collection, quoted in Jenny Matthews, student paper (in Jacquelyn Hall's possession).

13. For a vivid description of a similar experience, see Charles Marsh, *The Last Days: A Son's Story of Sin and Segregation at the Dawn of the New South* (New York: Basic Books, 2000), p. 248.

14. Scroggs Interview.

15. Lili Lai, student paper (in Jacquelyn Hall's possession).

16. Scroggs Interview.

17. Fred Hobson, *Tell About the South: The Southern Rage to Explain* (Baton Rouge: Louisiana State University Press, 1983).

18. By "rebbish," Caldwell means "unreconstructed" white southerners, those who sought to keep the "Lost Cause" of the Confederate rebels alive.

19. Personal exchange with Della Pollock.
20. John A. Powell, "A New Theory of Integrated Education: True Integration," paper delivered at the conference "The Resegregation of Southern Schools? A Crucial Moment in the History (and the Future) of Public Schooling in America," University of North Carolina Law School, Chapel Hill, NC, August 30, 2002 (in Jacquelyn Hall's possession).
21. Kit Leckerling, student paper (in Della Pollock's possession).
22. Melanie Kolasa, student paper (in Della Pollock's possession).
23. Williams paper.
24. Kit Leckerling, student paper (in Della Pollock's possession).
25. Richard Schechner, "Acting as Incorporation," *The Drama Review* 37.4 (1993): 64.
26. Leckerling paper.
27. Allen Tate, "Ode to the Confederate Dead," in Allen Tate, *Selected Poems* (New York: Charles Scribner's Sons, 1937).
28. James Agee and Walker Evans, *Let Us Now Praise Famous Men* (New York: Ballantine Books, 1941, 1960), p. 13. Parts of this paragraph are drawn from Hall, "Mobilizing Memory," p. B9.
29. Personal exchange with Della Pollock.

List of Contributors

Gretchen A. Case is a performer, writer, and public historian. She is a recipient of the White Scholarship in Medicine and Humanities from the University of California Humanities Research Institute and is a Ph.D. candidate. She is in the Interdisciplinary Program in Performance Studies at the University of California at Berkeley. She has given performances based on oral historical materials in numerous venues, including at annual meetings of the National Communication Association and the Oral History Association. Her essay on performing medical and personal history, "X-rays and Catholic Schoolgirls: Performing Medical and Personal History," appeared in a special issue of *Contemporary Theatre Review* (2001).

Rivka Syd Eisner is a doctoral student in Performance Studies in the Department of Communication Studies at the University of North Carolina at Chapel Hill. She received her M.A. in 2002 based on her performance-centered thesis, *And So There Are Pieces: Cuttings from the Life Memories of a Daughter of Vietnam*. She is a member of Wordshed Productions and was recently featured in *Nearly Finished*, short plays by Samuel Beckett; *Let Us Now Praise Famous Men*, adapted from the novel by James Agee and Walker Evans by Derek Goldman; and Brecht/Sophocles' *Antigone*. She is currently pursuing fieldwork in Vietnam as part of an intergenerational memory study of women in post-war Vietnam.

Natalie M. Fousekis is Assistant Professor of History at California State University, Fullerton, where she teaches courses in modern U.S. history, women's history, and oral history. Fousekis also serves as the Associate Director of the Center for Oral and Public History. She received her Ph.D. in U.S. history at the University of North Carolina at Chapel Hill (2000). She is currently working on a book-length manuscript entitled "Fighting for Our Children: Women's Activism, the Battle Over Child Care, and the Politics of Welfare, 1940–1971."

Michael A. Gordon is Associate Professor of History and Director of Graduate Studies at the University of Wisconsin-Milwaukee. He is also the coordinator of UWM's Public History Specialization. He is the author of *Orange Riots: Irish Political Violence in New York City, 1870 and 1871* (Cornell University Press, 1993). He has served on the editorial board of the *Oral History Review*, and was coeditor of the annual section on oral history in the *Journal of American History* (1996–2002). He has participated in numerous local public history projects involving theater, radio, exhibits, and oral history, and was the recipient of the Governor's Award for Excellence in Public Humanities Programming (2001).

Jacquelyn Dowd Hall is the Julia Cherry Spruill Professor of History at the University of North Carolina at Chapel Hill. She was the founding president of the Labor and Working Class History Association and is past president of the Southern Historical Association and the Organization of American Historians. She received a National Humanities Medal in 1999 for her leadership of the Southern Oral History Program at UNC and for her dedicated contributions to the study of the gender and class in the New South. Hall is the author of *Revolt Against Chivalry: Jessie Daniel Ames and the Women's Campaign Against Lynching* (1979), which won the Simpkins and Lillian Smith Awards and was reissued with a new introduction and epilogue in 1993, and coauthor of *Like a Family: The Making of a Southern Cotton Mill World* (1987), which received the Beveridge and Merle Curti Awards, and was reissued with an afterword by the authors and a foreword by Michael Frisch in 2000. Her current book project, *Writing a Way Home*, concerns the role of women writers and intellectuals in the interwar South.

Shannon Jackson is Professor of Rhetoric and of Theater, Dance, and Performance Studies at the University of California, Berkeley. She has published on a variety of aesthetic, political, and historical issues in *The Drama Review, Text and Performance Quarterly, Modern Drama*, and in other journals and collections. She is the author of *Lines of Activity: Performance, Historiography, Hull-House Domesticity* (2000) and *Professing Performance: Theatre in the Academy from Philology to Performativity* (2004).

Laurie Lathem is former Creative Director of the Berkeley Repertory School of Theatre and Director of Education for the Berkeley Repertory Theatre. She has conducted playwriting programs for incarcerated youth and for at-risk youth in South Central Los Angeles and at Alameda County Juvenile Hall. She is the teacher of the popular Go Solo Workshop at Highways Performance Space in Santa Monica, CA, and the director of the production, *Old Man in a Baseball Cap* by Fred Rochlin (HarperCollins, 1999). She wrote and performed in New York, Los Angeles, and London, "Is This America, Or What?" A playwright and screenwriter, she is currently at work on a book of memoirs.

D. Soyini Madison is Associate Professor in the Department of Communication Studies in the area of Performance Studies. She is the author of *Critical Ethnography: Methods, Ethics, and Performance* (Sage, 2005), coeditor, with Judith Hamera, of the *Handbook of Performance Studies* (Sage, 2005), and editor of *The Woman That I Am: The Literature and Culture of Contemporary Women of Color* (St. Martin's, 1994). She has published in the areas of performance studies and black diaspora studies in such journals as *Text and Performance Quarterly* and *Cultural Studies*. Madison has also adapted and directed ethnographic and oral historical materials for *I Have My Story to Tell* (1993), a performance reflecting the labor struggles of UNC service workers, and for *Mandelas, the Land, and the People* (1990).

Della Pollock is a Professor in the Department of Communication Studies at the University of North Carolina at Chapel Hill, specializing in the areas of Performance and Cultural Studies. She is the author of *Telling Bodies Performing Birth: Everyday Narratives of Childbirth* (1999), editor of *Exceptional Spaces: Essays in Performance and History* (1998), and coeditor of the journal, *Cultural Studies*. She has participated in several collaborative performance projects with the Southern Oral History Program at UNC, including a regional tour of performances based on Hall et al., *Like a Family: The Making of a Southern Cotton Mill World*, and, more recently, a public presentation of regional histories of desegregation, the basis of her essay, "Desegregation and the Inner Life of High Schools: Performance, Memory, and Histories of Change," *Handbook of Performance Studies* (Thousand Oaks, CA: Sage, 2005).

Alicia J. Rouverol has worked in the twin fields of folklore and oral history for nearly twenty years. She is former Assistant Director of the Southern Oral History Program at the University of North Carolina at Chapel Hill and former Associate Director/Acting Director of the Northeast Archives of Folklore and Oral History, and has taught oral history and life review at

UNC and Duke University. She is coauthor of *"I Was Content and Not Content": The Story of Linda Lord* and the *Closing of Penobscot Poultry* (2000). Her articles have appeared in the *Oral History Journal* (UK), *Journal of Applied Folklore*, and the *North Carolina Folklore Journal*. She is currently working on a book based on the Brown Creek Life Review Project, *Trying to Be Good: Lessons from a Penitentiary*.

Index

CPSIA information can be obtained
at www.ICGtesting.com
Printed in the USA
LVHW081123180722
723737LV00004B/40